AF845081

Power

A Practical Handbook

Consulting Editors **Munir Hassan** and **Rajan Phakey**

Featuring a Foreword by **Dame Fiona Woolf, DBE**

Consulting editors
Munir Hassan, CMS London
Rajan Phakey, Dentons

Managing director
Sian O'Neill

Power: A Practical Handbook
is published by

Globe Law and Business Ltd
3 Mylor Close
Horsell
Woking
Surrey GU21 4DD
Tel: +44 20 3745 4770
www.globelawandbusiness.com

Power: A Practical Handbook
ISBN 9781905783854

© 2017 Globe Law and Business Ltd

All rights reserved. No part of this publication may be reproduced in any material form (including photocopying, storing in any medium by electronic means or transmitting) without the written permission of the copyright owner, except in accordance with the provisions of the Copyright, Designs and Patents Act 1988 or under terms of a licence issued by the Copyright Licensing Agency Ltd, 6-10 Kirby Street, London EC1N 8TS, United Kingdom (www.cla.co.uk, email: licence@cla.co.uk). Applications for the copyright owner's written permission to reproduce any part of this publication should be addressed to the publisher.

DISCLAIMER
This publication is intended as a general guide only. The information and opinions which it contains are not intended to be a comprehensive study, nor to provide legal advice, and should not be treated as a substitute for legal advice concerning particular situations. Legal advice should always be sought before taking any action based on the information provided. The publishers bear no responsibility for any errors or omissions contained herein.

Table of contents

Foreword

Dame Fiona Woolf, DBE

Power is the focus of political and societal attention as governments and communities rise to the challenges of what the sector now calls the 'Trilemma'. Since the agreements of Kyoto in 1992 and Paris at the end of 2015, we have three imperatives – security of supply (and with it, serving unmet need), affordability (and with it, energy efficiency) and decarbonisation (and with it, long-term sustainability). Government policies, not just in developing economies, link the need for investment in efficient power infrastructure with economic growth and social development (health and education).

Having advised nearly 30 governments and the World Bank over nearly three decades of working in this sector, I have seen first-hand just how important having a well-functioning electricity sector is at all levels of society and how intensely political much needed reforms can become.

The sector is enormously dynamic, even where the first or second waves of reforms have been implemented. This is not simply because of changes in primary fuel markets and new technologies but because electricity markets are complex and effective demand-side participation is difficult to achieve. They are governed by the laws of physics as well as economics and require a truly multi-disciplinary effort. The good news is that we have nearly 30 years' experience to draw on. Those now involved in the sector do not have to reinvent the wheel. They can build on existing foundations and lessons learnt from early sector reforms while finding new ways to improve efficiencies and satisfy our insatiable demand for power. That will free up resources to innovate, to develop new technologies and to meet the inevitable new and unexpected challenges that arise.

At the end of the 20th century, many developed and developing countries were more focused on the societal and economic imperatives of a secure and reliable electricity supply at affordable cost than the role that the power sector needed to play in the transition to a low-carbon economy. This saw a large number of power stations and related infrastructure being built largely through centrally procured processes orchestrated by governments. Then a raft of market reforms swept the globe following the remarkable restructuring and market implementation in England and Wales. Having been fortunate enough to have advised on a large number of these reforms all over the world, I have seen an evolution to a more efficient electricity sector that is now capable of making scarce resources go further and to bring the benefits to a whole region and not just a single country or state.

As a result of the privatisation programmes and market reforms, whether in the

UK, Europe, Australia, the US or Latin America, market forces brought both cost-competitive operating rigour to the sector as well as a better allocation of risk. This has led to a development of complex legal and regulatory structures made up of intricate codes, licences and contractual arrangements, all of which need effective enforcement arrangements. This is the architecture on which much of the sector today builds and operates its power plants and networks, trades electricity and attracts investment for the future. Cleaner energy is no longer just a 'nice to have' and from the perspective of affordability, it is clear that it is more economic to invest in low-carbon infrastructure on a regional basis, resulting in the need for greater interconnection to enable low-cost, clean energy to be exported to higher-cost locations.

Since the end of the 20th century, government policies have encouraged the growth of renewable technologies and established clear evidence that investment will bring down the cost (solar and onshore wind being examples). However, there are many different policy approaches and some of them have come at a cost which has had to be borne by consumers or taxpayers. The right policy mix is still the subject of debate and there is no silver bullet. The good news is that none can ignore the global ambitions articulated through 180 countries signing the Paris climate change agreement in December 2015, or the groundswell of interest from the business community in investing in low-carbon infrastructure. This means that the era of cheap fossil fuels and unabated CO^2 emissions from our generating stations will be replaced with more sustainable sources, and the ageing networks replaced with 'smart grid' technologies capable of responding to new models of generating, delivering, trading and using electricity more efficiently.

This is an exciting time for the power sector. It is also a time when the level of complexity and challenge that this sector faces has never been higher. There is huge urgency for the key ingredients and the lessons that we have learnt to be understood so that governments, regulators, sector participants and their advisers can contribute (as they must) to the common economic and societal good in the face of continuing growth in global electricity demand.

This is why this book, *Power: A Practical Handbook,* is so important in bringing the insights and knowledge gained through working in the field to wider audiences. Like me, many of the contributors to this book have worked in this field for many years. They know from experience what it takes to create a recipe for success in this sector. There is no time to be lost!

Introduction

Munir Hassan
CMS London

Electricity has become an essential human need. Modern life is not possible without it. And demand for it is increasing, driven by industrialisation, rising populations, urbanisation, economic growth and an increase in global wealth.

For a sector that can no longer claim to be new, the electricity industry is not static, consistently evolving to meet the power needs and expectations of each subsequent generation. Recent changes in the sector have been unprecedented, driven less by increased demand and more by changing political, social and environmental objectives and by new technologies.

As advisers to the sector, we have to rise to the challenges that such changes represent: by being open to new ways of structuring the sector and arrangements within it; by being an informed voice in the debate, drawing on best practice from across different jurisdictions; and by guiding legal, regulatory, commercial and industry frameworks towards solutions that are coming up against the same issues for often similar reasons all over the world. There are many such issues.

Central generation from fewer larger plants is diminishing in importance, with distributed generation, smaller plants and consumer take-up of medium- and small-scale renewable technologies changing the number, nature and geographical location of engagement with the sector. Lines are blurring between generation and demand. Large customers play in wholesale markets, and small customers use smart meters to respond directly to price signals.

Networks are having to be more fleet of foot, as a largely stable coal, gas and nuclear fuel mix is eroded away and replaced by large numbers of plant with different characteristics and network requirements. Networks are challenged by the uncertainties of forecasting future need and smarter operations. Traditional long-term investment planning has given way to a flexible and reactive approach to the fast-paced and less predictable nature of future generation investments. Interconnectors with neighbouring markets, and sometimes even distant markets, play an increasing role in achieving efficient and least cost systems.

As the sector has changed, so have the players in the sector. The pace of technological change is a challenge and an opportunity for the brave. Traditional utilities remain important as a backbone to the sector. But there has been a tidal wave of new investors pursuing new technologies such as offshore and onshore wind, solar, tidal, wave, tidal lagoons, carbon capture, small modular nuclear, deepwater floating projects, offshore transmission and energy storage. Renewable technologies are displacing thermal generation, with the volatility of oil prices in recent years (prices having hit unexpected lows) and the resistance to new nuclear post-Fukushima playing their parts in driving forward the renewable agenda. The possibilities for large volumes of small-scale and distributed generation have thrown the sector wide open to these new entrants, from independents, financial investors, pension and insurance funds and renewables funds all the way to non-sectoral corporates keen to exhibit their sectoral credentials.

The power sector has always been important for project financing. However, renewables projects have driven the levels of activity in this area exponentially, with high capital expenditure and stable revenue projects becoming a staple diet for project financiers.

We would like to thank the contributors, who are all key advisers to the sector, for generously sharing their insights and experience and helping to demystify the power sector.

Power industries: structures and legal frameworks

Marianne Anton
Munir Hassan
CMS London
Dalia Majumder-Russell
Linklaters

1. Introduction

Many power sectors around the world have walked down the path of market liberalisation, restructuring, independent regulation, private sector investment and privatisation to varying extents and with varying degrees of success. Wherever they have ended up on that scale, the tramlines of reliable regulatory structures guide the sector in this endeavour. Ultimately the success of the sector in any jurisdiction or sphere will depend partly on the political will of the state governments to put in the necessary legislative and regulatory architecture and respond to the changes in the sector, as well as on the buy-in from the industry. Contracts are by their nature agreed positions of different stakeholders and laws, while ostensibly dictated by the Executive, in practice reflect a consensus reached by those regulating and being regulated.

The power sector is far from static and the law has had to keep pace with each transformational turn in the sector. Governments have had to adapt their legal and regulatory frameworks time and again, recognising that decisions being made now on how to replace ageing infrastructure or support the ravenous hunger for electricity of fast-developing economies will define the sector, and lock in technology choices, for decades. Market reforms are back in vogue in some places, but often look little like the economics-driven liberalisation programmes of the 1990s. Legal forms have diverged and the sector's approach has become increasingly fragmented, with often very different legal, regulatory and contractual arrangements being adopted for sub-sectors in the sector. And of course projects continue to have to deal with each country's specific industry arrangements, with each market change leaving behind a legacy of quirks and esoteric approaches that then frame the debate for the next change. Nevertheless, there are common component parts and general trends that can be identified across many jurisdictions. As noted, the structure of and drivers for power industries across the world varies, but there are also many comparable elements. This chapter provides an overview of the main elements and considerations in looking at legal and regulatory frameworks describing the key regulatory bodies involved, contracting and licensing structures and market arrangements. It could be considered as describing a kind of norm that may need to be adjusted to respond to the specific issues arising in any particular context.

2. Key bodies

Several key bodies play essential roles in the power industry. Because of the historically perceived nature of power networks as a natural monopoly, and with the sector in many countries being dominated by an incumbent utility, the power sector is a regulated industry (see the chapter on Regulating monopoly infrastructure). Governments usually set energy policy, environmental and planning bodies set out requirements that must be met for development of power networks and generation, regulators monitor and enforce compliance with laws and industry codes, system operators balance power networks, and industry bodies (generators, network owners, distributors, retailers) must comply with the legal framework to participate in power markets. Of course, there are many variations on this basic structure.

2.1 Government

The government ministry or department responsible for overseeing power normally sets the policy, targets and programmes to deliver the energy needs of the jurisdiction. This usually includes consulting with industry and economic experts, carrying out public consultations, and drafting laws. In the power industry, laws regulate participation (usually by granting licences or exceptions), applicable safety and security standards and measures, environmental protection measures, emissions targets and the government's and/or the sectoral regulator's powers to intervene in the market.

While governments are generally cautious about changing energy policy too frequently, there are examples around the world which serve as cautionary tales. The regulatory uncertainty engendered by too frequent or retrospective changes can deter investment in vital infrastructure, and undercut market confidence, leading to increasing power prices across all sections of consumption.

Case study: UK – Gone with the wind[1]

The Renewables Obligation was introduced in 2002 by the UK government to provide incentives for the deployment of large-scale renewable electricity in the UK, and was due to operate between 2002 and 2017. However, in June 2015, the government announced an end to new subsidies for onshore wind farms by legislating to close the scheme across Great Britain (but not Northern Ireland) one year early from 1 April 2016. The reasoning for this was:

We want to help technologies stand on their own two feet, not encourage a reliance on public subsidies. So we are driving forward our commitment to end new onshore wind subsidies and give local communities the final say over any new windfarms.

This change will likely have an impact on wind farm developments which have been held up through persistent litigations and continuous court appeals. This will have a particular impact in Scotland where there is a significant onshore wind energy sector, highlighting the tension between local political priorities which are supportive of onshore wind and national political agendas which prioritise budget control.

---

1 www.cms-lawnow.com/ealerts/2015/06/gone-with-the-wind?cc_lang=en.

The full impact of the swift about-face on the UK power sector remains to be seen. However, when balancing costs the government has the power to 'pick the winners', with the impact on solar and wind technologies being to deter future deployment.

2.2 Environmental and planning bodies

In addition to energy ministries and laws specifically designed to implement energy policy and regulation, government environmental and planning bodies (whether at national, regional or local levels) also have a role to play in the development of power markets. As with all major infrastructure projects, power generation projects and network expansions or reinforcements must obtain environmental and planning approvals.

Case study: European projects of common interest

In EU Member States, there has been an effort to ease the planning burden on key energy infrastructure projects (called projects of common interest or PCIs). According to the European Commission, PCIs may benefit from "accelerated planning and permit granting, a single national authority for obtaining permits, improved regulatory conditions, [and] lower administrative costs due to streamlined environmental assessment processes".[2]

PCIs are key infrastructure projects that will help EU Member States to physically integrate their energy markets, enable them to diversify their energy sources and help bring an end to the energy isolation some of them are facing. PCIs are expected to increase competition in energy markets and strengthen energy security while contributing to climate and energy goals by integrating renewables.

Updated every two years, the first list of PCIs chosen by the European Commission was published in 2013, with the next one due in 2017. The European Commission selects projects which it considers will "enable the EU to meet its energy policy objectives of market integration and sustainability through an integration of renewable energy", "boost security of supply through an increased grid resilience and flexibility", and "allow for the attainment of the 10% electricity interconnection target".[3]

2.3 Regulators

Before addressing the role of regulation in the power sector, it is worth considering briefly why power markets are regulated and the extent to which they are regulated (see the chapter on Regulating monopoly infrastructure). Power is a universal need, but the transmission and distribution networks are natural monopolies. Without regulation, the owners of these networks would potentially be able to affect entire economies, distort competition, limit access to the sector by competitors and make undeserved profits or at least operate to an extent independently of normal market forces. In addition, many generation technologies are inherently dangerous, and

2 https://ec.europa.eu/energy/en/topics/infrastructure/projects-common-interest.
3 http://europa.eu/rapid/press-release_MEMO-15-6108_en.htm.

therefore generators must adhere to technical and safety standards to keep the system safe. These considerations all feed in to the goal of protecting consumers' interests in:

- cost: keeping consumer bills as low as possible;
- access: making power accessible to all and ensuring secure supply through investment in maintaining and developing infrastructure; and
- safety: setting and enforcing safety standards.

While the detailed role of the regulator and its powers vary from jurisdiction to jurisdiction, in general, its role is to sit between the government, industry participants and consumers:

- implementing government policy;
- licensing and monitoring industry participants; and
- protecting the interests of consumers.

This is done through various measures, but can include monitoring, investigating and addressing anti-competitive behaviour, and assessing and reporting on risks to future security of supply to inform government decisions. Such powers are set out in sector specific laws, in licences and in quasi-statutory market participation rules. In some jurisdictions these functions could be split between a number of bodies.

Effective regulators, whether fully independent or a government department, share similar characteristics in that they are independent from industry, are fair and transparent, are clear in decision making (giving reasons and good justifications for actions), and are stable and predictable.

2.4 System operators

The role of a system operator can be undertaken by an independent entity, the owner of the power networks, a government entity, or an entity falling somewhere within the spectrum between fully government owned and fully independent.

Of its various functions, two functions of the system operator are considered particularly key: real time management of the system and long term planning (the latter role sometimes also involving other relevant entities such as network owner, regulator, or the government). Real time management entails balancing supply and demand on the network by despatching or constraining generation and by calling on a range of balancing services to maintain the frequency of the system within a specified safe range. A key task of the system operator is to avoid fluctuations or interruptions of power on the system both on a real time basis and also in the long term. Therefore, the system operator must also take a long term view, and carry out forecasting of demand and system planning, ensuring that investment is made where it is needed. This includes making provision for contingencies and emergencies, for example being able to call on reserves in case of high unanticipated demand, and by making arrangements for black start in case of widespread outages.

Case study: India's July 2012 blackouts

The network management function in India is carried out by Power System Operation Corporation Ltd, a wholly owned subsidiary company of Power Grid Corporation of India Ltd, the state-owned central transmission utility.[4] Grid management in India is carried out on a regional basis, with a regional load despatch centre in each of the five regions, and a national load despatch centre operating at the national level for overall coordination.

At the end of July 2012,[5] more than 700 million people in India were left without power in "the world's worst blackout of recent times". Three of India's five electricity grids failed at lunchtime, with power cuts affecting 20 of India's 28 states, along with the capital, New Delhi. The first grid to fail was the northern grid, which had also collapsed the previous day, quickly followed by the eastern grid, then the north-eastern grid.

The blackout caused widespread chaos, and led to fears that protests and even riots could follow if the country's electricity supply continued to fail to meet growing demand. The power minister blamed the collapse on states taking more than their allotted share of electricity.

An analysis compiled from investigation reports[6] set out the circumstances that led to the outages. A large number of lines were out of service near the interface between the western grid and the northern grid before the outage, resulting in system insecurity. Instructions from the northern grid load despatch centre to shed loads were not followed by states in the northern region.

The blackouts highlighted the need for India to invest in its power infrastructure to meet the needs of its 1.2 billion people. The situation may also have been avoided if the system operator had effective powers to incentivise 'good' behaviour and penalise 'bad' behaviour.

Generally, market participants will have to provide a range of balancing services, some mandatory and others optional. These are set out in industry codes that participants must accede to or in bilateral contracts, depending on the type of service being provided.

The system operator role is generally 'revenue neutral' whether or not it carries out other roles as well. This means that it does not itself bear the prudent costs of managing the system but recovers its costs through mechanisms in its licence, industry codes or bilateral contracts, either directly from the state and/or from users through network usage charges.

Where a market operator is needed, the role may be taken on by the system operator, or by a separate entity. The role of a market operator is to balance the system in real time against contracted positions made by participants. Where participants do not adhere to forecast or contracted positions and therefore use or consume too much or too little power, the market operator must take action to

4 www.powergridindia.com/_layouts/PowerGrid/User/ContentPage.aspx?PId=255&LangID=English.
5 www.theguardian.com/world/2012/jul/31/india-blackout-electricity-power-cuts.
6 www.slideshare.net/giridaran123/blackout-v2.

balance the system. Again, the market operator does not bear the costs of taking such actions, instead charging participants who caused the imbalance.

2.5 Industry participants

Finally, the power industry would not function without the key industry stakeholders which are regulated by the bodies described above where they are not all state-owned. Generators provide the required power, with investment in new stations carried out either by government or by private investors, depending on the structure of the market.

Network owners and distributors own the transmission and distribution lines. The distinction between transmission and distribution can vary and is not always clear cut; the distinction is sometimes made by reference to high voltage and low voltage lines, to regions or to function and purpose. As natural monopolies, these are key assets that are usually kept separate to varying degrees from generation and retail interests in order to avoid market distortion, for example through more favourable terms for companies related to the network owners.

Interconnectors are essentially network lines that carry power across borders, whether internationally (for example, across Europe) or across state lines (for example, across American states). Interconnectors are developed and operated either by independent companies or by network owners.

Finally, retailers purchase power from generators and sell it to end consumers. The power is conveyed across lines owned by networks owners who generally charge generators for use of the lines.

While there are usually exceptions or exemptions for small companies, each of these participants must usually hold a licence to carry out its activities. Regulators monitor compliance with licence obligations, carrying out investigations where necessary and taking enforcement action when breaches are discovered.

Case study: UK privatisation

The UK was at the forefront of liberalising its electricity sector starting from the mid-1980s when the Energy Act 1983 opened the supply market to beyond the 12 area boards existing at that time. In the privatisation programmes that followed in the 1980s and 1990s England and Wales were also pioneers in creating a wholesale market where electricity generators could sell the electricity in near real time to match demand on the supply side (the 'pool' system operated in England and Wales between 1990 and 2001). The privatisation programmes were carried out along jurisdictional lines:

- England and Wales. The restructuring and privatisation programme started in the early 1990s, and saw retail market opening introduced in phases in the period up to 1999.
- Scotland. The vertically integrated energy boards were privatised in 1991 and nuclear interests were privatised in 1996.
- Northern Ireland. The electricity industry was privatised between 1992 and 1993.

Following privatisation, the landscape of the UK electricity market has changed for a variety of reasons, not least to stay in line with changes arising out of EU legislation and in particular the principles of:

- free competition;
- transparency;
- free access to the network; and
- security of supply.

3. Structures

Power markets can be structured in many different ways, with responsibilities split between government, regulator, utilities and retailers. Common power market models are:

- centrally managed (with or without a single buyer);
- pool (another form of single buyer); and
- bilateral contracting (including power exchanges).

Whatever the model, there are common considerations:

- Who controls despatch of generation?
- What platform is used to carry out power trades? Is there a secondary (financial) market in power trades?
- How volatile are power prices? Are pricing mechanisms and signals accurate?
- How easy or complex is it to operate in or to understand the market?

3.1 Centrally managed

In the centrally managed model, the state owns or manages the procurement of all or most of the power in the power market. This still allows for many variations, for example the state could set up a single buyer of power that generators must sell to, and which will in turn supply all consumers. Alternatively, there may be no separate body acting as central buyer at all, with the system operator simply giving despatch instructions to ensure demand is met, while the state recovers costs through other means, for example by taxing consumers. Examples of centrally managed models include China[7] and India.[8]

The system operator has full visibility of all market information (costs, emissions, budgets, technical performance), and is therefore able to calculate marginal costs and despatch generation in the most economically efficient order. This information is not necessarily disseminated further down the power supply chain, as generators only need despatch instructions to ensure they know when and how to operate. Despatch may be done centrally on a state-wide basis, or broken down into regional areas. In centrally managed models, generators do not self despatch, and there is generally no trading platform, either for primary or secondary trades.

There are drawbacks to the model, as the performance of individual generation units may not be optimised, improved or effectively incentivised. Further, in a fully

---

7 www.sgcc.com.cn/ywlm/gsgk-e/zzjg-e/zzjg-e1.shtml.
8 http://indianpowersector.com/electricity-board/psus/.

state owned system, government capital is locked into the various companies and assets, and without outside stimulation provided by private investors, innovation and reduction in costs is likely to develop at a much slower pace. Prices are generally steady, but not necessarily cost-reflective.

3.2 Pool[9]

In a pool model, generators sell power into a notional pool, and retailers buy power out of the pool. Market participants may also reduce or increase generation or demand. In this model, the system operator or another nominated market operator usually acts as a single buyer, even if only temporarily, as it runs the pool into which power is sold and bought. The market operator matches these demands through a system of trades undertaken through bids and offers. The system operator determines price according to supply and demand, and may be responsible for scheduling centrally despatchable generation. An example of a pool model can be seen in Ireland and Northern Ireland.[10]

A pool can be mandatory or optional, with trades carried out through bilateral contracts in parallel. In an optional pool arrangement, some generation will be centrally despatched by the system operator, but generators operating outside the pool will generally self-despatch.

Pools may be seen as more expensive and complicated to implement and run and prices can be more volatile but more reflective of the relationship between supply and demand. However, pools may be more reliable, transparent and allow greater control over despatch of generation.

3.3 Bilateral contracting

In a bilateral contracting model, physical contracts (for the physical delivery of electricity) are entered between generators and retailers or large consumers. Parties may contract directly, or they may use brokers as intermediaries. Retailers and large consumers forecast their anticipated demand and enter into contracts with generators. This model can be seen in Great Britain.[11]

Generators self-despatch in order to meet their contracted demand and notify the market operator. The system operator may require generators to despatch otherwise than in accordance with their contracted positions in order to balance the system. If this happens, generators are generally compensated through market prices set through a balancing mechanism.

Alternatively, if generation or consumption deviates from what it had foreseen and notified, the system operator will be responsible for balancing the system. In such cases, parties could be exposed to imbalance charges, which incentivises them to forecast accurately and to meet those forecasts.

A power exchange may develop in parallel to a bilateral contracting model. In a power exchange, trades are offered on a day-ahead and intra-day basis, and

9 See the chapter on Market liberalisation and organisation.
10 www.uregni.gov.uk/market-overview/.
11 www.ofgem.gov.uk/electricity/wholesale-market/gb-electricity-wholesale-market.

transactions are undertaken by traders without the need for metered consumption or generation. Consequently, there is no exposure to imbalance charges.

3.4 Implications of structures

The structure of a power market will determine and be determined by the legislation that regulates it. A fully state owned and state run market will not necessarily require as many statutes, statutory instruments or quasi statutes as the state will be able to exercise powers set out for it in primary legislation or in contracts entered into with private sector participants such as independent power producers (IPPs). More liberalised models often require more legislation, guidance and oversight in order to incentivise behaviour that will ensure transparency and efficiency of participants.

In addition, new laws are sometimes introduced in order to break up state owned monopolies and set out new roles in transitional markets which are moving toward more liberalised models. These laws are not static, and are constantly developing even in very mature markets in order to cater to new needs – in particular, as we have seen in recent years, in relation to decarbonisation and promotion of clean and renewable energy.

Case study: Transitional markets – Mexican energy market reform

The Mexican energy ministry (SENER) is undertaking a reform of the electricity industry in Mexico, which is the biggest change to the Mexican electricity market in over 40 years. The current energy market reform aims primarily to promote investment, ensure transparency, and improve the competitiveness of the industry and commerce through reduced electricity rates, as well as establishing specific policies (such as clean energy certificates) to encourage the use and development of renewable generation.

Measures taken in the reform include the opening of electricity generation to the private sector, the creation of a wholesale electricity market, legal separation of the incumbent utility companies, market opening to the private sector, the introduction of clean energy obligations and many other major changes.

More specifically, the state owned utility, CFE, will operate under new horizontal and vertical divisions to ensure that it can compete in the different segments of the new market. CFE is to hold independent subsidiaries responsible for generation, transmission, distribution and retail supply to consumers.

Generation: Four different companies will be created to compete against each other and private companies in the new wholesale power market. SENER will determine which CFE power plants are assigned to each of these four companies, to ensure commercial viability and fair competition. Mexico's single nuclear energy power station will be controlled directly by CFE headquarters.

Retail: Residential and commercial retail business are being separated from the industrial business. A further business will be created to serve as supplier of last resort.

Transmission and distribution: CFE will remain the only market participant in these segments. Spin off companies will be formed to administer legacy contracts with independent power producers, the self-supply business, international purchases and sales and fuel procurement.

These changes have been introduced through establishing a new Electricity Law, new Electricity Market Rules (Bases del Mercado – published in the official journal of the Mexican government in September 2015), and a suite of Business Practice Manuals that contain the detail underlying the Market Rules. In addition, SENER has developed innovative model contracts which are entered into by successful auction participants.

On 29 January 2016, SENER announced the opening of the operational short term electricity market, a major step in the implementation of the reforms.[12]

Case study: Transitional markets – UK energy market reform

The UK government has, like many others, sought to incentivise investment in low carbon generation. However, with a mature market and a healthy pipeline of projects looking to construct plant and connect to the grid systems, the government needed an orderly transition from the then existing support mechanism for large renewable projects (under the Renewables Obligation) to the new support mechanism (the Contracts for Difference (CfD)).

There were broadly two routes the government took to assure investors of an orderly transition: (1) dual scheme projects; and (2) early CfDs.

First, for large projects which may build out in phases, the government recognised and expressly provided that it would be possible for different schemes to apply for those parts of the generating station that are subject to the Renewables Obligations regime versus those parts of the station that are subject to payments through the CfD regime. Appropriate metering and apportioning provisions were included in the regulations. While this is more administratively cumbersome, it permits projects to continue on existing construction programmes without undue disruption due to the wider regime changes.

Secondly, the government conducted an early round of CfD competitions through an early-CfD award process whereby certain projects which passed the prequalification requirements were able to enter into bespoke contracts directly with the government while it was putting the CfD regime in place. Accordingly, these projects were able to negotiate specific terms of the contract and raise issues which in turn informed the government's thinking for the final industry-standard CfD terms and allowed all parties to test out the terms and tease out their intentions.

4. Legislation

4.1 Power sector structure specific legislation

The nature of power as a universally required commodity that cannot be stored and which relies on monopoly infrastructure to reach consumers means that it is

12 www.gob.mx/sener/articulos/entra-en-marcha-el-mercado-electrico-de-corto-plazo-en-el-sistema-interconectado-nacional.

regulated through sector specific legislative measures. Sector specific legislation sets out the rules and requirements in relation to developing power infrastructure, participating in the power sector, safety standards, standards for providing services to consumers and sanctions for breaches. This legislation usually grants the powers required by the government and the regulator to oversee and manage the power sector, including (as applicable) powers to enforce legislation and market rules.

These laws may apply at different levels, for example at a federal level, or at regional or state levels. Local laws may also impose requirements for planning, consenting and development of power infrastructure.

Case study: Sanctions in the UK

Sanctions for breach of energy legislation can range in severity from financial penalties and orders to comply with licences, to criminal charges for serious contraventions.

A licence enforcement order is generally a 'warning shot', giving the licensee notice of an infraction and allowing a set period for compliance before more serious sanctions follow. Fines can and have been imposed in the UK and various jurisdictions for licence breaches, and this usually incentivises compliance from market participants. In England and Wales, a licensee can be fined up to 10% of its global turnover. The regulator, Ofgem, can and has imposed serious penalties, including:

- a £26m fine on a retailer in January 2016 for breaching licence conditions that required it to (i) maintain certain standards of service to customers, and (ii) follow its own complaints handling procedure;[13]
- a £28m fine on a generator in March 2015 for failing to achieve its statutory carbon emissions reduction obligations by the required deadline;[14]
- a £10.5m fine on a retailer in May 2013 for misleading sales practices which contravened its licence conditions.[15]

Criminal sanctions apply to a number of activities, including participating in transmission or distribution without a licence (fines),[16] insider dealing and market manipulation in relation to wholesale energy products (fines and/or imprisonment).[17]

13 www.ofgem.gov.uk/publications-and-updates/investigation-npower-s-compliance-standards-conduct-standard-licence-condition-25c-standard-licence-condition-27-provision-final-bills-and-gas-and-electricity-consumer-complaints-handling-standards-regulations-2008.

14 www.ofgem.gov.uk/publications-and-updates/notice-decision-impose-financial-penalty-following-investigation-compliance-drax-article-141-electricity-and-gas-community-energy-saving-programme-order-2009.

15 www.ofgem.gov.uk/publications-and-updates/notice-decision-impose-financial-penalty-sse-under-section-27a3-electricity-act-1989-and-section-30a3-gas-act-1986-following-investigation-compliance-marketing-obligations-0.

16 Electricity Act 1989, section 4: www.legislation.gov.uk/ukpga/1989/29/section/4.

17 Regulations 3, 4 and 11 of The Electricity and Gas (Market Integrity and Transparency) (Criminal Sanctions) Regulations 2015, www.legislation.gov.uk/uksi/2015/979/contents/made.

4.2 Wider legislative landscape

Participants in the power sector will have to comply with a wide variety of legislation, including in relation to:

- protection of the environment;
- planning and consent;
- competition and market dominance;
- market abuse; and
- behaviour and powers of public bodies.

Analysis of the full scope of legislation impacting the power sector is beyond the scope of this chapter. However, participants must be aware of and consider the wider legislative landscape of their jurisdiction.

4.3 Politically driven legislation

Legislation can also be used to further a number of political priorities and agendas. There are common themes around the globe, and those we will examine here relate to ensuring security of power supply and promoting renewable and clean energy.

Such subsidies must be considered in the context of the market they operate in, in particular if there are any competition law considerations. For example, any subsidies in EU Member States must be designed to be compliant with state aid laws that prohibit providing more favourable conditions to domestic companies as compared to companies from other Member States.

(a) Security of supply

Security of supply can be addressed through legislation or sector frameworks by, for example, mandating or promoting participation in capacity mechanisms, ensuring that there is sufficient power available at times of peak demand. This can be addressed both through giving the network additional options on the generation side, but also through demand response, reducing offtake of power where this is offered by large users of power.

Capacity mechanisms are designed to ensure sufficient investment in the overall level of reliable capacity (both generation and demand side) to meet peak demand. This is increasingly becoming an issue around the globe due to the rise of intermittent renewable power, the projected closure of old conventional plant, and the high levels of investment required to refurbish existing plant or to build new reliable plant.

The definition of 'reliable' will depend on the jurisdiction, and this may or may not include renewable energy. For example, wind power is intermittent and therefore considered not reliable for the purposes of a capacity mechanism, but geothermal power is much more constant and therefore considered reliable.

Capacity mechanisms can be structured in many ways, but the essential concept is simple: capacity providers are rewarded for maintaining the capacity to increase generation or reduce demand when called upon at times when the system is under stress and are penalised if they fail to do so.

Case study: EU Commission sector inquiry on capacity mechanisms

In April 2016, the European Commission adopted an interim report and a staff working document on the sector inquiry into capacity mechanisms ('sector inquiry') launched in April 2015. This inquiry considers the existing and proposed capacity markets in 11 EU jurisdictions – Belgium, Croatia, Denmark, France, Germany, Ireland, Italy, Poland, Portugal, Spain and Sweden – from the perspective of EU state aid rules.

The report's three main findings are as follows:

- the Commission recognises that capacity mechanisms may be necessary if electricity markets fail to deliver sufficient electricity supplies. However, they should not be a substitute for market and regulatory reform;
- there is concern that Member States have not carefully analysed the need for capacity mechanisms before introducing them; and
- capacity mechanisms in many Member States seem to benefit specific energy operators because they are only open to specific technologies or to energy operators within the borders of the Member State.

The Commission's views will inform any assessment of the current capacity mechanisms across Europe and their future evolution, even for those member states not investigated. Key issues to be considered include:

- potential EU-wide methodologies for determining generation adequacy and reliability standards;
- the emphasis on maintaining open and broad (and potentially cross-border) participation in capacity markets;
- favouring of competitive price determination and focus on avoiding over-compensation;
- ensuring that capacity penalties do not affect price signals from the wholesale market for cross-border trade; and
- capacity market designs would need to be different where addressing transitional capacity problems compared to those addressing longer term or general adequacy problems.

(b) Promoting renewable and clean energy

There has been an increase over the last decade of legislation used to promote renewable energy, drive efficiency, and reduce greenhouse gases and carbon emissions. This has mainly been achieved through implementation of subsidy schemes for renewable generation, which are set out in legislation. The purpose of these schemes is to attract investment in particular types of technologies in order to bring down costs and make them more widely available in the longer term. There are a number of common subsidy regimes of this type which are seen around the globe, including contracts for difference (CfDs), feed in tariffs (FiTs), green certificates and energy efficiency schemes.

CfDs are bilateral contracts between developers and a third party which are used to hedge power prices. The logic is that CfDs help to give investors more certainty over the level of returns they will receive, thereby encouraging investment in renewable generation or other 'clean' generation, for example, nuclear.

FiTs are payments made to households or small businesses for renewable or low carbon generation, generally for each MW generated. These are used to encourage take up of new technologies, and to encourage the private sector to invest in and develop renewable and low carbon technologies. In general, the high stability of long term FiT arrangements lends the structure well to small and medium scale projects deploying newer untested technologies, and they reduce or fall away once a technology becomes more established and more affordable. FiTs have been used to kick-start deployment in many countries around the world, including in Canada,[18] Germany[19] and the UK,[20] to name just a few.

Green certificates are tradeable certificates that attach to renewable or low carbon generation. Governments which implement green certificate schemes usually require either generators or retailers to submit green certificates to evidence that a certain percentage of the power that they produce or use comes from renewable or clean sources. Countries that have implemented such schemes include Italy,[21] Mexico (although the clean energy certificates operate somewhat differently),[22] and the UK (called Renewable Obligation Certificates).[23] Green certificates can work well, depending on their design, in promoting projects without overhauling the broader market framework. They can also mandate a deep engagement of retailers with the promotion of the renewables programme.

Energy efficiency schemes cover a broad range of measures taken to improve energy use. These can range from innovative financing schemes to introduce or retrofit efficiency measures to buildings (for example, improving the efficiency of air conditioners, heating and lighting), to smart metering and smart billing that allow demand side response, mandatory installation of efficient equipment, and obligatory energy savings for energy companies. A 2013 study[24] reviewed existing energy efficiency measures in 85 countries and drew conclusions on advantages and drawbacks of different policies with the aim of enabling "countries embarking on energy-demand management policies to benefit from the experience of the most advanced countries". The study acknowledged the importance of private contracts and economic incentives, but it recognised that regulations are increasingly used, in particular where the market fails to give appropriate signals.

4.4 Non-legislative authorisations

Authorisation for participation in the power market is generally granted through licences or concessions. Participants must adhere to the terms of their licences or concessions and also to market rules and industry codes. Industry codes set out the technical requirements that participants must meet to operate in the power sector.

---

18 http://fit.powerauthority.on.ca/.
19 http://energytransition.de/2012/10/renewable-energy-act-with-feed-in-tariffs/.
20 www.ofgem.gov.uk/environmental-programmes/feed-tariff-fit-scheme.
21 www.gse.it/en/qualificationandcertificates/GreenCertificates/Pages/default.aspx.
22 http://global-climatescope.org/en/country/mexico/#/details.
23 www.ofgem.gov.uk/environmental-programmes/renewables-obligation-ro.
24 World Energy Council, World Energy Perspective, Energy efficiency policies: what works and what does not, 2013, www.worldenergy.org/publications/2013/world-energy-perspective-energy-efficiency-policies-what-works-and-what-does-not/.

Case study: Energy storage – where does it fit?

Energy storage solutions have many benefits, including added system flexibility, reducing the need for system reinforcement, and the ability to offtake energy during low demand periods, thereby reducing energy prices for users. The potential of energy storage is huge, and it has been cast in the role of 'the next big thing' in the power sector. However, energy storage does not neatly fit into most legislative frameworks for power markets.

As an example, energy storage units are likely to fit into legislative definitions of users/customers and also generators. This could expose them to network charges twice:

- when importing power, and treated as end users, even though the power stored may later be exported back on to the network;
- when exporting power, and treated as generation units, though they may be unable to meet all of the technical requirements set out in industry codes.

These issues, among others, may disadvantage energy storage operators vis-à-vis other market participants. Given the benefits that can be offered, and the rapid development of viable large scale energy storage technology, these are issues that governments will need to address quickly.

5. Regional markets

5.1 The rise of regional markets

The last decade has seen a rise in integration of cross-jurisdictional energy markets. Regional markets have a wide variety of potential benefits, including more efficient use of existing resources (both generating plant and network infrastructure), flexibility to eliminate or reduce the impact of outages, reduced power prices through cross-border trade, and more efficient planning of network development. As expressed by the California system operator:

> *A regional energy market would better use resources, especially renewables, to reduce greenhouse gas emissions and costs. Enabling the ISO's sophisticated market and grid optimization systems to pick the lowest cost energy to serve demand and give preference to renewable resources across a wide geographic region also means grid planners can build a cleaner, more resilient energy generation and delivery network that will create tangible economic benefits.*[25]

5.2 Conflicting priorities

Despite the many potential benefits, regional energy markets also present a challenge in terms of balancing the needs of the state against the needs of the wider region. While not insurmountable, these challenges have delayed the development of regional energy markets around the world. Close cooperation and collaboration is required between governments, regulators and other industry participants. However,

25 www.caiso.com/informed/Pages/RegionalEnergyMarket/BenefitsofaRegionalEnergyMarket.aspx.

governments tend to consider energy security at a national level rather than a region-wide level, and this mind-set will need to shift if regional markets are to develop further.

Several examples are explored below, which highlight the tension between the potential widespread benefits that regional markets offer and the practical and political issues that may hinder their development.

5.3 North America

The American Federal Energy Regulatory Commission (FERC) is an independent entity that regulates interstate transmission of electricity in the United States of America at a wholesale level rather than retail sale to consumers.[26] According to the FERC, "[w]hile major sections of the country operate under more traditional market structures, two-thirds of the nation's electricity load is served in RTO regions".[27]

The FERC's 1996 Orders 888 and 889 (as amended) "suggested the concept of an Independent System Operator [(ISO)] as one way for existing tight power pools to satisfy the requirement of providing non-discriminatory access to transmission".[28] In 1999, Order 2000 introduced the concept of Regional Transmission Organisations (RTOs) whereby the FERC encouraged voluntary formation of RTOs to administer transmission on a regional basis throughout North America. Many RTO regions also extend into parts of Canada.

The Midcontinent ISO (MISO) and the Southwest Power Pool (SPP) are two examples of RTOs. The MISO works to deliver safe, cost-effective power across all or parts of 15 American states and the Canadian province of Manitoba. As an RTO, "MISO assures consumers of unbiased regional grid management and open access to the transmission facilities under MISO's functional supervision".[29] The SPP "oversees the bulk electric grid and wholesale power market in the central United States on behalf of a diverse group of utilities and transmission companies in 14 states" and aims to "ensure the reliable supply of power, adequate transmission infrastructure, and competitive wholesale electricity prices for a 575,000-square-mile region including more than 60,000 miles of high-voltage transmission lines".[30]

According to the ISO/RTO Council (IRC), a North American industry-wide body, nine ISOs/RTOs "serve two-thirds of electricity consumers in the United States and more than 50 percent of Canada's population" and "IRC regional markets consistently outperform those in areas under monopoly control".[31]

5.4 Europe

In Europe, the Agency for the Cooperation of Energy Regulators (ACER) is tasked with "working towards a single energy market to the benefit of all EU consumers".[32]

---

26 www.ferc.gov/about/ferc-does.asp.
27 www.ferc.gov/market-oversight/mkt-electric/overview.asp.
28 www.ferc.gov/industries/electric/indus-act/rto.asp.
29 www.misoenergy.org/ABOUTUS/Pages/AboutUs.aspx.
30 www.spp.org/about-us/.
31 www.isorto.org/about/irchistory.
32 www.acer.europa.eu/en/the_eu_energy_market/Legislation/Pages/default.aspx.

Current EU wide legislation[33] provides common rules for internal markets in electricity and gas, including rules for interconnection between Member States. Europe has been working toward an 'energy community' for over 10 years, with the European Regulators' Group for Electricity and Gas, ACER's predecessor and an adviser to the European Commission, launching the Electricity Regional Initiative (ERI) in spring 2006. The ERI set up seven regional electricity markets across Europe as a first step toward creation of a single electricity market for the whole European Union. The regions were tasked with identifying and implementing practical solutions to overcome barriers to competition and trade within the EU.

5.5 Southeast Asia

Rapid economic and demographic growth across the Association of Southeast Asian Nations (ASEAN) has driven corresponding growth in energy demand in the region. A 2015 report[34] on the energy outlook in Southeast Asia highlighted four key issues that will shape its energy system: power grid interconnection, energy investment, energy access and fossil-fuel subsidies. The report sets out the benefits of a regional market:

> *Greater integration of Southeast Asia's energy networks can deliver strong benefits across the region. Building on existing cross-border cooperation, timely implementation of new plans and projects to connect the region's markets, such as the ASEAN Power Grid and the Trans-ASEAN Gas Pipeline, can help to catalyse development of remote or high capital cost energy resources, facilitate more efficient use of the region's resources and enhance energy security. Region-wide energy market development and integration could help to achieve balanced and equitable economic growth for all Southeast Asian countries.*

While historical development of electricity systems across the region has had a national focus, the perspective is shifting toward integrated power grids and the benefits they can offer. The report identities potential benefits including "increased energy security and power system reliability, economic advantages and opportunities to enhance access and sustainability, especially by integrating higher shares of renewables".

The report goes on to cite a "particular interest in tapping the hydropower potential in Cambodia, Lao PDR and Myanmar for domestic use and cross-border interconnections to supply growing demand in Thailand, Malaysia, Singapore and Vietnam, as a means of facilitating trade and underpinning development of a regional power market". While the report preceded the creation of the ASEAN Economic Community (AEC)[35] in 2015, it anticipated that the AEC would create "further momentum towards enhancing and expanding interconnections throughout the region".

---

33 The suite of EU energy market legislation comprises two Directives and three Regulations, and is known as the Third Package. It aims to "improve the functioning of the internal energy market and resolve structural problems". Full information about the Third Package is available at: https://ec.europa.eu/energy/en/topics/markets-and-consumers/market-legislation.

34 World Energy Outlook Special Report 2015: Southeast Asia Energy Outlook 2015, www.iea.org/publications/freepublications/publication/world-energy-outlook-special-report-2015-southeast-asia-energy-outlook-2015-.html.

35 www.asean.org/asean-economic-community/.

6. Conclusion

Development of legal and regulatory frameworks has gone hand in hand with the development of power projects. While the roles and risk allocations are often similar across many jurisdictions, the evolving nature of the sector and the competing pressures on national governments to deliver their particular aims has meant that this is a lively area of law. While each jurisdiction has over time developed its own systems, industry arrangements and markets, there are common themes that run through the regulation and key principles that are the cornerstones of the energy sector and industry.

All in all, one message is clear: the importance of clear, enforceable and well understood legal frameworks with distinct roles for the various stakeholders cannot be overstated. In this ever evolving climate of commercial and technological developments, the success and societal benefit in particular of private sector power projects is rooted in the solid foundations that the rule of law, well-functioning markets and clear contractual and industry frameworks provide.

Market liberalisation and organisation: an economic perspective

Nick Elms
Frontier Economics

1. Introduction

As we saw in the chapter on Power industries: structures and legal frameworks, the power sector was first established in the late 19th and early 20th century by competing private sector enterprises. However, by the mid-20th century the organisation of the sector had largely changed. A combination of market forces and government intervention had integrated the sector vertically and horizontally, and in many cases the industry had also been nationalised. Several reasons have been given for the change:

- Economies of scale. One or few firms would be more efficient at producing and delivering electricity than multiple firms. Only large firms would have the capital and human resources required to plan and develop the very large coal, nuclear and hydro power stations needed to generate electricity cheaply. In addition, electricity networks were (and still are) considered natural monopolies, making it impractical and inefficient to have network firms compete to serve customers in the same region.[1]
- Benefits of coordination. Common ownership would help to coordinate investment and operations within and between the generation, transmission, distribution and retail segments of the sector.
- Consumer protection. Government ownership was thought to be an appropriate way to protect consumers from the problem of private firms exploiting their position as natural monopolies.
- Strategic industry. Government ownership was considered necessary for an economically strategic industry as well as to help attain social objectives.

During the 1980s a change of thinking came about regarding the possible organisation of the sector, partly as a result of technological change. Smaller and cheaper power plants such as combined cycle gas turbines (CCGTs) were developed. This reduced economies of scale in electricity production, potentially allowing smaller firms to plan, develop and operate power stations. In addition, improvements in information technology allowed for coordination between

1 A natural monopoly may exist where economies of scale are large relative to the size of the market, meaning that a single firm serving the market has lower average costs than multiple firms serving the market. Economies of scale occur when average costs fall with increasing scale.

disaggregated segments of the industry. These developments allowed vertical and horizontal unbundling and competition to be introduced in the sector.

Chile pioneered power sector liberalisation with unbundling and the introduction of competition to the sector in the 1980s. The US Public Utility Regulatory Policies Act (PURPA) 1978 introduced aspects of competition to generation by forcing utilities to buy power from other producers if the cost was below the utility's own avoided cost.[2] The US Energy Policy Act 1992 went further by giving large end users the right to choose their electricity retail supplier and requiring utilities to provide those retail suppliers with access to their networks. Great Britain (GB) unbundled the Central Electricity Generating Board (CEGB) into competing generation firms and a separate transmission company in 1990 and established the electricity pool as the wholesale market for electricity. During the next 10 years Great Britain separated retailing and distribution, introduced competition in retailing and privatised the sector. In 1996, the European Union issued its first Electricity Directive which took steps towards network unbundling and the introduction of competition in retailing. Two further Electricity Directives (2003 and 2009) strengthened unbundling requirements and competition. During the 1990s, other countries such as Norway, New Zealand and Australia also began to unbundle the power sector and introduce competition.

Power market liberalisation has not stopped there. Most developed and many transitional and developing countries have now taken steps towards liberalisation. In addition, liberalisation is an on-going process with countries taking steps forwards or backwards on the path to liberalisation as politics and factors such as the climate change debate influence policy makers.

This chapter considers the economics of market liberalisation. It starts by describing objectives of liberalisation. It then explores where competition can be introduced to the sector. Finally, it considers how to organise competition in wholesale markets and why some regulation or managed competition may be required even in the potentially competitive segments of the industry.

2. Objectives of market liberalisation

It is important to understand the objectives of market liberalisation because they influence both the transition to liberalised markets and the final outcome of liberalisation. A policy maker would typically have a range of different objectives in mind when liberalising its country's electricity market, including:

- Providing financing for the sector. Liberalisation can be used to help finance the power sector in two ways:
    - liberalisation can be used to create the commercial framework for the sector that protects consumers and provides investors with the certainty required to allow privatisation, with the funds from privatisation being used to invest in the sector; and

---

2 Avoided cost is an important term in economics that refers to the savings in not undertaking an activity. In this context it refers to the cost savings a utility makes in response to buying electricity from another firm. Depending upon the timeframe considered, avoided costs could be limited to short run costs (the costs of generating electricity, eg fuel costs, emissions costs and variable operations and maintenance cost) or include short and long run costs (including the costs of generation capacity).

- tariffs can be adjusted as part of liberalisation to a level that allows efficient firms (private or public) to fund their ongoing operations while making an adequate return on investments.
- Reducing the need for government to finance the sector is cited as the main reason for reform in Indonesia, Pakistan, the Philippines, Cameroon, Chile, Peru and Ukraine.[3]
- Raising money for government. Governments may use liberalisation as a means to allow privatisation, with the funds from privatisation being used to supplement the state's budget. The Argentine government used the proceeds from privatisation (including privatisation of the power sector) to reduce its budget deficit in the early 1990s.[4]
- Privatisation (as an ideology). Governments may liberalise as a means to allow privatisation, with privatisation being an objective in itself. The UK's power sector reforms of 1990 are considered by some to have been driven by privatisation as an ideology.[5]
- Increasing efficiency. Liberalisation may be used as a way to reduce costs and improve service quality and, in some countries, to broaden the provision of power. The California reforms, legislated for in 1996, aimed at reducing costs since California had higher than average electricity tariffs.[6]

While difficult to prove conclusively, several studies have shown that power market liberalisation is beneficial. Newbery and Pollitt estimate the net social welfare benefits of GB privatisation and liberalisation at between £6 billion and £12 billion (1995), which is equivalent to a permanent reduction in prices of between 3.2% and 7.5%.[7] Toba estimates that the Philippine power sector reforms and privatisation resulted in a net benefit of US$10.4 billion (1999).[8] Fabrizio et al estimate that investor owned US generation companies in states that restructured their power markets reduced labour and non-fuel operating expenses by 3–5% compared to those in states that did not restructure.[9]

Irrespective of the prime reason for initiating liberalisation, one may expect that the organisation of power markets would over time tend to move towards a form that maximises social welfare, since this could be expected to be the aim of government.[10] Economic efficiency and social welfare are linked. If economic efficiency is achieved,

---

3 World Bank Group, *Private Sector Development in the Electric Power Sector: A Joint OED/OEG/OEU Review of the World Bank Group's Assistance in the 1990s*, p5.

4 M Pollitt, *Electricity Reform in Argentina: Lessons for Developing Countries* (2004).

5 K Gratwick and A Eberhard, "Demise of the standard model for power sector reform and the emergence of hybrid power markets" (2008) 36 *Energy Policy* 3948–3960.

6 J Besant Jones and B Tenenbaum, *The California Power Crisis: Lessons for Developing Countries* (The World Bank Group, April 2001), p18.

7 D Newbery and M Pollitt, *The Restructuring and Privatization of the UK Electricity Supply – Was It Worth It?* (The World Bank Group, April 1997).

8 N Toba, *Welfare Impacts of Electricity Generation Sector Reform in the Philippines* (Asian Development Bank, 2003).

9 K Fabrizio, N Rose and C Wolfram, "Do Markets Reduce Costs? Assessing the Impact of Regulatory Restructuring on U.S. Electric Generation Efficiency" (2007) 97(4) *American Economic Review*.

10 In practice this movement may not happen for many different reasons including opposition from vested interests, political considerations, etc.

this means social welfare has been maximised across time. The remainder of this chapter therefore focuses on market liberalisation from the perspective of economic efficiency.

The key issue is how to organise the power market such that the actors in the market (producers and consumers) have incentives to behave in a way that maximises economic efficiency. To understand how economic efficiency can be achieved it is useful to separate the concept of economic efficiency into two elements:

- *Allocative efficiency.* Allocative efficiency means there is an optimal distribution of goods or services. In the power sector, this means that prices are set equal to marginal cost[11] such that the power stations with the lowest production costs produce electricity, they produce the amount of electricity consumers are willing to pay for and the electricity produced is consumed by those consumers willing to pay for it.
- *Productive efficiency.* Productive efficiency means that no more outputs can be achieved from the given set of inputs over time. This means that the best investment decisions are made (for example, in power stations and distribution and transmission networks) and that, in the long run, firms are operating at or close to the lowest point on their average total cost curve.

Policy makers tend not to describe objectives for the power sector in terms of economic efficiency. Rather, they use terms like consumer protection, security of supply and environmental sustainability.[12] However, these terms are all consistent with economic efficiency. Consumer protection means having access to power at efficient prices both today and in the future. To the extent that CO^2 emissions or other emissions cause costs, it is economically efficient to avoid those emissions so long as the marginal cost of doing so is less than the marginal cost imposed (both locally and globally) by an incremental emission. If consumers value security of supply, it is economically efficient to improve security so long as the marginal benefit of the improvement exceeds the marginal cost.

Policy makers may also consider fairness and other social objectives. These are subjective measures which can be considered within the framework of economic efficiency if one assumes different value weights for the social welfare of different consumers, for example, some policy makers might argue for higher weights to be placed on the social welfare of low income consumers.

3. Organisation of the sector – when to regulate

As described in the chapter on Power industries: structures and legal frameworks, the power sector is typically described as comprising four segments: generation,

11 Marginal cost is an important economic concept that refers to the change in the total cost of producing one more unit of a good or service. The related terms 'short run marginal cost' (where the capital stock is assumed to be fixed) and 'long run marginal cost' (where all costs may vary) are also important terms. In the case of power generation, short run marginal cost includes the costs of items such as fuel, emissions and variable operations and maintenance. Long run marginal cost includes those costs and the costs of building the power station and fixed operations and maintenance.

12 Ofgem (the GB regulator for electricity and gas) has summarised its principal objective as being to protect the interests of consumers, present and future, including their interests in the reduction of greenhouse gases and in security of supply. Similarly, the European Commission's energy policy objectives are sustainability (in an environmental sense), affordability and security of supply.

transmission, distribution and retail supply. One can observe that some of these segments are usually regulated while other segments are open to competition. It is worth understanding why this is the case.

Competition and the workings of a free market are generally presumed to be good things in terms of promoting economic efficiency. Under perfect competition,[13] prices reflect the costs of production, costs are at an efficient level and the profit incentive encourages actors[14] to reduce costs further, provide innovative products, improve quality and undertake the appropriate level of investment.

Regulation is costly and the costs include the direct costs of the regulator and the indirect costs of regulation. The information requirements of the regulator are intensive, information about regulated firms is costly to gather and regulations may have unintended consequences due to the incentives they impose on the regulated firms.

This implies that regulation should only be imposed where there are identifiable market failures and where the costs of regulation are smaller than the benefits of regulation in reducing the economic detriment arising from the market failures. This thinking is reflected in the requirements in many countries to undertake an impact assessment before imposing new regulations.[15]

There are four main types of market failure which may justify regulation:

- Monopoly power. A monopoly is the sole provider of a good or service in a market. It maximises profit typically by setting prices above the marginal cost of production and producing less than it would under perfect competition. Unlike a firm in a market with perfect competition, a monopoly can raise price knowing that no other firm can enter the market and gain market share. Regulators may be concerned that the pricing and production decisions of a monopoly cause a reduction in social welfare compared to the perfectly competitive outcome and a redistribution of welfare from consumers to producers (see Figure 1).
- Externalities. An externality occurs if an entity, when producing or consuming a product, causes additional costs or benefits to be incurred by others. Two examples relevant for the power sector are as follows:
  - pollution – if a power station produces environmental pollution (eg, NOx, SOx or CO^2 discharged into the atmosphere) the vast bulk of any damage caused by the pollution would fall on others; and

---

13 Perfect competition is another important economic concept. Characteristics of a market with perfect competition include an infinite number of consumers and producers willing to transact at any price, producers and consumers are free to enter or leave the market, producers and consumers have perfect information about prices and the quality of the good or service, no transaction costs in buying and selling the good or service, firms seek to maximise profits etc.

14 An actor refers to a market participant. Actors in the power sector include fuel supply companies, generation companies, transmission companies, distribution companies, retail supply companies, end consumers, etc.

15 For example, the Reagan administration introduced legislation requiring US federal agencies to produce a regulatory impact assessment (RIA) for all proposed major regulations. In GB, the gas and power sector regulator Ofgem states: "Ofgem regulates only where necessary to protect consumers' interests and we carefully consider whether any regulatory requirement we are proposing to introduce is proportionate and necessary to protect consumers … [and] are committed to setting out the costs and benefits, as well as the social and environmental impacts of all major decisions, through Impact Assessments." Similarly, the European Commission states: "[b]efore [it] proposes new initiatives it assesses the potential economic, social and environmental consequences that they may have."

- network effects – if a generation firm's power station suddenly stopped producing electricity, causing the frequency of the power system to fall, this would affect all users of the network including users that are not customers of the generation company.[16]
- Public goods. A public good is one where its consumption does not deprive others of consuming the good and no one can be excluded from consuming the good. The result is that users will tend to underpay for the good and there may be difficulty in incentivising investment. This is closely related to the issue of externalities. An example of a public good relevant to the power sector is the environment – whereby a power station 'consumes' the environment if it discharges pollutants into the air or water.
- Information asymmetries. Information asymmetry could manifest itself as adverse selection (eg, a vertically integrated utility developing a new power station based on private information about where its transmission arm plans to expand transmission capacity) or moral hazard (eg, the transmission arm of a vertically integrated utility takes a line out for maintenance, forcing a power station of a competing entity offline at an inconvenient time).

Social issues such as concerns about fuel poverty or a universal service obligation might also prompt regulation.

Factors that contribute to monopoly power include economies of scale, which if sufficiently large could mean that it is more efficient for one firm to serve a market than for multiple firms to do so, a high share of the market and barriers to expansion or entry by competitors.

Electricity transmission and distribution networks have large fixed and sunk costs related to the establishment of the network and relatively low marginal costs of connecting and serving an additional customer. When the network is not congested, the network related cost of serving additional consumption from existing customers is related to energy losses in the network. Large fixed and sunk costs combined with low marginal costs mean that average total costs fall over a wide range of possible output of the network, as shown by Figure 2. This means that it is not economically efficient to duplicate the network in a given region, that is, the network is a natural monopoly. In practical terms, this means that it is cheaper for a single distribution company to be used to deliver electricity to all households on a street than to have competing distribution companies.

Since an existing network has lower average total costs than a potential competitor, an unregulated network operator could price slightly under the cost of entry (ie, the average total cost of the entrant) or at the monopoly level, if this were lower than the cost of entry, and thereby deter entry. Pricing at either the cost of

16 The system operator would normally organise for some generation capacity or demand that can be curtailed voluntarily to be held in reserve to be activated quickly to replace the lost generation. Therefore, any reduction in system frequency would be transient although the system may be vulnerable to a second plant failure until the reserve can be replaced.

17 In practice the price elasticity of demand for network services is likely to be low, which means the social welfare loss due to pricing above the efficient level would be low. However, regulators are likely to be concerned about the transfer of social welfare from consumers to producers.

Figure 1: The monopoly's incentive to raise price and reduce output would reduce social welfare

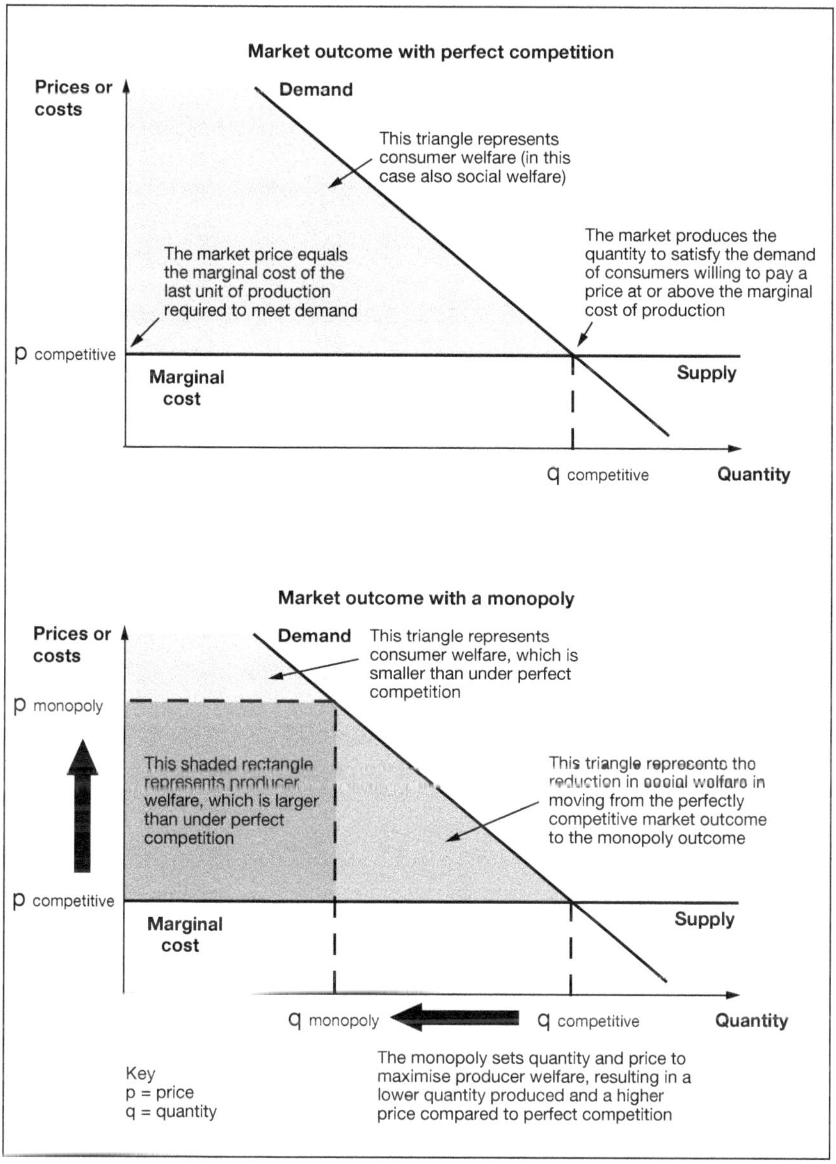

entry or the monopoly level reduces social welfare compared to the perfectly competitive market outcome since prices would be above the efficient level and the quantity of network services consumed below the efficient level.[17]

Transmission and distribution networks are therefore typically regulated with respect to the prices they charge (or revenues they are allowed to earn), quality and

Figure 2: A network is a natural monopoly because its average total costs fall over a wide range of possible output

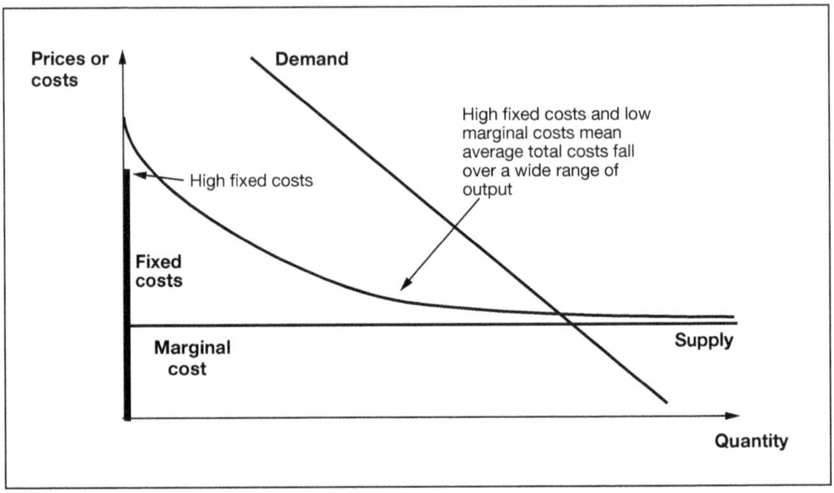

Source: Frontier Economics

the terms and conditions of access. The chapter on Regulating monopoly infrastructure: an economic perspective takes a more in-depth look at the historic approach to such regulation, and more recent trends.

Power generation and retail supply do not typically exhibit characteristics of a natural monopoly and are therefore potentially competitive. General competition law would be relied upon to protect consumers and new entrants in the absence of any regulation in generation and retail supply. However, if competition law were considered inadequate, some form of regulation of these segments may be called for.

In deciding whether and how to regulate the generation and retail segments, policy makers would look for characteristics that did not allow competition to function adequately, and to focus regulation on addressing those characteristics or their effects. For example, some barriers to entry that may be perceived to exist include:

- *Sunk costs*. A new entrant generation company or new entrant retail supply company must expect to recover its sunk costs (for example, the capital cost of developing a power station or the capital cost of developing a customer management and billing system) if they enter the generation or retail supply segment. This means the generation company must expect power prices to be above its marginal costs of production at least some of the time and the retail supply company must expect retail margins to exceed its marginal costs of retail supply. Depending on the extent of competition in the market, the short run operating profits required to induce entry may not be available or may not be perceived to be available, for example due to Bertrand competition[18] or the threat of aggressive competition by incumbents.

- *Customer inertia.* In electricity retail supply the incumbent may have a large customer base. If switching rates are relatively low, it may take many years before an entrant is able to attract sufficient customers to attain a minimum efficient scale. The regulator could help overcome this issue by providing customers with information about alternative sources of retail supply and by imposing behavioural constraints on the incumbent until the entrant achieves a certain market share.
- *Price control on the incumbent in potentially competitive activities.* Regulators may impose a price control on the incumbent at the same time as allowing entry. If the price control is too tight, this could deter entry as it limits the available profit. This is an example of the trade-off between static and dynamic issues: lower prices in the short term v establishment of a competitive market and the relaxation of regulation in the long run.
- *Raising rivals' costs.* A vertically integrated incumbent may have the incentive and ability to raise rivals' costs in the generation and retail supply markets by raising network access charges for rivals while maintaining low prices for its own generation and retail arms. This could be solved by regulating network access terms and conditions (although this is potentially open to abuse through cross-subsidy and discrimination) or requiring unbundling of the incumbent's network businesses from generation and retail supply.

In summary, the need for regulation and the potential for competition depend on the structure of each segment of the power sector. While transmission and distribution networks will require ongoing regulation, regulation of generation and retail supply might be narrower in scope or might only be required while competition is in the process of forming as part of the transition to a liberalised market. For example:

- In GB, Ofgem regulates the allowed revenues of transmission and distribution networks. While it doesn't regulate the revenues of generators and retail suppliers it uses a licensing regime to place certain obligations on them with an aim of increasing effective competition.
- The EU Electricity Directive[19] requires that national regulatory authorities or other equivalent national bodies regulate the sector within Europe. It also requires unbundling of networks from generation and retail supply, non-discriminatory access to the networks based on published tariffs, and the freedom for end users to choose their retail supplier. The EC Cross-Border Electricity Regulation[20] aims to improve coordination of the power market across Europe. It provides for the development of legally binding network codes that would apply throughout the EU and be aimed at non-

18 Bertrand competition refers to a market model whereby firms compete on price. With this model consumers switch all of their consumption to the firm with the lowest price, and the market outcome is that prices equal marginal cost. Supply constraints, imperfect information and other factors may mean that real world market outcomes differ from this model of competition.

19 Directive 2009/72/EC of the European Parliament and of the Council of 13 July 2009.

20 Regulation (EC) No 714/2009 of the European Parliament and of the Council of 13 July 2009.

discrimination, effective competition and the efficient functioning of the electricity market across Europe. It also requires that network charges are cost reflective.

4. Wholesale power market

The electricity sector has certain physical characteristics that may lead regulators, competition agencies and policy makers to apply a form of managed competition even when the market structure in the potentially competitive segments would imply a competitive market in other industries. These characteristics are:

- *Supply and demand must be balanced in real time.* Electricity cannot be stored economically in large quantities (with the exception of energy stored in the form of water in hydro reservoirs to use for future electricity generation). This means that a system operator must control the system supply and demand balance continuously and must establish rules in the form of a grid code[21] and other codes such as a market code[22] as to how this is achieved.
- *Inelastic demand.* In the short term consumers tend not to change significantly their consumption in response to changes in electricity prices. This is due to several factors including a lack of real time information about prices, a lack of substitutes for electricity and the high value that consumers place on the consumption of electricity. Consequently, power markets may be more susceptible to the exercise of market power for a given ownership concentration than markets for other goods or services.[23]
- *Lack of real time information about price.* Since supply and demand must be continuously balanced, the value of electricity varies continuously. Prices in wholesale electricity markets are typically set for quarter-hour, half-hour or one-hour settlement periods, with real time prices normally established after the electricity has actually been delivered.[24] This means it is difficult for generators and consumers to respond to real time price information. The system operator cannot rely on price alone to incentivise generators to respond in order to balance the system. Since it is difficult for most consumers to voluntarily reduce consumption in response to short term high prices, an administratively set price, called the Value of Lost Load (VoLL), is often used to establish the market price when consumers are involuntarily disconnected. The rationale is that if consumers had real time price

21 A grid code sets out the technical rules for connecting to and using the transmission network, covering the development, maintenance and operation of the network. Both the transmission operator and transmission users would need to comply with the grid code.

22 Depending on the legal framework, the rules governing the operation of the electricity market may be set out in a market code, addressing how electricity is traded in the wholesale market and possibly also the retail market.

23 Other issues such as the length of time and perceived effort to switch between retail suppliers may affect the efficient functioning of the retail market.

24 Markets for trading contracts for delivery on the following day are sometimes referred to as spot markets. However, these markets are forward markets whose prices reflect expectations as to what will happen when power is delivered in real time. While the price signals from forward markets provide some information as to likely demand and supply in real time, changes to demand and generation availability between when the forward market is run and real time delivery may mean that the forward market prices do not reflect actual market demand and supply.

information and the ability to control consumption, they would prefer not to consume electricity than to pay a price above the administered price.

Other efforts to address this lack of information include 'smart metering', which is being rolled-out in various jurisdictions. The EU requires that Member States implement smart metering by 2020 so long as to do so would bring positive net benefits for the Member State. As of 2014, Austria, Denmark, Estonia, Finland, France, Greece, Ireland, Italy, Luxemburg, Malta, the Netherlands, Poland, Romania, Spain, Sweden, and the UK had committed to the widespread roll-out of smart meters by 2020.[25]

There have been many studies of demand side response and smart metering. A study undertaken for the recently disbanded Department of Energy and Climate Change (DECC) in the UK concluded that:[26]

- *Consumers do shift electricity demand in response to economic incentives (such as the application of higher prices during peak demand periods) even if these incentives are accompanied by only basic information on the prices being applied, however the size of the shift can vary significantly. Basic information may include provision of fridge magnets displaying peak hours and/or prices, information sheets, and basic bill inserts.*
- *Interventions to automate responses deliver the greatest and most sustained household shifts in demand where consumers have certain flexible loads, such as air conditioners or electric heating.*
- *After automation, a combination of economic incentives and enhanced information generally delivers the greatest demand response. Enhanced information includes both bespoke information (for example enhanced billing which breaks consumption down into different tariff periods), and technologies or accessories that provide real-time interactive information (such as in-home displays) ...*

- *Network effects*. It is impossible to identify the ownership of electricity as it flows around the network and the actions of a network user affect all network users, not just those users with which the user has a contract. This means that arrangements must be put in place to settle differences between the electricity injected onto the network by generators and the power taken off the network by their customers.

All of these characteristics must be taken into account when designing power market arrangements. In the remainder of this section, we discuss several aspects of the organisation of wholesale power markets: wholesale trading, generation investment decision making, internalising the cost of externalities such as pollution, and market ownership structure.

4.1 Wholesale trading

If the electricity sector is organised as a single vertically integrated company, arrangements do not need to be put in place to trade electricity, aside from the sale

25 See http://ses.jrc.ec.europa.eu/smart-metering-deployment-european-union.
26 DECC, *Demand Side Response in the domestic sector – a literature review of major trials* (August 2012).

to consumers. However, when third party access to the network is provided, trading arrangements must be put in place. The electricity produced by a generator cannot be tracked as it makes its way around the network to consumers. Furthermore, the consumption of electricity by a consumer is not directly linked to the production of electricity by the generator from which it has contracted to buy the electricity (or the generator from which the consumer's retail supplier has contracted to buy electricity).

Trading arrangements must be put in place to keep track of what electricity has been injected into the system by whom, what electricity has been taken off the system by whom and who should pay or receive what for any imbalance between what they have contracted to inject or take off and what they actually inject into or take off the system.

Two main forms of trading arrangements have been applied in liberalised power markets around the world: the power pool and the bilateral contracts model. We describe both below, presenting the two models as very distinct choices. However, some features of the models are similar, for example, the need to have a centrally operated cash out mechanism and for the system operator to have ultimate control over system dispatch. In addition, different variants of the models blur the distinction between the two.

(a) *Power pool*

In a power pool generators inform some central agency such as the system operator (SO) or market operator (MO)[27] of their availability to produce electricity and their willingness to generate, expressed as a price (eg, \$/MWh). Retail suppliers may provide information about the quantity of consumption and the price at which their customers are willing to consume electricity. Alternatively, the SO or MO may clear the market (ie, match supply and demand to determine the price) based on forecast demand or clear the market ex-post using actual demand information.

The SO or MO selects the cheapest way to meet demand from the generation offers available to it, consistent with maintaining a balance of supply and demand. Price is set equal to the offer price of the marginal generator (or dispatchable demand offer) required to equate supply and demand.[28]

There are many variations around the basic pool model. However, the important feature of a pool is that a central agency decides on the cheapest way to meet demand from the available generation and sets the market price. The SO would typically instruct power plants as to their output levels.[29] Although it would try to minimise the differences between the actual dispatch and the market clearing

---

27 The roles of system operator and market operator are interrelated and are often undertaken by the same entity. A system operator is responsible for the physical operation of the transmission system, ensuring a continuous balance of supply and demand and managing power flows. A market operator is responsible for the commercial operation of the market, including receiving bids and offers from market participants, setting market prices and determining how much money should be paid to and paid by parties.

28 The marginal generator is the generator with the lowest short run marginal cost of production (expressed as the generator's offer price) able to respond to a small increase in demand.

29 It is possible to have a pool whereby the generator is responsible for taking some dispatch decisions such as when to start a power plant.

dispatch, some differences are inevitable. Generators would normally be compensated for such differences to provide them with an incentive to follow the SO's instructions.

In a gross pool, all power plants are paid the market clearing price for their output and all retail suppliers pay the market clearing price for their consumption. In a net pool, the dispatch would typically be the same as for a gross pool. However, the MO would take account of notified contract quantities during settlement. Generators are paid the market clearing price for their output less their net contracted sales. Retail suppliers pay the market clearing price for their consumption less their net contracted purchases.

With a pool, the market clearing price is intended to be set equal to the short run marginal cost of electricity at any point in time. All generators that should be running in order to meet demand at least cost are incentivised to run, given the clearing price. All generators that should not be running to meet demand at least cost are incentivised not to run, given the clearing price. A pool is therefore intended to be consistent with allocative efficiency. A concern expressed about pools is that the price setting mechanism may be non-transparent and the price may not necessarily reflect the true marginal cost of electricity.

Many jurisdictions have organised their wholesale power markets in the form of a power pool, including Greece, Ireland[30] and Spain in Europe, PJM, New York, New England and Texas in the US, Australia, New Zealand and Singapore. In some cases the power pool determines a single power price for each settlement period that applies to a region or country and in other cases the pool determines a price for each settlement period for each individual node on the transmission network.

(b) *Bilateral contracts model*

Under a bilateral contracts model, generators enter into contracts for the delivery of power with retail suppliers, other generators and traders such as commodities trading companies and banks. The delivery volumes and timing under these contracts are notified to a market operator or settlement administrator. Generators decide what electricity they want to produce and when and notify these plans to the SO. The SO will ensure that supply and demand balances and manage flows on the transmission network by requesting (or in some cases mandating) changes to generators' production plans. These changes would normally be paid for through ancillary services contracts or through specially designed market mechanisms such as the balancing mechanism under the GB trading arrangements, BETTA.[31]

The settlement administrator compares contracted sales and purchases of power that have been notified to it with the amount of electricity actually delivered onto and taken off the network. It does this comparison for each balancing group, which may comprise a single company or multiple companies.[32] The difference between the contracted and physical quantities of electricity delivered onto the network and

30 At the time of writing, Ireland was in the process of redesigning its power market, with the new market due to be implemented in late 2017.

31 British Electricity Trading and Transmission Arrangements.

32 In Britain, the comparison is done separately for generation and for retail supply.

taken off the network in a given settlement period for the balancing group is called an imbalance. Depending on whether the imbalance volume is an over-delivery or an under-delivery, the producer, retail supplier or trader will need to be paid or make a payment. The imbalance volume is said to be 'cashed out' at an imbalance price. Typically (but not always) the imbalance price for surplus power is below the market price and the imbalance price for a shortage of power is above the market price. In this way, incentives are placed on parties to closely manage their imbalances.

A key feature of the bilateral contracts model is that generators take their own decisions about what to produce. In a perfect market the outcome of the bilateral contracts model would be the same as a pool. If any expensive power station were running while a cheaper power station were idle, the expensive power station would theoretically choose to meet any obligation to supply by purchasing power from the cheaper power station in preference to generating to meet its obligation.

The market price that results from the trading of power contracts under this model can be expected to broadly reflect the marginal cost of electricity, that is, this model may also be consistent with productive efficiency.[33] Although each generator receives the price agreed for each of its sale transactions and each retail supplier pays the price agreed for each of its purchase transactions (ie, this is what is often referred to as a 'pay as bid' pricing mechanism) the price of transactions will tend to cluster closely around the view of the 'market' price at the time of the transactions.[34]

A concern with the bilateral contracts model is that some productive efficiency may be lost if generators do not make all of the trades required to arrive at the cost minimising dispatch, that is, if a power station is running when a cheaper power station is idle. The power pool does away with the need for these transactions to take place bilaterally by centrally coordinating the dispatch decision.

Most countries in Europe have organised their wholesale power markets as the bilateral contracts model, including Germany, France, Great Britain, Belgium, and the Netherlands.

4.2 Investment decision making

Investors will make decisions about whether or not to build a new power station based on a comparison of their expectations of the future operating profit of the power plant and the fixed costs of the power plant, including an adequate return on investment.

The level of demand varies from hour to hour within a day, from day to day and from season to season. Some power plants will be utilised almost continuously throughout the year when they are not out of operation for maintenance. Other power plants will be used rarely, for example to meet the high demand during cold winter evenings or hot summer afternoons.

Different types of power stations have different cost structures. Nuclear plants have very high fixed costs but very low short run marginal costs of production. At the other extreme, open cycle gas turbines (OCGTs, also known as combustion

---

33 Here we do not address issues such as the exercise of market power which could mean that under a bilateral contracts model or a pool model prices do not reflect marginal costs.

34 Under this model, in many countries contracts for the delivery of power may also be bought and sold through auctions whereby all transactions are undertaken at the market clearing price.

turbines or CTs) have low fixed costs but high short run marginal costs of production.

The choice as to which type of power plant is most appropriate (cheapest or most profitable) to build to meet demand depends on the expected utilisation of the power plant and on the cost structure of the power plant. This is illustrated by the graph at the top of Figure 3. Here we plot the total annuitised cost of different types of power station with a notional capacity of 1 MW that operate at full output for a different number of hours in a year, creating an efficient frontier for electricity production by running hours. In this hypothetical example, nuclear plants are the cheapest option if operating for most of the year, coal plants are cheapest if operating between about a third and three-quarters of the time during the year, and CCGT and OCGT plants are cheapest if operating less frequently. For a few hours of each year it is cheapest to allow prices to rise to VoLL and to cut off some consumers involuntarily.

Figure 3: Incentives to build capacity

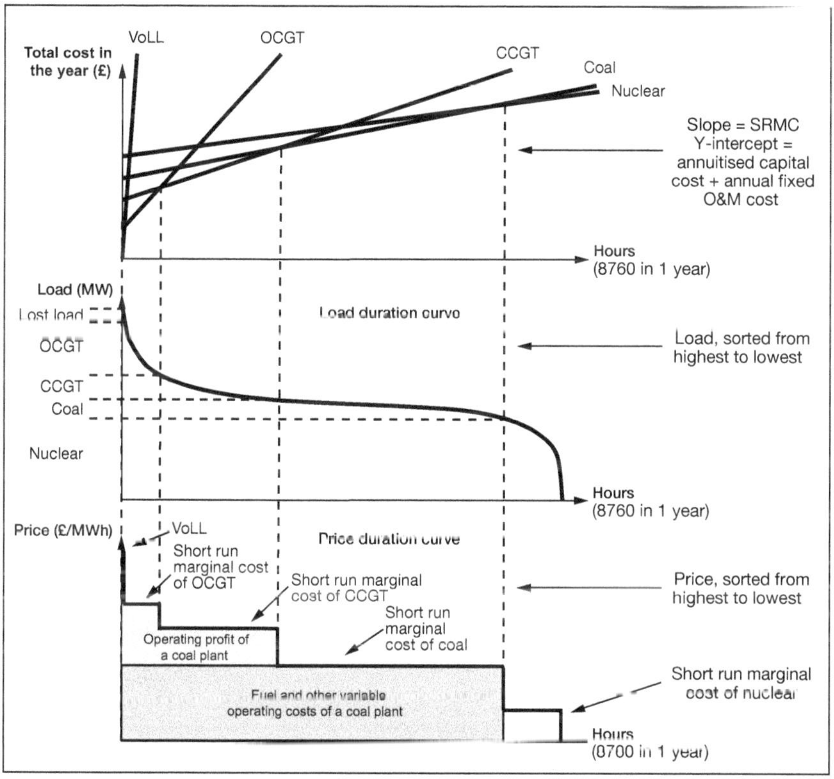

How much capacity of each type of power plant should be built in this perfect market depends on how many hours of each year any given level of demand is exceeded. By ranking the level of demand from highest to lowest and plotting the result we create a load duration curve (LDC), shown in the middle graph of Figure 3. Mapping the corner points from the efficient frontier of electricity production (ie, the top graph of Figure 3) onto the LDC tells us how much capacity of each type of plant to build.

(a) ***Energy only wholesale market***

In the lower graph of Figure 3, we show the market prices resulting from this plant mix. The height of each flat step of the price duration curve (PDC) is equal to the slope of the line for the corresponding power station in the upper graph of Figure 3. When a power station is running, the PDC shows that it always at least recovers its short run marginal costs of production. Only when a power station with a higher short run marginal cost of production is running will the plant make a contribution towards its fixed operating and capital costs.[35]

In this perfect market, each type of power station will precisely recover its variable costs and fixed costs through the wholesale electricity price, that is, the energy price. However, this requires that prices rise to VoLL for a few hours each year or perhaps every few years. Investors in all power plants (not just investors in OCGTs) rely on revenues during periods when prices are set to VoLL to recover their fixed costs.

Outcomes in this perfect market are allocatively and productively efficient. The role of the regulator or policy maker is simply to decide on the appropriate level for VoLL. Market forces (the profit motive) incentivise the perfect market outcome.

In the perfect power market, the higher the VoLL the fewer the number of hours during which some customers will be cut off to balance supply and demand. Conversely, the lower the VoLL the greater the number of hours when customers will be cut off. This illustrates an important point about wholesale power markets. If prices are artificially capped at too low a level (eg, by policy makers nervous about high prices even during short periods) investors may not be incentivised to build sufficient generation capacity.

Energy only wholesale electricity markets such as that described above are used in many countries around the world, including in Germany, the Netherlands and the NEM of Australia. At the time of writing France was in the process of introducing a capacity mechanism to become effective during the winter of 2016/17, and in 2014 both GB and Belgium introduced capacity mechanisms.[36]

(b) ***Capacity mechanism***

In the real world, investors need to take a view as to market outcomes over many

---

35 Figure 3 illustrates a conceptual approach to power sector planning. In practice this concept would need to be applied simultaneously over many years into the future, taking account of intermittent and energy constrained power plants such as wind, solar and hydro powered generation, demand uncertainty, fuel price uncertainty, interconnector flows to and from adjacent power systems and the pre-existing mix of power plants.

36 GB introduced what is known as a 'market wide' capacity mechanism and Belgium introduced a targeted capacity mechanism known as a 'strategic reserve'. In 2012 Germany introduced a mechanism aimed at meeting generation capacity shortfalls in specific grid locations, which it calls a 'winter reserve'. Since the winter reserve is for specific locations, it is not incorrect to say that Germany has an energy only wholesale market.

years in light of uncertain costs (eg, fuel prices), uncertain plans of other investors, uncertain demand and uncertainty about the future regulatory and political environment. This uncertainty, if systematic, may raise the threshold for the return on capital that investors expect to make before they commit to developing a new power plant.

These market imperfections mean that policy makers may be unconvinced that the type of energy only market described above will achieve a secure power system. In addition, policy makers may be reluctant to allow prices to rise to VoLL during periods of shortage or they may simply be reluctant to allow for a system which relies on some periods of shortage in order to incentivise investment.

For these reasons policy makers sometimes introduce a capacity mechanism to provide an incentive for investors to develop power stations beyond those provided by the energy market alone. The basic feature of a capacity mechanism is that a generator is paid for a power station to be available even if the power station never runs.

One approach to a capacity mechanism would be for a central planner (eg, the SO) to decide upon the level of capacity necessary to achieve a secure power system.[37] The SO could then run a tender for that capacity, with both existing and planned power stations able to participate (the tender would need to be run several years in advance of delivery to allow time for the planned power stations to be built). If participants anticipated that the future system would comprise the efficient plant mix described above and the SO procured sufficient capacity such that the price would never rise above the short run marginal cost of an OCGT, the result of the tender in the perfect market would be that the annual capacity price equalled the annuitised fixed cost of an OCGT. All participants selected in the tender would receive the capacity price so long as their plants were available when required.

Arguably, such a mechanism may not be consistent with productive efficiency since it would have been cheaper to cut off some load during very high demand periods and avoid the cost of building and operating some OCGT plants.

Different types of capacity mechanisms have been included in wholesale markets around the world, including in Finland, Ireland, Spain, Sweden, New England, New York, PJM, Belgium, GB and, from 2016/17, France.

4.3 Internalising the cost of externalities

Policy makers may introduce mechanisms which force generators to incur the cost of their negative externalities. This increases economic efficiency since generators would now include those externalities in their decision making and pricing.

As an example, the CO^2 emitted by a power station is a negative externality if the cost of the contribution of the emissions to the damage from global warming (or the marginal CO^2 abatement cost) is not included in the running costs of the power station. Policy makers have in some countries attempted to internalise this cost by

37 A policy maker may need to decide on the definition of a secure power system, for example in terms of the expected number of hours during which a consumer is involuntarily cut off each year due to a shortage of generation.

placing a price on each tonne of CO^2 (or equivalent) emissions through a tax or a cap and trade mechanism such as the European Union Emissions Trading Scheme (EU ETS).

Consider again the graph at the top of Figure 3. Placing a cost on the amount of CO^2 emitted increases the running cost of a power station. The short run marginal cost of production from lignite and hard coal fired power stations, with high CO^2 emissions per MWh of electricity produced, will increase by more than the short run marginal cost of production from CCGT power stations, with lower CO^2 emissions rates. The short run marginal costs of nuclear plants would be unaffected since they do not emit CO^2 when generating.

By raising the short run marginal cost of production of a power station, its slope in the graph at the top of Figure 3 becomes steeper. If the short run marginal cost of hard coal increases by more than that of CCGT and nuclear, less hard coal capacity and more nuclear and CCGT capacity would be built in the ideal plant mix. The production of electricity from hard coal plants would fall while the production from nuclear and CCGT plants would increase, thereby reducing CO^2 emissions.

4.4 Market structure

A concern about power market liberalisation is that generation companies may be able to capture excess profit by exerting market power. As described previously, the lack of demand side response to a change in price combined with the inability to store electricity means that the power market may be more susceptible to market power than markets for other goods or services.

A generator could exert market power by raising price or withdrawing capacity. In Figure 4 we show the effect on price and operating profit of withdrawing generation capacity. The top graph of the figure shows the competitive market outcome. The generator that owns all of the hard coal plants makes operating profit 1.

By withdrawing a small amount of coal fired capacity, as shown in the middle graph, the price jumps and the generator's operating profit increases. Although not shown on the graph, the operating profits of the nuclear, lignite and CCGT operators also increase. In deciding whether or not to withhold capacity, the coal fired generator would compare operating profit 2 and operating profit 1. It is trading-off the loss of revenue from withdrawing capacity against the increase of revenue for all of its in merit plants due to the price increase following withdrawal. Since the operating profit from withdrawal is greater, the generator has an incentive to withhold capacity.

The larger the portfolio owned (or contracted) by a single player, the greater that player's incentive to withdraw capacity.[38] The bottom graph of Figure 4 shows that a generator's operating profit would increase significantly if it owned both the coal and lignite plants, even though it withdrew the same amount of coal fired capacity from the system.

Some ability to raise price above the short run marginal cost of production is often tolerated by some regulators and policy makers so long as entry or expansion

38 Here we do not consider collusion.

Figure 4: Incentives to withdraw generation capacity

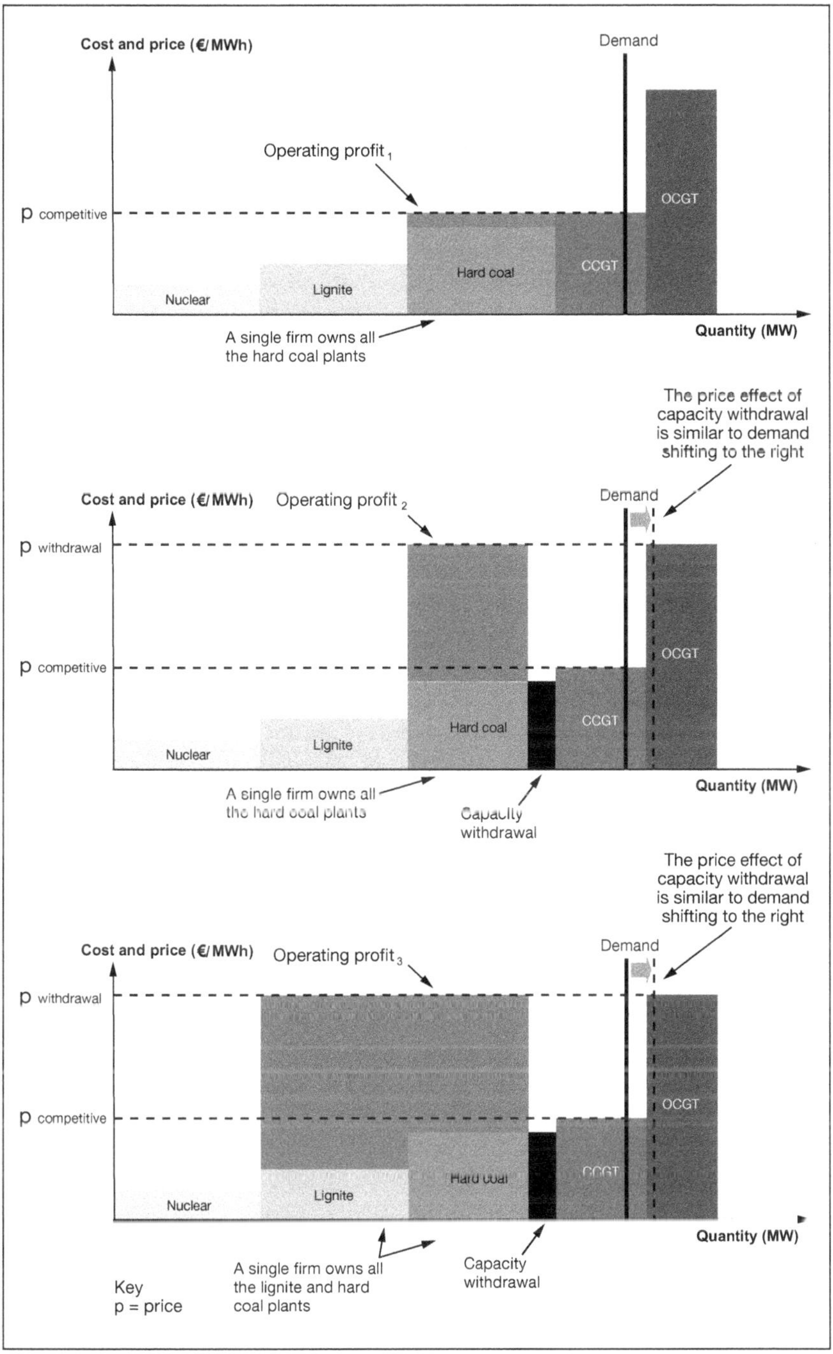

in the generation market can occur. However, since it takes several years to build a new power station other policy makers do not consider the threat of entry or expansion sufficient to constrain incumbent generators' behaviour. In response, some policy makers impose structural or behavioural constraints on firms.

When designing market liberalisation, policy makers often address the issue of market power. There are many ways to address this, including creating multiple competing generation firms, regulating the pricing behaviour of generators in the wholesale market and imposing long term sale contracts on generation companies at vesting. If a generation firm sells power through a long term contract whose price is independent of the spot market price, the generator does not benefit in the short run from an increase in the market price with respect to its generation production that is covered by the contract. The greater the quantity of power sold under long term contracts with a price independent of the spot market, the lower the incentive to raise the market price in the short run.

In response to a merger or perceived issues of market power, anti-trust authorities might impose a divestment or they might force a firm to sell power through contracts as a way to mitigate market power.

The extent of market power is important since, as illustrated by Figure 1, the more a firm acts like a monopolist, the greater the loss of social welfare compared to the perfectly competitive market outcome. By addressing issues of market power, authorities therefore address economic efficiency and the allocation of social welfare between consumers and producers.

5. Conclusion

In this chapter we have described some of the key objectives of liberalisation and the design of power markets more generally, and in doing so have emphasised economic efficiency. We then described ways in which power markets can be organised to help meet this objective.

A key point of the chapter is that competition cannot be allowed to reign freely over the power sector. The transmission and distribution network segments of the sector require regulation and even the potentially competitive segments of generation and retail supply may need some regulation or managed competition to help ensure or encourage efficient outcomes.

However, we also stress that a properly functioning competitive market is preferable to a regulated market. Therefore, the positive and potentially negative effects of regulation should be carefully considered before taking a decision as to whether and how to intervene in a potentially competitive market.

We described how power station investment decisions are made under an energy only market and under a market with a capacity mechanism. Both types of market can result in efficient investment decisions. However, in the case of energy only markets this requires authorities to allow short run market prices to rise to reflect scarcity. Non-market risks faced by investors in conventional generation such as unexpected changes to schemes that support renewable generation, which would affect future market returns for the conventional plants, are difficult to mitigate and may serve to raise entry costs of conventional generation. Capacity mechanisms are an approach used to help address this type of issue, by removing from the investor some of the risk related to investing in generation capacity.

We touched on power station operations, comparing the way operating decisions are taken under the pool model and under the bilateral contracts model. In theory the dispatch outcome so as to meet demand at least cost should be similar under the two models although the approaches to achieving the outcome differ. With the pool model, dispatch decisions are normally centrally coordinated whereas in the bilateral contracts model decisions are decentralised, with trading between generators being an important means to help the system arrive at something approaching the least cost dispatch outcome.

Power plant investments and operations are inherently linked since power plants make a contribution towards their fixed costs when running at times when their short run marginal cost of production is below the wholesale price of electricity.

The cost of negative externalities such as CO^2 emissions can be internalised within power plant investment and operating decisions by placing a price on the emissions. A CO^2 price raises the short run marginal cost of more polluting plants by more than it does less polluting plants. This has two effects that serve to reduce emissions. First, if this were to cause a shift in the ranking of power plants by short run marginal cost it would reduce the expected generation of more polluting plants and increase the expected generation of less polluting plants. Secondly, all else being equal, the contribution towards fixed costs of more polluting plants would tend to decline while it would tend to increase for less polluting plants. The result would be more investment in less polluting plants.

Finally, we described that electricity wholesale markets are susceptible to market power due to inelastic demand and the time taken to expand or enter the generation market. We saw how the ownership structure of generation affects the ability and incentive for generation companies to raise price. When liberalising power markets, authorities should therefore consider not just the design of the market rules but also the ownership structure and whether specific interventions are required to address concerns about market power.

Introduction to nuclear power

Rupert Cowen
Jonathan Leech
Prospect Law

1. Introduction

Historically nuclear power has polarised opinion like no other generating technology. Over the 60 years that nuclear power has contributed to global power generation it has gone from "epoch making"[1] to "energy source of last resort".[2] It does appear that public perception has gradually become more positive in recent years.[3] This may be the result of nuclear costs and risks being placed in context of global threats from climate change and growing recognition of the positive role of nuclear power in supporting political and financial stability through enhanced security of energy supplies. Notably, in some countries, such as China, nuclear energy is experiencing rapid growth. Nuclear plants that are currently under construction will, when completed, more than triple China's 2009 nuclear electricity-generating capacity (although, even in China, local opposition has resulted in cancellation of nuclear projects).

The controlled release of energy from a nuclear chain reaction harnesses the most concentrated source of energy known to man, providing reliable carbon-free base load generation. Nuclear power makes a major contribution to global power generation and is now widely recognised as a significant component in many diversified energy strategies. As of October 2015 International Atomic Energy Agency statistics indicate that there were 440 grid-connected commercial reactors operating in 31 countries with a combined generating capacity of 381 GW(e).[4] This equates to approximately 11% of global electricity generation[5] with virtually no carbon emissions. A further 66 commercial reactors were shown as under construction.

Nuclear power does carry risks associated with containment and control, challenges of long term inter-generational management and disposal of spent fuel and other waste products and, of course, perceived association with the uniquely destructive power of nuclear weapons. It is for these reasons that exploitation of nuclear power is the most highly regulated activity in human history, with unprecedented levels of international cooperation and oversight. In addition to the numerous development and environmental licences and permits required to develop

1 Lord Privy Seal, R A ('Rab') Butler, commenting on the opening of Calder Hall nuclear power station in 1956.
2 President Carter, 7 December 1979, response to the Kemeny report into the Three Mile Island incident.
3 UK Energy Research Centre, Public Attitudes to Nuclear Power and Climate Change in Britain Two Years after the Fukushima Accident, 19 September 2013.
4 IAEA Power Reactor Information System.
5 World Nuclear Association, Nuclear Power in the World Today (updated February 2015).

a traditional coal or gas fired power station, depending on jurisdiction the developer of a nuclear power station will be required to justify introduction of a practice involving the use of ionising radiation, provide extensive information in support of submissions required under the EURATOM treaty, establish and demonstrate the capability of the proposed site operator (with management structures and resources to comply with all requirements relating to safety, security, emergency preparedness and other regulatory obligations), put in place a funded decommissioning programme, obtain a nuclear site licence and submit to the detailed inspection and control of the nuclear safety regulator.

Extensive regulatory control coupled with the complexity and high capital costs of developing new nuclear generating capacity inevitably present significant economic hurdles to new nuclear development. Private sector investment must be underpinned by stable power markets with predictable long term revenue streams, such as that intended to be provided by the 'contract for difference' mechanism developed in the UK. Any case for investment will also require a supportive policy framework covering all aspects of project delivery from planning, licensing and permitting through to waste management and decommissioning.

2. Benefit and detriment: a special case

There is no mature commercial generating technology that does not entail a balance of benefit and detriment. In the context of nuclear power, that balance involves a unique equation. The benefit of nuclear generation in providing virtually carbon free base-load power is clear. The detriment is different in nature from the constant carbon emissions of conventional gas and coal fired power generation or the colonisation of swathes of countryside with onshore wind farms providing intermittent power. With some important exceptions (such as the impact of waste heat on the marine environment), the immediate environmental impact of nuclear power generation is limited and closely controlled. Instead the primary detriment comes in the form of risk:

- risk that a nuclear incident will cause widespread contamination;
- risk that spent fuel and other hazardous waste products will not be managed and disposed of safely now and for generations to come; and
- risk that nuclear materials may be used to cause deliberate and devastating harm.

Each of these risks must be managed on a technical, political and legal basis.

Arguably, risk from the nuclear industry to the population of any state in the developed world is best managed by that state contributing positively to nuclear regulation and technology. We are better off benefitting from a vibrant and well-regulated global nuclear industry, safely deploying third and fourth generation reactor technology in a closely regulated environment. The alternative is an increased risk of nuclear incidents from a marginalised and under-funded industry operating in states where economic circumstances may drive a more liberal attitude to risk.

3. Development of commercial nuclear power

The foundations of the modern nuclear industry were laid in the years following World War II, with development of a range of reactor technologies and establishment of the international organisations and conventions now seen as essential to safe nuclear generation. Early commercial exploitation of nuclear power was led by the US, the UK, Canada, France and the former Soviet Union.

The world's first nuclear power was generated in the Soviet Union by the 5 MW(e) Obninsk generating station, which came online in 1954 and preceded the first significant nuclear power generation in the US by a year. The US experimental Borax III reactor started generation in 1955, providing power for a population of 1,200 people in Arco, Idaho. The accolade for the first industrial scale nuclear power station was claimed by the UK. Calder Hall in Cumbria began supplying power to the national grid on 27 August 1956 with the connection of the first of four 60 MW(e) Magnox units. It continued in operation until 2003. Calder Hall was designed with a dual purpose: power generation and production of plutonium for the UK's nuclear weapons programme, so perpetuating the link between military and civil nuclear applications.

Calder Hall was the first of a rapid succession of commercial reactors.

- In the US the 60 MW(e) Shippingport pressurised water reactor (PWR) in Pennsylvania started up in 1957 (continuing in operation until 1982), followed in 1960 by the 175 MW(e) Yankee Rowe PWR in Massachusetts (continuing in operation until 1992) and the 250 MW(e) Dresden-1 boiling water reactor (BWR) (continuing in operation until 1978).
- The first of the Canadian CANDU (short for 'Canada Deuterium Uranium') units, the 20 MW(e) Nuclear Power Demonstration reactor came online in 1962, followed in 1968 by the first full scale 220 MW(e) CANDU reactor at Douglas Point.
- In 1964 France started up the 70 MW(e) EDF1 in Chinon (continuing in operation until 1973), using the 'Uranium Naturel Graphite Gaz' design.
- The first two commercial Soviet units started generating in 1964, with a 100 MW(e) boiling water graphite channel reactor in Beloyarsk (Urals) (continuing in operation until 1983) and a 210 MW(e) PWR in Novovorenzh (Volga Region) (continuing in operation until 1988).

The 1960s and 1970s saw a dramatic increase in both numbers and capacity of commercial reactors. In the space of two decades installed capacity rose from just over 1 GW(e) in 1960 to 133 GW(e) in 1980.[6] The first 1000 MW(e) reactors, the US Zion twin 1040 MW(e) PWR units, began generating power in 1973 and 1974. Annual construction starts reached a peak of 43 in 1976. Connection of new nuclear capacity peaked in 1984 with the addition of just under 31 GW(e) of new capacity in a single year, reflecting in part the long construction periods taken to bring new reactors on line.

The seemingly inevitable and inexorable expansion of nuclear power generation

6 Nuclear Power Reactors in the World, IAEA, Reference Data Series No 2, 2014 Edition.

was thrown off course in the 1970s. A combination of factors brought new reactor development to a virtual standstill.

- The economic impact of the OPEC oil embargo of 1973 resulted in a dramatic reduction in the rate of growth in power demand in the US, the UK and parts of Europe in particular.
- Increased concerns over accumulation of plutonium stocks and proliferation of nuclear weapons, including use of CANDU technology in India to produce weapons material and the 1974 Indian nuclear weapons tests, pushed public opinion against nuclear power and resulted in the US ban on reprocessing of spent fuel.
- The 1979 partial meltdown of one of the two reactors operating at Three Mile Island in Pennsylvania galvanised negative public opinion. Although the incident did not itself result in any significant release of radiation, it had a dramatic impact on public perception and confidence in the nuclear industry and triggered substantial regulatory changes. Commenting on the Kemeny report into the incident, President Carter stated on 7 December 1979 that "in this country nuclear power is an energy source of last resort".

Following the 1976 peak, construction starts declined rapidly with just one construction start in 1996.[7] The decline in decennial growth in nuclear generating capacity is striking.

Decade	% growth in installed nuclear generating capacity
1960s	1,524%
1970s	653%
1980s	139%
1990s	10%
2000s	7%

For the past decade installed capacity has remained relatively static with new reactor connections barely matching shut downs. In the period between 2010 and 2014, IAEA statistics indicate that installed nuclear capacity has hardly changed at all, growing by less than 0.5%. The contribution of nuclear power to global generating capacity has dropped from a peak of 17.59% in 1996 to 10.76% in 2013.[8]

Despite the dramatic decline in growth, construction of new reactors has never stopped entirely. In every year from 1954 to the present day, construction work on

7 Nuclear Power Reactors in the World, IAEA, Reference Data Series No 2, 2014 Edition.
8 Based on BP Statistical Review of World Energy 2014, historical data.

at least one new commercial reactor has started. The number of reactors in operation continued to rise every year until 1989 (reaching 420) and installed nuclear capacity continued to grow every year until 1997, reflecting increased unit output.

The 440 commercial reactors listed by the IAEA as operational as at October 2015 is close to the all-time highs of 441 shown for 2005 and 2010. Installed capacity (at 381 GW(e)) has never been higher. These figures must however be read in context of the IAEA's definition of 'operational'. A reactor is considered to be operational until permanently shutdown or declared as 'long-term shutdown'. The IAEA list of operational reactors therefore includes a number of reactors that are not generating and, in some cases, have not generated for a considerable period of time.

Notably, 43 reactors in Japan are listed as operational (with one in long-term shutdown and 16 permanently shutdown, including the six Fukushima Daiichi units). As at October 2015 just two of the 43 'operational' reactors are generating power (Sendai units 1 and 2, which restarted in August and October 2015 respectively under new safety standards). Of the 41 'operational' reactors that are not currently generating, two have not generated since 2013, six have not generated since 2012, 30 have not generated since 2011, five have not generated since 2010 and three have not generated since 2007. Japan's restart programme remains subject to significant uncertainty. As of October 2015 restart applications have been submitted to the Japanese Nuclear Regulatory Authority (NRA) for a total of 25 reactors. Three of those (including Sendai 1 and 2 and Ikata 3) have received final NRA and local government approval. A further two (Takahama units 3 and 4) have NRA approval but await local government approval and removal of a court injunction.[9]

Analysis of the status of the world nuclear industry must also take into account the age profile of the reactor fleet. As of October 2015 application of IAEA statistics puts the mean average age (from first grid connection) of operational commercial reactors at 28.5 years, with 250 operational reactors aged 30 years or over and 68 operational reactors aged 40 years or over.[10] This is a legacy of the historic peaks in construction activity in the 1970s and early 1980s. Investment in new reactors will need to increase significantly if capacity is to be maintained as more of these reactors reach the end of their operational lives.

4. International cooperation

Foremost amongst international organisations underpinning the nuclear industry is the International Atomic Energy Agency, created by the United Nations in 1957 to control and promote the safe, secure and peaceful use of nuclear power. The IAEA was foreshadowed in President Eisenhower's 1953 'Atoms for Peace' speech. It now has 166 Member States and is "the world's centre for cooperation in the nuclear field".[11]

The IAEA delivers on its mission through development of standards to ensure

9 World Nuclear Association Information Library, Country Profiles, Japan.
10 Based on data contained in IAEA Power Reactor Information System.
11 www.iaea.org/about/about-iaea.

safety and security, underpinned with inspection and monitoring and promotion of cooperation and scientific development on application of nuclear technology. The agency provides extensive guidance and standards for the development of national infrastructure required to support a safe nuclear power industry, including requirements relating to safety, the environment, regulatory frameworks, safeguards, security, the fuel cycle and radioactive waste. IAEA guidance and standards are particularly significant as new states seek to develop nuclear generating capacity.

The IAEA is also responsible for administration of international agreements such as the Vienna Convention on Civil Liability for Nuclear Damage and the Nuclear Non-Proliferation Treaty, which is the primary international agreement aimed at ensuring that civil nuclear materials are used only for peaceful purposes and do not add to the proliferation of nuclear weapons.

The Non-Proliferation Treaty entered into force in 1970 and in 1995 was extended indefinitely. It now has 190 state parties (191 if North Korea is included, although on 10 January 2003 North Korea announced its withdrawal from the treaty). In 1970 there were five nuclear weapon states: the US, the former Soviet Union, the UK, France and China. Since that date Israel, India and Pakistan have also acquired nuclear weapons. This represents a dramatic improvement on early fears as to likely levels of proliferation. The treaty objectives are implemented by extensive safeguarding arrangements administered by the IAEA. Those arrangements include declarations of movements and transactions of nuclear materials, inspection, analysis and auditing of materials inventories. The Non-Proliferation Treaty also restricts transfer of sensitive nuclear technologies and equipment, such as enrichment and processing technologies.

Other organisations at the heart of international cooperation within the nuclear industry include the OECD's Nuclear Energy Agency, the World Association of Nuclear Operators and the International Commission on Radiological Protection.

- The OECD Nuclear Energy Agency's mission is to "assist its member countries in maintaining and further developing, through international cooperation, the scientific, technological and legal bases required for a safe, environmentally friendly and economical use of nuclear energy for peaceful purposes ...".[12] It is a forum for pooling expertise and developing technical consensus. Current membership stands at 31 countries, spanning Europe, North America and the Asia-Pacific region.
- The World Association of Nuclear Operators (WANO) is a voluntary organisation bringing together operators of nuclear plant. Its mission is to "maximise the safety and reliability of nuclear power plants worldwide by working together to assess, benchmark and improve performance through mutual support, exchange of information and emulation of best practice".[13] Membership carries commitments and obligations to address performance issues and provide resources to support WANO's mission.
- The International Commission on Radiological Protection works to protect

12 www.oecd-nea.org/nea/.
13 www.wano.info/en-gb/aboutus/ourmission.

the environment and to prevent negative health consequences associated with exposure to ionising radiation. Founded in 1928, it has developed a globally recognised International System of Radiological Protection, which provides a common basis for radiological protection standards and practice. It is an independent organisation made up of volunteer members who are recognised as leaders in radiological protection.

5. Reactor designs and operational reactors

Reactor technologies are generally defined by the fuel used, the moderator employed to control the chain reaction and the coolant that transfers heat from the reactor core to drive generating turbines. The IAEA Power Reactor Information System classifies reactors using the following reactor types.

Boiling Water Reactor (BWR)	Boiling water reactors are water cooled and moderated, using enriched uranium fuel. The reactor core heats water, producing steam to drive turbines.
Fast Breeder Reactor (FBR)	Fast breeder reactors are liquid metal (typically sodium) cooled, using uranium or plutonium fuels and no neutron moderator. In a fast breeder reactor the chain reaction produces more fissile material (in the form of plutonium) than is consumed by fission, addressing early concerns that supplies of natural uranium would be exhausted.
Gas Cooled Reactor (GCR)	Gas cooled reactors use carbon dioxide or (in some more recent designs) helium as a coolant with a graphite moderator. Uranium fuels range from natural uranium through to relatively high enrichment levels.
Light Water Graphite Reactor (LWGR)	Light water graphite reactors are water cooled but graphite moderated, using either natural or enriched uranium fuel. Also referred to as 'RBMK' or 'High Power Channel-type Reactor' in the context of Russian designs.
Pressurised Heavy Water Reactor (PHWR)	Pressurised heavy water reactors are heavy water (deuterium oxide (D^2O) as opposed to normal water (H^2O)) cooled and moderated, using natural or mildly enriched uranium fuel.
Pressurised Water Reactor (PWR)	Pressurised water reactors are water cooled and moderated, using enriched uranium fuel. The coolant water is maintained under high pressure (to prevent boiling) and heat is transferred to a secondary coolant circuit via a heat exchanger.

In the decade following the end of World War II the US was extremely protective of its uranium enrichment technology. This was a key factor in the development of reactors fuelled with natural uranium in Canada, the UK and France. The Soviets succeeded in developing enrichment technology and used relatively low levels of enrichment in early commercial reactors.

- Of the 440 commercial reactors the IAEA identifies as operational as at October 2015, the vast majority (359) are ordinary (or 'light') water cooled, comprising 281 Pressurised Water Reactors and 78 Boiling Water Reactors, 49 are Pressurised Heavy Water Reactors, 15 are Gas Cooled Reactors, 15 are Light Water Graphite Reactors and two are Fast Breeder Reactors.
- Development of the Pressurised Heavy Water Reactor was pioneered in Canada. The majority of the 49 operational Pressurised Heavy Water Reactors are CANDU units (19 in Canada, three in Argentina, two in China, four in South Korea, one in Pakistan and two in Romania). India also has 18 operational PHWRs. These are indigenous units but are to a significant extent the legacy of early collaboration with and technology transfer from Atomic Energy of Canada Ltd.
- The 15 operational Gas Cooled Reactors are all in the United Kingdom, reflecting the UK's early commitment to gas cooled reactor technology that started with the four Calder Hall Magnox units. Of the UK's first generation Magnox units (of which the last, Wylfa in Anglesey, ceased operations in December 2015) just two examples were exported. These were the 160 MW(e) Italian Latina reactor and the 166 MW(e) Japanese Tokai-1 reactor. The UK's second generation Advanced Gas Cooled Reactors (AGRs) have never been exported. The UK itself abandoned Gas Cooled Reactor technology for its most recent reactor, Sizewell B (which went into operation in 1995), echoing France's earlier switch to Pressurised Water Reactors.
- The 15 operational Light Water Graphite Reactors are all in Russia and commenced operation between 1973 and 1990. The design is generally considered unlicensable elsewhere in the world. Operational instabilities and shortcomings in safety systems were exposed to devastating effect in the 1986 disaster involving reactor 4 at Chernobyl, Ukraine. Despite modifications made to all operational LWGR reactors following the Chernobyl disaster the design remains a source of concern.
- The two Fast Breeder Reactors listed as operational are in Russia and China. The Russian 600 MW(e) Beloyarsk 3 was connected to the grid in 1980 and continues to generate. The Chinese FBR listed is the 20 MW(e) China Experimental Fast Reactor (CEFR), which was connected to the grid in 2011 but has generated minimal power (being primarily a research and development facility).

6. Reactors under construction and projected growth

Projected electricity demand growth, particularly in developing countries, coupled with concerns over carbon emissions, long term fuel price instability and security of energy supplies is driving many states to pursue new nuclear power as a major component of energy policy. This includes both renewed interest within existing nuclear states and significant numbers of potential new entrants into the market.

For example, following the recent review of Hinkley Point C, the current political consensus within the UK remains that introduction of new reactors will achieve the diverse generation mix sought by the UK government, increasing the resilience of the UK's electricity system. Sufficient uranium is available to fuel existing and potential new power stations. The relatively small volume of nuclear fuel required for electricity generation means that nuclear fuel can be stockpiled if future supply becomes uncertain. For these reasons, the proposed introduction contributes significantly to the UK's energy security.

The security consensus is underlined by carbon reduction benefits. In response to the strong scientific consensus that human activities are causing global climate change by adding greenhouse gases to the atmosphere, the UK has established legally binding climate change targets requiring an 80% reduction in greenhouse gas emissions from 1990 levels by 2050. This will require the UK to make significant reductions in its dependence on fossil fuels. Nuclear power is a low carbon-generating technology, with emissions across the entire life cycle of a nuclear plant comparable to those from renewable resources. Fulfilment of the UK's carbon reduction obligations is therefore perceived as a further major benefit of nuclear power.

When data relating to the costs of nuclear energy is compared with cost data for other generation technologies, the political consensus in the UK is that nuclear is expected to remain a competitive form of generation, particularly when compared with other low carbon technologies. Furthermore, the current Electricity Market Reform policy and proposals provide a mechanism for the UK government to determine, through its negotiations with individual nuclear developers, whether it considers that an individual project will represent value for money and be a cost effective addition to the UK generation mix.

The IAEA predicts growth in global nuclear generating capacity of between 1% and 66% by 2030.[14] These predictions are lower than those prior to the Fukushima disaster, but remain significant. The highest growth is projected in China and South Korea. Eastern Europe and Russia are also identified as having strong growth potential. Notably, predictions for Western Europe show the greatest uncertainty, ranging from a decline of approximately 45% to (almost) maintaining the status quo with a decline of approximately 2%. Predictions for the US show similar uncertainty, ranging from a decline of approximately 18% to an increase of approximately 25%.

Of the 66 reactors identified by the IAEA as under construction as at October 2015, 42 are in Asia, with 24 of those in China and Taiwan. The IAEA classifies a reactor as under construction from the first major placing of concrete, usually for the base mat of the reactor building. The list does not include planned reactors or those, such as EDF's Hinkley Point C in the UK, where only earthworks and other preparatory site works have commenced.

For the vast majority of reactors currently classed as under construction,

14 Based on Energy, Electricity and Nuclear Power Estimates for the Period up to 2050, 2015 Edition, Table 3.

construction commenced between 2007 and 2014, but in some cases reactors have been under construction for considerably longer. The record is held by Watts Bar unit 2 in the US, which has been under construction since 1972, albeit with a 19-year hiatus from 1988. The US Nuclear Regulatory Commission finally issued an operating licence on 22 October 2015. It entered commercial operation in October 2016. Reactor units in Slovakia and Ukraine with construction starts in 1986 and 1987 have also been subject to protracted stoppages, with completions now scheduled between 2016 and 2020. Two units are included as under construction in Japan: Shimane 3 and Ohma. Construction of both units was suspended following the Fukushima disaster. Despite official approval for construction to proceed doubt remains as to whether either will ever enter operation.

The World Nuclear Association (the international trade association for the nuclear industry) also maintains detailed country by country analysis of reactors under construction, adding further details of reactors classed as 'planned' and 'proposed'.[15] As of July 2015 that analysis shows that 43 countries have 'planned' a total of 166 reactors (with capacity of 187 GW(e)) and a further 322 (with capacity of 365 GW(e)) are classed as 'proposed'. These figures are in addition to reactors currently classed as under construction. Reactors identified as 'planned' are those where approvals, funding or major commitments are already in place. Reactors that are 'proposed' are the subject of specific programme or site proposals. Taking Turkey as an example, the four Russian supplied AES-2006 units to be constructed at Akkuyu are classed as planned, whereas four Atmea 1 units at Sinop are currently classed as proposed. Turkey is also considering a third site, but as yet no specific proposals for this are included.

For the UK, the World Nuclear Association shows four reactors as planned with a further seven proposed.

- The planned units are the four EPRs for EDF's sites at Hinkley Point C and Sizewell C. Significant progress has been made in relation to the Hinkley Point C units (to be constructed by EDF with equity participation from China General Nuclear Power Corporation (CGN)). Construction was postponed due to negotiation of an investment contract with the UK government and commissioning is now planned for 2023. The investment contract effectively guarantees a minimum price for power generated. It does this by means of a 35-year contract for difference, with a 'strike price' of £89.50 per MW/h (increased to £92.50 per MH/h if Sizewell C does not go ahead and first of a kind costs cannot be shared). The agreement was modified following a European Commission decision on compliance with EU State Aid rules and now includes requirements to share gains with the UK government for the full 60-year projected plant life if returns are higher than expected. Any savings in construction costs will also be shared.
- Horizon Nuclear Power (now owned by Hitachi) has proposals for two GE-Hitachi Advanced Boiling Water Reactors (ABWR) at Wylfa and a further two units at Oldbury, both sites being adjacent to old Magnox reactors.

15 World Nuclear Association, World Nuclear Power Reactors and Uranium Requirements, 31 July 2015.

- NuGen (now a 60:40 joint venture between Toshiba and ENGIE) has proposals for three Toshiba AP1000 reactors on a site known as Moorside next to the existing Sellafield site.

Whilst the IAEA predictions anticipate highest growth in countries that already have commercial reactors in operation, both the IAEA and World Nuclear Association anticipate development of significant nuclear capacity in states that do not yet have commercial nuclear power industries. Of the 43 countries identified by the World Nuclear Association as actively pursuing development of new nuclear power, 17 are new nuclear states with no previous commercial nuclear power generating capacity. In July 2012 the United Arab Emirates became the first country in 27 years to begin construction of a debut nuclear power plant (Barakah-1), rapidly followed by the start on a second unit in May 2013 and a third in September 2014. Belarus has now also commenced construction of its first reactor units, with construction starts in November 2013 and April 2014.

In contrast, of the existing nuclear states Germany and Belgium are actively pursuing the phase out of all nuclear power generation. Spain and Sweden have no current plans or proposals for further commercial reactor development, although Sweden announced a consultation process in 2014. Italy is uniquely placed as the only country to have fully abandoned nuclear power with no plans for future development. Following a referendum in the wake of the Chernobyl disaster and the subsequent decision to shut down remaining operational reactors in 1990, Italy is the only G8 member with no nuclear generating capacity (and is also the world's largest net importer of electricity).

Construction of new reactor units is of course only part of the equation in maintaining and increasing nuclear generating capacity. Increasing the capacity of existing plant can provide a cost effective solution. This approach has been pursued extensively in many countries, including Belgium, Finland, Germany, Russia, Spain, Sweden, Switzerland and the US. Capacity increases in the range of 4–15% are common. In some cases greater increases have been achieved. For example, the net capacity of the two original Olkiluoto reactor units in Finland has been increased by 33% in a series of incremental steps, taking capacity from the original 660 MW(e) to 880 MW(e). A capacity increase of 185 MW(e) (29%) is planned to the 638 MW(e) Oskarshamn-2 reactor in Sweden. This increase has been postponed due to delays in the modernisation of safety systems and is now planned for 2017.

7. Waste management and decommissioning

When considering radioactive waste it is important to distinguish between the legacy of experimentation and pioneering development in the earlier years of the nuclear industry and current approaches to decommissioning and waste management. Despite negative public perceptions, the amount of waste now produced by the nuclear industry is relatively small and carefully managed. It also presents a hazard that diminishes with time due to radioactive decay (albeit in some cases over very long periods).

- The vast majority of waste by volume is either exempt waste or Very Low

Level Waste (VLLW), consisting mainly of soil and demolition materials. It is generally considered safe for disposal with non-radioactive wastes and not to be harmful to people or the environment (paradoxically much VLLW is currently caught within international nuclear liabilities provisions, a position that is at best unhelpful in developing cost effective disposal options and offers little tangible benefit).

- The next step up is characterised as Low Level Waste (LLW), which includes lightly contaminated clothing, filters, metals and other materials generated by the nuclear industry, non-nuclear industries and hospitals. Low Level Waste does not require shielding during handling and transport. Options for management include incineration, surface treatment and melting of metals, compaction and ultimately disposal in designated surface or near surface facilities. VLLW and LLW together make up approximately 93% by volume of all radioactive waste from the nuclear industry.
- Intermediate Waste is more radioactive and may require shielding. It may include fuel cladding, contaminated resins and sludges and contaminated reactor components. Intermediate Waste makes up around 6.5% of radioactive waste by volume.
- High Level Waste comprises spent fuel and wastes arising from fuel reprocessing. High level waste makes up approximately 0.02% of radioactive waste by volume but accounts for over 95% of total radioactivity.

The total volume of high level waste produced by the global nuclear industry each year is estimated to be approximately 10,000 cubic metres. Used fuel is generally stored in specially designed storage ponds 7–12 metres deep, either on reactor sites or at central facilities. Wet storage provides both shielding and cooling. Radioactivity and heat fall dramatically in storage for four to five decades. High level waste can be vitrified, encapsulated and stored for eventual disposal.

All currently available high level waste facilities are designed for interim storage only. As yet there is no facility available to the civil nuclear industry for final disposal of high level wastes, although proposals for deep geological repositories are well advanced in a number of countries. Both Finland and Sweden have selected sites. The US had selected and carried out extensive studies and works at the Yucca Mountain site in Nevada, but has since abandoned the plan.

Current reactor designs have been developed to facilitate decommissioning. Most countries also have arrangements in place that seek to ensure that funds will be available to cover the costs of decommissioning even if an operator becomes insolvent. In the UK, for example, any new nuclear generating facility must have a Funded Decommissioning Programme in place from the outset. This is, in effect, a pension fund for the reactor, intended to avoid costs of decommissioning and waste disposal ultimately falling to the taxpayer.

The position is very different in relation to the costs of dealing with the legacy of the early nuclear industry. Many reactors were one-off designs, developed with little thought to ultimate decommissioning. Facilities for storage of historic high level wastes are ageing and hazardous, with significant uncertainties surrounding their contents. Characterisation, removal and processing of that waste requires solutions that are innovative and expensive. The latest estimate from the UK Nuclear Decommissioning Authority is that the cost of decommissioning the UK's 17 legacy nuclear sites, dating back to the 1940s, will be in excess of £115 billion spread over 120 years or so. In recognition of the numerous uncertainties that remain, the Nuclear Decommissioning Authority gives a likely range of £90 billion to £220 billion.[16]

8. Nuclear liabilities conventions

The need for international nuclear liabilities conventions stems from the uniquely destructive power of nuclear energy. The potential for a nuclear incident to have a devastating impact over very considerable distances creates liability risks within the civil nuclear industry that are in many ways unique, both in terms of magnitude and the number of jurisdictions that may be affected. Those liability risks have a very low probability of manifesting but have a potential impact that cannot easily be carried on the balance sheet of any private sector organisation.

Nuclear liabilities conventions have a dual purpose – to protect parties suffering injury or damage as a result of a nuclear catastrophe and also to enable the private sector to invest in the nuclear industry without exposure to unquantifiable liability risks. This is a balance. An injured party gains a right to compensation from the operator of a nuclear facility for damage caused by a nuclear incident at that facility. There is generally no need to prove fault and the injured party can be certain that financial provision is available to pay compensation. The nuclear industry gains greater certainty as to who carries liability risks, the types of loss recoverable and the maximum amount that can be claimed. This channelling of liability to nuclear site operators is designed to allow insurance capacity to be focused on a relatively small group of liability holders whilst alleviating balance sheet risks that may deter entry for others.

There is unfortunately no single coherent international nuclear liabilities regime. Instead groups of states have worked together to address nuclear liability issues. There are, broadly, two international nuclear liabilities groups. These are the OECD's Paris Convention (accompanied for some members by the Brussels Supplementary Convention) and the IAEA's Vienna Convention. The Paris/Brussels Conventions have members predominantly from Western Europe, whilst the Vienna Convention originated with members drawn from Eastern Europe. Membership of both groups remains open to new states. As with any members' club, club rules apply only between members. Additional or changed rules under the various amending protocols only apply to members that have signed and ratified those protocols. There is also a Joint Protocol which seeks to link the two groups, but not all members have signed up.

In theory at least, all states that are signed up to the same international nuclear liability convention apply equivalent rules, so national liability regimes work together consistently where nuclear related damage crosses international boundaries.

16 www.nda.gov.uk/2015/02/explaining-the-nuclear-provision/.

In reality, because of the different ways that states have chosen to implement convention principles in national law, significant inconsistencies exist. Some states have developed their own unique regimes, such as Price Anderson in the US. Others, such as China, have no specific nuclear liabilities regime.

The result is a complex web of often inconsistent regimes. Added to this, significant elements of those regimes are untested. For example, in the history of the nuclear industry to date there has not been an incident involving nuclear substances in the course of carriage that has led to liabilities under any of the international nuclear liabilities conventions.

Both the Paris/Brussels and the Vienna Conventions apply similar principles:

- Liability for nuclear damage is channelled to an identified site operator.
- The operator's liability is strict, removing any need to establish fault.
- The operator's liability is limited in time and amount (although some jurisdictions impose unlimited operator liability).
- The full extent of liability must be insured against or covered by some other financial instrument or state guarantee.
- No person other than the site operator is liable for nuclear damage.
- The courts of the state in which an incident occurs have exclusive jurisdiction over claims arising from that incident.
- Compensation is to be available without discrimination between victims on the grounds of nationality, domicile or residence.

The scale of damage caused by the Chernobyl disaster in 1986 led to a reassessment of the adequacy of compensation available under international nuclear liabilities conventions. It was this reassessment that resulted in agreement of the 1997 protocol to the Vienna Convention and the 2004 protocols to the Paris and Brussels Conventions. In essence, the protocols require that more compensation is available to more people for more types of loss. The 2004 protocols are still not in force, although the UK and other European states are edging closer to ratification (now expected during 2017).

In addition, in 1997 the IAEA established the Convention on Supplementary Compensation for Nuclear Damage, intended as a free-standing arrangement open to all states. The convention provides for an additional layer of compensation funded by contracting states collectively and, crucially, contains provisions for allocating jurisdiction in relation to a nuclear incident as between contracting states. To enter into force the convention required ratification by a minimum of five states with a minimum of 400,000 units of installed nuclear capacity. With ratification by Japan in addition to existing signatories with installed nuclear capacity (Argentina, Romania and the US) and others with no current installed capacity (Montenegro, Morocco and UAE) the Convention on Supplementary Compensation entered into force on 15 April 2015. Canada also has plans to ratify in the near future.

Potential gaps in the scope of losses covered by each of the international liabilities conventions coupled with risks of claims in jurisdictions that may not be party to the same, or any, convention mean that the nuclear industry is still some way from a mature global approach to management of nuclear liability risks.

9. Nuclear incidents

The safety significance of nuclear incidents is categorised in accordance with the International Nuclear Events Scale developed by the IAEA and the Nuclear Energy Agency of the OECD. The scale comprises seven levels, from 'anomaly' to 'major accident'. The scale takes into account the impact of an incident on: (i) people and the environment; (ii) radiological barriers and controls; and (iii) 'defence in depth', where measures intended to prevent or manage an incident fail or are compromised. Each level is intended to represent an increase in severity of an order of magnitude (ie, a tenfold increase over the previous level).

The following table summarises the criteria for rating nuclear incidents within the scale.[17]

INES level	People and environment	Radiological barriers and controls	Defence in depth
Level 7 Major accident	• Major release of radioactive material. Widespread health and environmental effects.		
Level 6 Serious accident	• Significant release of radioactive material.		
Level 5 Accident with wider conse-quence	• Limited release of radioactive material. • Several deaths from radiation.	• Severe damage to reactor core. • Release of large quantities of radioactive material within an installation. High probability of significant public exposure.	

continued on next page

17 Based on Table 1 as included in *The International Nuclear and Radiological Events Scale User's Manual*, 2008 Edition.

INES level	People and environment	Radiological barriers and controls	Defence in depth
Level 4 Accident with local conse-quence	• Minor release of radioactive material. • At least one death from radiation.	• Fuel melt or fuel damage resulting in release of > 0.1% of core. • Release of significant quantities of radioactive material within an installation. High probability of significant public exposure.	
Level 3 Serious incident	• Exposure in excess of 10 x statutory annual limit for works. • Non-lethal radiation dose-related health effects.	• Exposure rates > 1Sv/hr in an operating area. • Severe contamination. Low probability of significant public exposure.	• Near accident. No safety provisions remaining. • Loss or theft of highly radioactive sealed source. • Misdelivery of highly radioactive sealed source without adequate radiation procedures.
Level 2 Incident	• Exposure of a member of the public > 10mSv. • Exposure of a worker in excess of statutory annual limits.	• Radiation levels in an operating area > 50 mSv/hr. • Significant contamination.	• Significant failures in safety provisions. • Found highly radioactive sealed source device or package with safety provisions intact. • Inadequate packaging of a highly radioactive sealed source.

continued on next page

INES level	People and environment	Radiological barriers and controls	Defence in depth
Level 1 Anomaly			• Exposure of member of public in excess of statutory limits. • Minor problems with safety components. • Theft or loss of low activity source, device or transport package.

There have been very few incidents at the upper end of the scale. The Chernobyl disaster in 1986 and Fukushima disaster in 2011 are the only two events to have reached Level 7. The Kyshtym disaster in 1957 is the only event to have been classified as Level 6. Both the Windscale fire in 1957 and the Three Mile Island accident in 1979 were classified as Level 5.

10. The future and fusion

Nuclear power is currently delivered by large scale reactor units that are expensive to construct and require a ready and stable power market to sustain what are predominantly fixed running costs over many decades. We have seen advances in power output and safety systems and also in designing in eventual decommissioning, but some would argue that the fundamental concepts underlying large capacity uranium fuelled light water reactors are inconsistent with future smart distribution grids. At the other end of the spectrum, small modular reactors (SMRs) offer the prospect of affordable, mass produced reactor units that can be deployed in locations and within power markets where traditional large scale reactors would not be viable.

SMRs are a type of nuclear fission reactor. They are manufactured off-site and brought to site for final assembly. Small reactors are defined by the International Atomic Energy Agency as those with an electricity output of less than 300 MW(e). Because SMRs allow for reduced on-site construction activities, increased containment efficiency and heightened security for nuclear materials, their construction offers opportunities for reducing construction risks sufficient to encourage traditional project financing. There are now initiatives in the UK, the US and Russia aiming to deliver viable SMRs for deployment within the next decade.

The ultimate goal may still be viable commercial scale fusion reactors, producing clean sustainable power from plentiful fuel sources without the quantities of highly radioactive spent fuel and waste produced by fission reactors. International collaboration on the ITER project in southern France, with a tokamak twice the size of any other in existence, offers a tantalising prospect of a viable fusion power plant. ITER is designed to be capable of producing ten times the power it consumes and is intended as a key step towards a demonstration project. Commercial applications are, however, probably still decades away.

Conventional power plants: technical and commercial issues

Milagros Miranda Rojas
Former policy director at the World Coal Association

1. Introduction

Fossil fuels, coal in particular, have powered the industrialisation of developed and developing countries alike. Energy is an enabler of development and electricity in particular is critical for economic growth, industrialisation and competitiveness of businesses and countries.

There are 1.1 billion people in the world without access to electricity. Rising demographic and urbanisation pressures are to substantially increase the world's energy demand and most of this surge is expected to happen in developing and emerging economies, particularly Asia and Africa. Southeast Asia alone is expected to increase its energy demand by 80% by 2040.

While there has been significant progress since the 1990s, energy poverty continues to be a serious challenge. The UN global sustainable development agenda seeks to improve the situation with the sustainable development goals (SDG). SDG 7 calls for ensuring access to affordable, reliable, sustainable and modern energy for all and SDG13 calls for taking urgent action to combat climate change and its impacts.

How countries respond to these and other global challenges will to a large extent depend on the choices they make for their energy matrix and the technologies they decide to use. These decisions will also impact their response to climate change challenges and, consequently, the way they implement the Paris Agreement.

The Paris Agreement is the first universal agreement aiming at responding to climate change. The historic agreement sets the ambitious global goal of keeping global temperature rise well below 2°C of pre-industrial levels, while pursuing efforts to limit temperature increase to 1.5°C above pre-industrial levels. It contains provisions on mitigation, adaptation, loss and damage, financial support and a transparency system and global stock-take accounting for climate action. It was adopted in December 2015 by the Conference of the Parties (COP) of the UN Framework Convention on Climate Change (UNFCCC) and entered into force on 4 November 2016.

In this chapter, we will present the current situation concerning the use of fossil fuels, with an emphasis on the generation of electricity and associated technologies. Advanced technologies are positively impacting the way countries use fossil fuels. In the case of coal using countries, for instance, a shift to high efficiency low emissions (HELE) coal technologies, such as supercritical and ultra-supercritical technologies, is driving changes in regard of energy efficiency and emissions reductions.

The chapter will also introduce some of the commercial issues and trends affecting those resources. In the last section, we will evaluate the role of fossil fuels in addressing the global challenges of energy poverty and climate change.

2. What do we understand by conventional power?

By 'conventional power' we understand that electricity is generated through the use of fossil fuels – that is, coal, oil and gas. They are containers of energy that will be converted into electricity through thermodynamic technologies. Fossil fuels, nuclear and renewables are also known as the primary forms of energy, while electricity is considered as secondary form of energy.

3. Current technologies used in the generation of electricity from fossil fuels

Technologies used in the generation of electricity affect not only levels of energy efficiency, and consequently the consumption of the finite conventional power resource, but also the supply cost, the electricity market, the fuel choice and water consumption levels.

The use of energy is the largest source of greenhouse gases (GHG) in the world, accounting for 68% of GHG, and the majority of it corresponds to the use of fossil fuels. Fossil fuels represented 82% of total primary energy supply (TPES) by 2014.[1]

TPES by coal has increased from 24.5% in 1973 to 28.6% in 2014. Electricity generated by coal has increased from 38.3% to 40.8%, in the same period of time.[2] By 2014, coal was responsible for 46% of the world's total CO^2 emissions.[3]

In 2009 China and the US coined the term '21st century coal' referring to the importance of developing modern clean coal technologies through strategic international partnerships. Cleaner coal technologies are those that allow for substantial reduction in carbon emissions. They constitute a key step in a global low carbon roadmap.

These technologies are known as High Efficiency Low Emissions (HELE) coal technologies and include a range of technologies designed to increase the efficiency of coal-fired power plants, whilst simultaneously reducing greenhouse emissions, principally carbon emissions (CO^2), other greenhouse gases emissions (GHG) and non GHG emissions, such as nitrogen oxide (NOx), sulphur dioxide (SO^2) and particulate matter (PM). Increasing the efficiency of such power plants results in less energy spend and less resource used, per unit of generated energy output, and also reduced emissions, reduced pollution and less water consumption. A 1% improvement in the efficiency of a conventional pulverised coal combustion plant could result in a 2–3% reduction in CO^2 emissions.[4]

HELE coal technologies are classified in supercritical, ultra-supercritical,

---

1 IEA, *Key CO^2 Emissions Trends 2016. Excerpt from CO^2 Emissions from Fuels Combustion*, www.iea.org/publications/freepublications/publication/KeyCO2EmissionsTrends.pdf, pp1–6.

2 IEA, *Key World Energy Statistics 2016*, www.iea.org/publications/freepublications/publication/KeyWorld2016.pdf, pp6 and 25.

3 IEA, *Key CO^2 Emissions Trends 2016. Excerpt from CO^2 Emissions from Fuels Combustion*, www.iea.org/publications/freepublications/publication/KeyCO2EmissionsTrends.pdf, p6.

4 www.worldcoal.org/sites/default/files/Hele%20Factsheet%20landscape_0.jpg.

advanced ultra-supercritical and integrated gasification combined cycle.[5] Subcritical technologies are not considered to be HELE because they do not meet the efficiency performance required to be described as such.[6] HELE technologies can be used with pulverised coal combustion system or steam cycle technology, integrated gasification combined cycle and Fluidised bed combustion.

By 2012, however, according to the IEA, almost three quarters of operating coal power plants were using subcritical technologies (not HELE) and more than half of operating plants were older than 25 years. A recent study by the World Coal Association found that around 18% of coal fired capacity currently under construction or under development will use subcritical technology and that by 2040, coal fired-power capacity using subcritical technologies could comprise 43% of incremental coal-generation capacity.[7] The same study suggests that associated technologies costs and the lack of financing sources for modern technologies might be behind countries opting for subcritical technologies, as initial capital investments costs are higher for HELE coal plants than for subcritical ones. As an example, "a new 1,000MW subcritical coal generation plant in South East Asia currently costs around $1 billion, while an equivalent ultra-supercritical plant costs around $1.5 billion".[8]

The difference between subcritical and HELE technologies lies mainly in the water steam temperatures and the different components required for that purpose. With supercritical technologies, steam is generated at a pressure above the critical point of water (373.946°C), hence there is no need to separate water from steam. Whilst subcritical technologies can reach average efficiencies of 33% and currently reach a worldwide average of around 30%, HELE technologies can potentially reach efficiencies of up to 50% (advanced ultra-supercritical)[9] by 2020 and currently achieve 45% efficiency levels (for example, ultra-supercritical unit 2 of Isogo plant in Japan).[10]

Ultra-supercritical technologies operate at even higher temperatures than supercritical technologies. They operate at greater levels of steam temperatures and may reach temperatures of 600°C. Ultra-supercritical technologies typically achieve efficiencies of 45%. Advanced ultra-supercritical technologies operate at steam temperatures of 700–760°C and can achieve efficiencies of 50%. Supercritical and ultra-supercritical HELE technologies are currently commercially deployed and operating throughout the world – for example, in Germany, Italy, India, South Korea, Japan, Poland, Malaysia, Indonesia, Czech Republic, Netherlands, Slovenia, USA, Australia, South Africa and particularly in China.

---

5 IEA, *Technology Roadmap: High-Efficiency Low-Emissions Coal-Fired Power Generation* (2012), www.iea.org/publications/freepublications/publication/TechnologyRoadmapHighEfficiencyLowEmissionsCoalFiredPowerGeneration_WEB_Updated_March2013.pdf, p14.

6 *Ibid.*

7 World Coal Association (WCA), *The Case For Coal The Power Of High Efficiency Coal Reducing Emissions While Delivering Economic Development And Reliable Energy* (2016), www.worldcoal.org/sites/default/files/The%20Power%20of%20high%20efficiency%20coal%20-%20WCA%20-%200316.pdf, p6.

8 *Ibid*, p7.

9 www.worldcoal.org/file_validate.php?file=Hele%20Factsheet%20landscape.jpg.

10 Dawn Santoianni, "Setting the benchmark: The world's most efficient coal-fired power plants" in *Cornerstone* (The official journal of the coal industry) Spring 2015, p41. http://cornerstonemag.net/setting-the-benchmark-the-worlds-most-efficient-coal-fired-power-plants/.

Pulverised coal-fired technology (PC):[11] works by pulverising coal into a fine powder and mixing it with air for combustion. The mixture is blown into the boiler where welded tubing recovers heat from water evaporation. Combustion temperatures range from 1300 to 1700°C.[12] The steam in turn feeds a steam turbine power generation device.

Around 90% or more of the coal fired power plants in the world operate with PC technology.[13] This technology can be applied to a wide variety of coals, however experts advise that it is not always appropriate to use it with coals that have a high ash content.[14]

There has been significant progress in the development of PC technology and it currently operates with subcritical, supercritical and ultra-supercritical conditions. Supercritical steam cycles became commercially available at the beginning of the 1960s, and currently can achieve overall thermal efficiencies ranging between 43% and 45%.[15] Ultra-supercritical pulverised coal combustion is the most efficient HELE technology, reaching efficiencies of 45% or more (LHV[16] net) and reducing emissions to 740 grams of CO^2 per kilowatt hour.[17]

Circulating fluidised bed combustion (CFBC):[18] with CFBC, different sizes of crushed coal are placed on a bed of minerals. This is suspended in motion by the constant injection of combustion air. Compared to the conventional burners used with PC technology, the CFBC boilers require larger amounts of air for combustion. The combusted material is transferred from the furnace to a high temperature cyclone that separates the gas from the solid material, such as any unburned coal. The solid material is redirected to the furnace while the gas is transferred to a boiler. For the separation, absorbing chemicals such as limestone are added in order to absorb sulphur pollutants that, in turn, impact the quality of the steam. There are two CFBC methods, circulating fluidised bed or bubbling bed – the latter is the most used.[19]

Around 90–95% of SO^2 (sulphur dioxide) emissions can be reduced with CFBC. Also, the fluidised bed boilers operating at temperatures of 850–900°C suppress thermal emissions of nitrogen oxide (NOx), which contributes to efficiency.[20]

Compared to PC, CFBC offers several benefits as it can use a wider range of coal, including lignite, anthracite, waste coal and biomass; the quantities and sizes of fuel to be burned are wider; also, SO^2 and NOx, emissions are significantly lower, without the need for flue gas emission control systems.[21] CFBC also uses post-combustion capture for reducing CO^2.

---

11 www.iea-coal.org.uk/site/2010/database-section/ccts/pulverised-coal-combustion-pcc?
12 *Ibid.*
13 *Fossil Fuel – Fired Power Generation* (2007), p27.
14 www.iea-coal.org.uk/site/2010/database-section/ccts/pulverised-coal-combustion-pcc?
15 www.iea-coal.org.uk/site/2010/database-section/clean-coal-technologies.
16 LHV (Lower Heating Value) refers to the net heat production during combustion.
17 IEA, *Technology Roadmap: High-Efficiency Low-Emissions Coal-Fired Power Generation* (2012), www.iea.org/publications/freepublications/publication/TechnologyRoadmapHighEfficiencyLowEmissionsCoalFiredPowerGeneration_WEB_Updated_March2013.pdf.
18 www.iea-coal.org.uk/site/2010/database-section/clean-coal-technologies.
19 *Ibid.*
20 *Ibid.*
21 IEA, "Profiles. Developments in fluidised bed-combustion". N 13/7. June 2013, www.iea-coal.org.uk/documents/83172/8753/Developments-in-circulating-fluidised-bed-combustion,-CCC/219.

PC and CFBC boilers can also utilise biomass up to around 20% of the total fuel input. When used with biomass, the power plants can reduce carbon emissions as well as NOx and SO2, with minor reductions in efficiency.[22] Both technologies have utilised biomass in Denmark, the UK and the Netherlands. For example, the Eemshaven Power station, operative since the summer of 2015, has ultra-supercritical technologies and reaches efficiencies of 46%.[23]

Integrated gasification combined cycle (IGCC):[24] uses a combination of gas and steam turbines to produce electricity. Coal is converted into synthesis gas (syngas) in a gasifier, followed by a cleaning process that removes particulate matter, mercury and other pollutants. Once cleaned, the syngas goes into a combustion gas turbine generator to produce electricity. The steam generated from the gas turbine in turn drives a steam turbine to generate electricity.

This technology is flexible as it allows for the use of solid and liquid fuels (typically coal, petroleum coke, biomass, or a combination) and although the use of high ash and high moisture coal might reduce efficiency, IGCC plants currently can achieve efficiencies of 50% (LHV, net), when using the latest 1,600°C-class gas turbines.[25]

Besides the combined cycle, natural gas is used to generate electricity through steam generation and a simple cycle. Steam generation plants use gas to heat water and the produced steam spins an electricity generation turbine. With the open or simple cycle (Open Gas Cycle Turbine – OGCT) natural gas is burnt to produce a high pressure gas that spins the turbine. Because these technologies are not very efficient in their ability to convert heat into electricity, their use is limited to periods of high demand.[26]

TPES by natural gas has increased from 16% in 1973 to 21.2% in 2014.[27] In the same interval of time, electricity generated by natural gas has increased from 12.1% to 21.6%.[28] By 2014, gas accounted for 19% of total world CO2 emissions. Gas use is expected to increase significantly in the coming decades, having as one of its driving forces the shale gas revolution in the US.[29]

Combined heat and power or co-generation: is designed to provide flexibility so that the use of a steam turbine can drive an electricity generator and/or the steam can be used directly for district heating. This technology can use gas or coal (either PC or CFBC) as fuel.[30] In 2012, co-generation of heat and power reached global average efficiencies of 58%, nevertheless it only represented 9% of global electricity production.[31]

---

22 IEA, "Coal Industry Advisory Board. 21st Century Coal. Advance Technology and Global Energy Solution. Insights Series 2013". OECD/IEA, p29.
23 www.rwe.com/web/cms/en/1772148/rwe-generation-se/locations/netherlands/eemshaven-power-plant/.
24 www.iea-coal.org.uk/site/2010/database-section/clean-coal-technologies.
25 IEA, NEA and OECD, *Projected Costs of Generating Electricity* (2015),www.oecd-nea.org/ndd/egc/2015/, p148.
26 www.aep.com/about/IssuesAndPositions/Generation/Technologies/NaturalGas.aspx.
27 IEA, *Key World Energy Statistics 2016*, www.iea.org/publications/freepublications/publication/KeyWorld 2016.pdf, p6.
28 *Ibid*, p25.
29 IEA, *World Energy Outlook* (2015). Executive Summary. www.iea.org/Textbase/npsum/WEO2015SUM.pdf.
30 www.iea-coal.org.uk/site/2010/database-section/clean-coal-technologies.
31 IEA, *Energy Technology Perspective 2015. Mobilising innovation to accelerate climate action*, p110.

In the case of oil, TPES by oil has decreased from 46.2% in 1973 to 31.3% in 2014.[32] In the same period of time, electricity generation has declined from 24.8% to 4.3%.[33] Its contribution will be substantially decreased by 2040.[34] Political instability in some of the main oil suppliers and regions, rising costs of production and a prolonged period of lower prices are the main factors affecting the decline in oil production and use.[35] Conventional steam, combustion turbines and combined cycle technologies are used to generate electricity from oil.

Oil demand is mainly concentrated in the transport and industrial sectors, particularly petrochemical.

4. Technical issues: LCOE and other costs related to electricity generation technologies

With a range of policy aims including energy access and energy security, policy makers need to consider a variety of factors in deciding which energy sources and technologies to use, in addition to efficiencies. Amongst those factors are the resource availability, associated investment costs, levelised costs of electricity (LCOE), the impact of the market and prices of fossil fuel and other alternative resources, as well as the level of GHG emission reductions to address international and domestic policies.

By 2012, overnight costs associated with HELE supercritical technologies were estimated to be between US$700/kW and US$2,310/kW. For ultra-supercritical units, overnight costs were calculated from US$800/kW to US$2,530/kW and for IGCC, overnight costs ranged from US$110/kW to US$2,860/kW. In comparison, subcritical technology costs of a unit were from US$600/kW to US$1,980/kW, around 10–20% cheaper than the cost incurred in a supercritical unit.[36]

The EGC 2015 dataset also indicates that overnight costs for combined cycle gas technology ranged between US$627/kWe and US$1,289/kWe. For open cycle gas technology, the costs were between US$500/kWe and US$933/kWe. For coal, overnight costs ranged from US$813/kWe to US$3,067/kWe and for co-generation, overnight costs were between US$926/kWe to US$15,988/kWe.[37]

Prices vary not only between different technologies but also depending on the country where the investment occurs. The same data points out that overnight costs also vary considerably within the OECD[38] area and between OECD and non-OECD countries. Ultra-supercritical plants overnight costs in China are estimated at

---

32 IEA, *Key World Energy Statistics 2016*, www.iea.org/publications/freepublications/publication/KeyWorld2016.pdf, p6.

33 *Ibid*, p25.

34 IEA, *World Energy Outlook* (2015), p85.

35 IEA, *World Energy Outlook* (2015). Executive Summary. www.iea.org/Textbase/npsum/WEO2015SUM.pdf.

36 IEA, NEA and OECD, *Projected Costs of Generating Electricity* (2015), p14. Please note that overnight costs are defined in this study as "the cost of a power plant minus any interest incurred during construction, ie as if the plant were completed overnight".

37 IEA, NEA and OECD, *Projected Costs of Generating Electricity* (2015), www.oecd-nea.org/ndd/egc/2015/, p37. Please note that overnight cost includes pre-construction (owner's), construction (engineering, procurement and construction) and contingency costs, but not interest during construction). All figures are given in 2013 US dollars and the assumed commissioning date is 2020.

38 OECD = Organisation for Economic Cooperation and Development.

US$813/kWe, in South Africa at US$2,222/kWe, while they are calculated at US$2496/kWe in Japan and US$2,660/kWe in the Netherlands.[39]

In order to choose a technology, policy makers and investors also looked at the LCOE.[40] If we take, for example, Belgium to compare the LCOE of different technologies in one OECD country, we will find that the LCOE for CCGT ranges between US$98/MWh and US$106.19/MWh. For ultra-supercritical coal plants, it ranges between US$72/MWh and US$94.02/MWh.[41]

In China, LCOE for CCGT ranges between US$90.17/MWh and US$95.13/MWh and for ultra-supercritical coal, LCOE ranges between US$73.61/MWh and US$81.57/MWh.[42] These costs are expected to fall by 2030 with LCOE for advanced ultra-supercritical coal at around US$58/MWh.[43]

From 2000 to 2013, OECD countries spent an average of US$30 billion per year on new natural gas-fired generators (combined cycle and open cycle) and an average of US$12 billion per year in coal power generation. These figures contrast with the investments in non-OECD countries which invested around US$16 billion per year on natural gas power generation and US$43 billion per year on coal power generation.[44]

Besides overnight costs and LCOE, it would be important to know what other factors are driving those investments. It would also be important to compare those figures with the LCOE for renewables in the mentioned regions, as these technologies are becoming more cost-competitive and are usually portrayed not only as the main competitors but in some cases as the panacea or solution for energy problems.

In this regard, a recent study found that while developed economies have reduced their investments in renewables from US$141.6 billion in 2014 to US$130.1 billion in 2015, developing countries' investments have increased from US$131.5 billion in 2014 to US$155.9 billion in 2015.[45]

Currently, one of the most competitive renewable sources is solar photovoltaic (PV). Its cost has declined substantially and it can achieve levels of efficiency around 28%. Costs vary: the LCOE for PV in Belgium ranges from US$142.29/MWh to US$311.77/MWh, while in the Netherlands it ranges from US$101.02/MWh to US$167.90/MWh. In China, it ranges between US$54.84/MWh and US$95.69/MWh, while in South Africa LCOE varies between US$139.27/MWh and US$243.09/MWh.[46]

39 IEA, NEA and OECD, *Projected Costs of Generating Electricity* (2015), www.oecd-nea.org/ndd/egc/2015/, pp38–39.

40 IEA, NEA and OECD *Projected Costs of Generating Electricity* (2015), www.oecd-nea.org/ndd/egc/2015/, indicate that "LCOE is calculated by summing all plant-level costs (investments, fuel, emissions, operation and maintenance, dismantling, etc) and dividing them by the amount of electricity the plant will produce, after an appropriate discounting. The LCOE represents the average lifetime cost for providing a unit of output (MWh) for a given capacity factor, often the average capacity factor achievable by the power plant or a common value typical of baseload plants", p163.

41 IEA, NEA and OECD, *Projected Costs of Generating Electricity* (2015), www.oecd-nea.org/ndd/egc/2015/, p49.

42 *Ibid.*

43 *Ibid*, p148.

44 IEA, NEA and OECD, *Projected Costs of Generating Electricity* (2015), www.oecd-nea.org/ndd/egc/2015/, p38.

45 FS-UNEP "Global Trends in Renewable Energy Investment 2016" (2016), UNEP & Bloomberg: New Energy Finance, http://fs-unep-centre.org/sites/default/files/publications/globaltrendsinrenewableenergyinvestment2016lowres_0.pdf, p20.

46 *Ibid*, pp50–51.

These figures show that LCOE for coal ultra-supercritical technologies is lower than other technologies, including PV. This comparison applies to OECD and non-OECD countries.[47]

Similar conclusions are reached by the World Coal Association (WCA). In a recent analysis[48] of the LCOE of HELE technologies in ASEAN countries plus India, Bangladesh, Sri Lanka and Pakistan, the WCA found that HELE coal technologies costs are less than for other technologies, including gas. According to this study, HELE technologies costs range from US$55/MWh to US$60/MWh, whereas OCGT almost doubles this cost. In China, the comparative cost advantages of coal generation seem to be clearer, according to the same study, with LCOE of HELE coal technologies at around US$50/KWh, or a third of the LCOE of OCGT.[49]

Despite LCOE differences, investment in renewable technologies has grown substantially. This might reflect not only the declining costs of renewable technologies, but also the effect of subsidies, compared to other technologies, as well as the low prices of fossil fuels that discourage investment. How subsidies are reflected or not in LCOE might be another important question for investors, along with other questions regarding country-specific factors and situations, like the availability and reliability of the resources, grid infrastructure, energy demand, fuel and labour costs, regulatory standards, amongst others. In the US, for example, the EPA clean power plan programme[50] has set important regulatory standards that are affecting future coal use.

Furthermore, international policy commitments might have an important bearing on decisions. Mitigation pledges made by countries in their Intended National Determined Contributions (INDC) in the run up to the COP21 signalled intentions to diversify the energy mix with more investment in renewables in some cases, and a transition to cleaner technologies that allow the continued use of fossil fuels with reduced CO^2 emissions like HELE coal technologies.[51] Recent WCA analysis indicates that 19 countries representing 44% of global CO^2 emissions have stated within their INDCs that they will use HELE coal technologies as important tools to fulfil their mitigation commitments.[52]

5. Electricity demand and commercial issues related to conventional power

Energy is an enabler of development and fossil fuels have been at the source of energy and electricity generation for centuries. They have played a dominant role since industrialisation.

---

47 IEA, NEA and OECD emphasise that an explicit comparison of LCOEs for different technologies among countries can be misleading, due to the different set of risk profiles for every country (see p47). See also *ibid*, Chapter 8.

48 World Coal Association (WCA), *The Case For Coal The Power Of High Efficiency Coal Reducing Emissions While Delivering Economic Development And Reliable Energy* (2016), www.worldcoal.org/sites/default/files/The%20Power%20of%20high%20efficiency%20coal%20-%20WCA%20-%200316.pdf, p5.

49 WCA, *ibid*, p5.

50 EPA (United States Environmental Protection Agency), www.epa.gov/cleanpowerplan/clean-power-plan-existing-power-plants.

51 http://unfccc.int/focus/indc_portal/items/8766.php.

52 WCA. www.worldcoal.org/coal-important-part-paris-agreement.

53 IEA, *World Energy Outlook 2015*.

The IEA predicts[53] that by 2040, fossil fuels will account for 79% of the world primary energy demand. In all scenarios in this prediction fossil fuels remain the dominant source of energy supply, although they see their share in the global energy mix reduced as the share of renewables increases. BP's 2016 Energy Outlook largely agrees with that projection. It adds that fossil fuels represented 86% of total energy supply by 2014 and will still account for almost 80% by 2035.[54]

Industrialised country economic growth has been based on high levels of energy intensity (the amount of energy required per unit of GDP) and developing countries have followed. Increases in world population and urbanisation will increase energy demand. The global population reached 7.3 billion in mid-2015, and UN analysis indicates that by 2050 the figure will exceed 9 billion, with the majority of this increase in Asia and Africa.[55] The IEA indicates that between 1990 and 2013, world primary energy demand increased by 55% and from 2013 to 2040 it will increase by 32% (New Policies Scenario). BP's Energy Outlook 2016 projects an increase by 34% between 2014 and 2035. In both analyses, the majority of this increase will happen in non-OECD countries.

It is clear that the world has relied on fossil fuels for energy and electricity supply and that they will continue to play a role, despite the substantial increased investment in renewable sources.

Oil will continue to play a role in the energy supply, particularly in the transport and petrochemical sector. Oil demand is forecast to increase by 15% in the IEA's New Policies Scenario, reaching 103.5 million barrels per day in 2040,[56] although it will account for less than 4% in the global energy mix. Oil prices have declined since mid-2014, after a period of stable high prices, going from around US$115/barrel to US$40-60 in 2015, with a projection to remain low until the 2020s when it is predicted to rise and stabilise at around US$80/barrel.[57] The IEA states, "the collapse in prices was driven by a marked slowdown in demand growth and record increases in supply, particularly tight oil from North America, as well as a decision by the Organization of Petroleum Exporting Countries (OPEC) countries not to try to rebalance the market through cuts in output".[58]

The US, the world's largest oil consumer is predicted to reduce its oil demand by 25% by 2040. China will replace the US as the largest consumer, with India being the second largest. Asia, as a whole, is expected to increase its oil demand by around 35% by 2040.[59]

When looking at the role of oil in energy supply, it is always important to consider political risks that affect energy security. Iraq and Iran are amongst the major oil producers and face political and institutional instability that creates energy security concerns and affects oil demand.

54 BP 2016 Energy Outlook, p15 (www.bp.com/content/dam/bp/pdf/energy-economics/energy-outlook-2016/bp-energy-outlook-2016.pdf).

55 UN-DESA World Population Prospects. 2015 Revision, p1. (http://esa.un.org/unpd/wpp/publications/files/key_findings_wpp_2015.pdf).

56 IEA, *World Energy Outlook 2015*, p62.

57 *Ibid*, pp46–50.

58 *Ibid*, p46.

59 *Ibid*, p63.

Concerning the price of gas, the IEA states that there is no global benchmark for natural gas but instead three regional markets: North America, Asia-Pacific and Europe, each with different pricing mechanisms and market conditions.[60] Production and transport infrastructure are amongst the most important factors influencing production and price, even if markets are more interconnected. As the IEA points out, "one-fifth of the projected rise in global demand consists of gas transported over long distances via very capital-intensive pipeline or LNG projects. Keeping these project costs under control (contrary to numerous recent examples of overruns) will be vital to the future competitive positioning of gas".[61]

In the New Policies Scenario, gas consumption increases by 47% and reaches 5160 billion cubic metres in 2040, with non-OECD markets accounting for 85% of the rise in demand, and China and the Middle East as the drivers in production and consumption.[62] This increase will mean that by 2040, gas, oil and coal have similar shares in the global energy mix. By 2040, gas accounts for 23% of the world electricity generation, becoming the second largest fuel in the energy mix. Most of the increase in gas demand occurs in the electricity sector that accounts for around 40%.[63]

Around half of the increase in gas demand comes from countries increasing imports of liquified natural gas (LNG). However, this trend might be affected as LNG has high capital infrastructure costs and its price is linked to the oil price.[64]

Unconventional gas supply is also to increase substantially in the coming years and is expected to represent around 60% of the total gas production by 2040, nevertheless its growth beyond North America might not be significant. China's potential to produce unconventional gas is still uncertain despite encouraging policies, due to geology issues, accessing the gas and the underdeveloped domestic pipelines, amongst others.[65]

Within OECD members, only North America is expected to increase its gas demand. Within OECD members overall gas production is expected to decline, with production declining in Norway, the Netherlands and the UK. Globally, new actors will develop in the Caspian region, Africa and Latin America.[66]

Gas is the fastest growing energy source. Its low carbon emissions levels have contributed to seeing gas as a viable replacement for more carbon-intensive fuels, in particular coal. This, added to the versatility of the fuel for supporting the integration of renewables into the energy mix, has made gas "a good fit for a gradually decarbonising energy system".[67] Nevertheless, gas competitiveness positioning still faces some important challenges such as its oil-linked prices, efficiency policies and infrastructure related investment costs, amongst others.[68] Also, as mentioned in the

60 *Ibid*, p51.
61 *Ibid*, pp24–25.
62 *Ibid*, p66.
63 *Ibid*, pp196–201.
64 *Ibid*, Chapter 5. This chapter explains in detail the major variables affecting the cost of new LNG liquefaction facilities.
65 *Ibid*, p229.
66 *Ibid*, pp84–85.
67 IEA, *World Energy Outlook*. Executive Summary, pp4–5. www.iea.org/Textbase/npsum/WEO2015SUM.pdf.
68 *Ibid*.

previous section, LCOE of gas technologies are not that competitive when compared with other technologies and its methane emissions are a source of great concern.

Coal is the largest source of power generation. Its share in the global energy mix increased from 23% in 2000 to 29% in 2015. According to IEA projections, from 2013 to 2040 global coal demand will rise by a further 12% reaching around 6300 million tonnes of coal equivalent (Mtce). Coal currently contributes around 41% of the world electricity generation and by 2040 it will still contribute 30%. While coal demand is expected to decrease by about 40% in OECD countries, it will dramatically increase in non–OECD countries, in particular in Southeast Asia.

In its special report on Southeast Asia, the IEA forecast that by 2040, the region will experience an 80% increase in its energy demand, with coal being the fuel of choice. The region will increase coal demand by around 50% by 2040 and 4.8% per year until 2035.[69]

Coal prices have declined mainly due to overcapacity and major supply investments in Australia, Colombia, Indonesia and South Africa. Currently coal prices (including transportation costs) are below the production costs of the marginal producers. Nevertheless, as IEA's analysis shows, "in all of the scenarios, the international coal market returns to balance by 2020"[70] and by 2040 the coal price is expected to be around US$110/tonne.[71]

Despite these price predictions, by 2040, installed power generation capacity from coal will reach 2843 GW[72] compared to 1805 GW today. It is expected that 75% of installed capacity and generation will be in non-OECD Asian countries. Other studies indicate that around 910 GW of additional coal-fired generation capacity will be built globally, with China accounting for almost 70%.[73]

In India, demand for coal power generation will almost triple and production will grow more than in any other country, "making India by a distance the largest source of growth in global coal use".[74] India will become the second largest worldwide coal producer and, in 2020, the largest importer, overtaking Japan, the EU and China.[75] By 2030 in India coal will account for more than 50% of primary energy demand and 73% of electricity generation, with power consumption rising from 1340 TWh in 2015 to 3,300 TWh.[76]

The increase in coal demand in developing countries, due to the availability, affordability and reliability of the resource might be driving a "renaissance of coal" as many developing countries use it to meet their energy needs. That renaissance might be driven by China and India but will not be limited to them.[77]

69 IEA, *Southeast Asia Energy Outlook 2015*, World Energy Outlook Special Report. Executive Summary.
70 IEA, *World Energy Outlook 2015*, p52.
71 *Ibid.*
72 WCA analysis of Platts Power Plant Database in IEA, *World Energy Outlook 2015*. New Policies Scenario equivalent is 2468GW.
73 CIAB/Wood McKenzie, Presentation to CIAB, June 2015.
74 IEA, *World Energy Outlook 2015*, p22.
75 *Ibid.*
76 CIAB/Wood McKenzie, Presentation to CIAB, June 2015.
77 "Drivers for the renaissance of coal", Proceedings of the National Academy of Sciences of the United States of America, 6 July 2015, pE3776.

Nevertheless, coal faces important sustainability challenges mainly related to its high carbon emissions levels and current low efficiency, as well as through environmental policies. These challenges and concerns have been at the forefront of the divestment campaign that does not see a role for fuel in a low carbon future.

6. International policy challenges to the use of fossil fuels

National and international policies and commitments play an important role in the evolution of the energy sector. In this context, it will be important to see how the Paris Agreement and the UN Sustainable Development Agenda, in particular the Sustainable Development Goals (SDGs), will be implemented.

The Paris Agreement sets a goal of limiting global warming to rises of well below 2°C and 1.5°C by the end of the century. A successful Paris Agreement will depend on the effective implementation of the Intended National Determined Contributions (INDC) – to become National Determined Contributions (NDC) once the agreement enters into force. INDCs contain countries' commitments, in particular in the areas of mitigation and adaptation.

Energy is the sector that contributes the most to greenhouse gas emissions, but to respond to climate change and to achieve the Agreement's goals all sources of GHG emissions will need to be addressed.

Coal is the fossil fuel that emits more CO^2, while gas emits more methane than CO^2. As countries continue their economic development, and due to the demographic changes discussed above, they will increase their energy and coal demand, even if contemplating China reaching a plateau in its coal use.

As fossil fuels will continue playing an important role in the energy and electricity generation in developing countries, it is critical to support those countries in achieving their INDC if there is to be a chance of success for the Paris Agreement.

Today, 1.1 billion (17% of the world population) people lack access to electricity. Ten countries account for 63% (677 million people) of that deficit: India (263 million), Nigeria (75 million), Ethiopia (67 million), Bangladesh (62 million), DRC (55 million), Tanzania (40 million), Kenya (33 million), Uganda (30 million), Myanmar (25 million) and Sudan (25 million).[78]

SDG7 aims to ensure access to affordable, reliable, sustainable and modern energy for all. In order to achieve this goal, countries will need to use all available and affordable resources, and particularly those that can provide a reliable base load for electricity.

The challenge for countries is therefore to achieve universal access to energy to meet their population and industrialisation demands, whilst fulfilling international commitments to reduce GHG emissions. A key piece in this puzzle is the future use of fossil fuels. Whether there is the opportunity to use them in synergy with a sustainable development plan or not, the answer to this dilemma will come on a country-by-country basis.

As every country implements the Paris Agreement's commitments and their INDC into national laws, they will need to decide if they will use fossil fuels or not

---

78 www.se4all.org/sites/default/files/SE4All-Advisory-Board-Finance-Committee-Report.pdf, p11.

and how to use them; whether it has the capacity to invest in renewables and if those resources alone can meet their energy demand. This might be the biggest conundrum of our times.

There is a strong campaign to divest from fossil fuels, in particular coal. For this campaign, the world needs to eliminate fossil fuels because they are responsible for climate change. Under this view a move towards sustainable energy systems implies a transition away from fossil fuels.

This seems to be a radical proposition or a carefree approach.[79] In 2015, while coal produced 109 days and fossil fuel combined produced 313 days of the world's annual primary needs, wind and solar energy produced the equivalent of nine days of global primary energy needs. An extremist approach of eliminating fossil fuels might be ignoring the consequences of limiting fossil fuels, such as restricting access to electricity to those that currently do not have it. "To put this problem into context – the energy used by Christmas lights in the US in an average festive season is more than the national electricity consumption of many developing countries, such as El Salvador, Ethiopia, Tanzania, Nepal or Cambodia".[80]

Perhaps the answer does not lie in a 100% fossil fuel or 100% renewable production, but in a more efficient use of those resources and more diversified energy mix, depending on the particular situation and need of every country.

The decline in the use of fossil fuels for energy purposes has been notorious in Europe, precisely where the industrial revolution started, based on coal. This has taken a long time and a marked change of perspective, if we take into account that the European Union started with the European Coal and Steel Community, which has as one of its main objectives to create a common market for coal.

What is the situation in non-OECD countries? India, the third largest economy in the world, accounts for only 6% of global energy use. With 1.295 billion people, 263 million lack access to electricity. India is undertaking a profound transformation of its energy system. It currently relies on coal for 60% of its electricity generation. In its INDC it has pledged to transition to supercritical and ultra-supercritical technologies, given that coal will continue to be at the core of its economic and energy development. India has also pledged to increase the share of renewables in its energy mix. Many other developing countries have made similar pledges to use more efficient technologies and increase the use of renewables.

Renewables competition with fossil fuels has grown in the past decades, and is expected to continue increasing, but renewables are not yet a substitute for fossil fuels. According to the IEA, by 2040 renewables-based generation will reach 50% in the EU, around 30% in China and Japan, and above 25% in the United States and India. In contrast, coal will be just 13% of the electricity supply outside Asia.[81]

As previously mentioned, prices are one factor to be taken into account. In India, for example, a recent opinion indicates that PV solar might soon become more

79 Brendan Pearson, "Carefree ignores the consequences of limiting supply of fossil fuels" *The Australian*, 12 April 2016, www.theaustralian.com.au/opinion/carefree-ignore-consequences-of-limiting-supply-of-fossil-fuels/news-story/0ad3fc06412c829d62c475d8be19d675.

80 *Ibid.*

81 IEA, *World Energy Outlook 2015*, p53.

competitive than coal, "[t]his year, solar energy prices in the country dropped to around parity with coal for the first time ever, hitting 4.34 rupees (about 6 US cents) a kilowatt-hour (kWh), while coal tariffs usually range between 3–5 rupees/kWh (about 5–8 US cents)".[82]

Can renewables provide the necessary base load power and deliver affordable and reliable electricity? By 2040, India's electricity demand is forecast to be almost 3300 TWh, the equivalent to today's power consumption of Japan, the Middle East and Africa combined. Can renewables alone offer the answer? This seems very unlikely.

There are still many challenges concerning the use of renewables. As one study explains, "[a] large-scale penetration of renewables into the power grid would require: significant overbuilding of generation to meet demand, costly grid upgrades and storage expansion, storage that might not be available in time and huge build-out of transmission infrastructure".[83]

In a transition towards a near-zero emissions and diversified energy mix, all sources might be necessary, especially to provide the continuous and reliable provision of electricity, and all low-carbon technologies will need to play a role.

Besides prices and LCOE considerations, industries and investors need to evaluate the impact of subsidies, labour costs and regulatory issues affecting upstream and downstream operations, as well as carbon pricing markets. Equally important is the energy uptake amongst consumers and the level of access to electricity that can be provided.

Electricity consumption is expected to rise by more than 70% by 2040, however this does not mean that universal access to electricity has been achieved.

In this context, it is critical to support developing and coal-using countries transitioning towards HELE technologies. HELE technologies are an important tool to address mitigation commitments embedded in the INDCs. Today, there are 900 GW of coal capacity in development in non-OECD countries. Only 500 GW are planned to use HELE coal technologies. By 2040, under IEA's New Policies Scenario, there will be around 2.6 TW global installed coal-fired generation capacity, which equals 12,000 TWh of electricity generation. Of that installed capacity, 75% will be in non-OECD Asia and 43% of the incremental coal-fired generation plants will still use subcritical technologies – non-HELE – if no investment in HELE technologies is made.[84]

How much does it cost to transition to HELE? WCA analysis indicates that to shift 400 GW of coal capacity from subcritical to supercritical or ultra-supercritical technologies in non-OECD countries will cost around US$31 billion. This conversion can save six billion tonnes of CO^2 from 2015 to 2040. Furthermore, to move 400 GW of subcritical and 300 GW of supercritical to ultra-supercritical will cost US$81 billion and will save around 13 billion tonnes of CO^2 from 2015 by 2040.[85]

HELE technologies are also important as a key first step towards the deployment

82 http://ieefa.org/blogs-india-solar-power-now-cheaper-coal/.

83 IEA, India Energy Outlook. World Energy Outlook Special Report (2015), www.iea.org/publications/freepublications/publication/IndiaEnergyOutlook_WEO2015.pdf, pp82–84.

84 World Coal Association (WCA), *The Case For Coal The Power Of High Efficiency Coal Reducing Emissions While Delivering Economic Development And Reliable Energy* (2016), www.worldcoal.org/sites/default/files/The%20Power%20of%20high%20efficiency%20coal%20-%20WCA%20-%200316.pdf, p9.

85 *Ibid.*

of carbon capture and storage (CCS), as they reduce the volume of CO^2 to be captured and reduce the cost of CO^2 abatement. HELE coal technologies also have lower operating costs for CCS, hence retrofitting supercritical and ultra-supercritical plants is less expensive than retrofitting subcritical plants. As retrofitting existing power plants with CCS might impose some efficiency penalties, it is better to integrate CCS in the new plants.

Given the existing level of deployment of subcritical coal power plants it would important to increase efficiency through the use of HELE technologies before incorporating CCS. As noted by the IEA Clean Coal Centre (IEA-CCC), "HELE with CCS represents the ultimate clean coal power plant, at comparable cost to most alternative low and zero carbon technologies".[86]

While HELE technologies can substantially contribute to the reduction of carbon emissions, the achievement of climate goals will be highly unlikely without deployment of CCS.

CCS is important for reducing carbon emissions in the power sector and also in the industrial sector. It can achieve around 90% of carbon emissions reductions from coal-fired power plants.

The Intergovernmental Panel on Climate Change (IPCC) has already pointed out that without CCS, it will be 138% more expensive to achieve the 2°C scenario and the IEA has estimated that the exclusion of that technology would increase mitigation costs by around US$2 trillion by 2050.[87] The Global Carbon Capture and Storage Institute (GCCSI) expects a 40% cost increase in the decarbonisation of the power sector without CCS.[88]

Moreover, CCS has been recognised within the UNFCCC Clean Development Mechanism as a recognised project activity and the Addis Ababa Action Agenda that sets the UN framework for finance for development emphasises the importance of investment on CCS.

Despite awareness of the vital importance of CCS for achieving climate objectives, the high capital cost of the technology and the lack of appropriate policy support have limited the required level of deployment.

CCS urgently needs an intensification of commercial-scale deployments and appropriate policy support. Additional research, demonstration and deployment and learning-by-doing would reduce costs over the period to 2040.[89]

Political will and commitment, as well as policy parity between CCS and renewables are also important. Between 1994 and 2013, US$1929 billion was invested in renewables compared with US$20 billion investments in CCS.[90]

Concerning carbon pricing, while there has been a growing development of national carbon markets supported by an increasing international support for a global carbon price,[91] current prices are considered to be too low to incentivise the investment in low-

86 www.unece.org/fileadmin/DAM/energy/se/pp/clep/ge11_ws_oct.2015/3_Minchener.pdf. Slide 18.
87 www.globalccsinstitute.com/news/high-cost-not-deploying-ccs-globally.
88 *Ibid.*
89 IEA, *World Energy Outlook 2015*, p44.
90 www.worldcoal.org/sites/default/files/andrew_purvis_gccsi%2811_12_2014%29.pdf.
91 See, for example, the Carbon Pricing Leadership Coalition: www.carbonpricingleadership.org/leadership-coalition.

carbon technologies. Article 6 of the Paris Agreement does not refer specifically to a global carbon pricing but it is understood to lay the ground for further development.

According to the World Bank, there are 66 jurisdictions implementing emission-trading programmes or carbon taxes but only 12% of global greenhouse gas emissions are covered by carbon prices.[92]

7. Concluding remarks and final thoughts

This chapter has briefly presented the current electricity generation technologies from fossil fuels and the main technical and commercial issues arising out of their utilisation. It has also presented the main political challenges associated with conventional power.

It seems clear from the data and analysis reviewed that to meet electricity demands while achieving climate objectives will require significant investment in cleaner power generation across the entire value chain, particularly to increase energy efficiency and energy access while accomplishing mitigation objectives. Electricity market reforms are also important elements to consider regarding future use of fossil fuels for power generation, in particular on-grid and off-grid capacity and distribution issues.

Given the role that fossil fuels have played and continue to play in powering industrialisation and development, a more reasonable and realistic approach might be to promote investment in low carbon technologies that will allow for a more efficient and sustainable use of those fuels such as HELE coal technologies and CCS, instead of simply calling for them to be removed from the energy mix. This is of particular importance for developing countries that have decided to continue using coal.

Considering that countries, in particular developing ones, have to juggle many development objectives, restrictive investment policies for cleaner coal power plants might be unnecessarily penalising those countries. It would be important for financing conventional power projects to consider not only competitiveness-related issues such as prices and LCOE, but also the feasibility of developing alternative power sources vis-a-vis the countries' needs. While a dominant renewable energy mix might be desirable, it might not be achievable in the short term or it might not suffice to achieve energy access objectives. Equally, as much preference as there is for gas as a replacement for coal, consideration of infrastructure requirements, costs and timing need to be considered.

This also highlights the important role of public-private partnerships, international cooperation programmes and governmental responsibility to provide enabling investment frameworks.

An energy transition towards a near-zero emissions pathway requires focusing on all available low emissions technologies in all sectors, not necessarily the elimination of certain fossil fuels from the energy mix. CCS should be a global priority. Perhaps, as the World Economic Forum suggested in its recommendations to policy makers,

---

92 www.worldbank.org/en/news/speech/2016/04/21/carbon-pricing-panel---setting-a-transformational-vision-for-2020-and-beyond.

regulators and business,[93] in order to follow a more efficient path to achieve energy goals, it will be important to develop an optimal balance of conventional and renewable resources, central and distributed, depending on national needs, circumstances and indigenous resources and investments in the right energy efficiency technologies.

While every country will decide on the best available and most affordable composition of its energy mix, international public and private support, especially public-private partnerships will play an important role in the effective implementation of INDC conducive to a successful Paris Agreement.

In the transitional period until the Paris Agreement's goals are achieved, supporting countries that rely on fossil fuels for electricity generation is of the utmost importance. Those countries need to implement their INDC and at the same time achieve universal access to electricity. As the global UN agenda for sustainable development calls for a universal access to electricity by 2030, there will be a certain pressure to deliver on time. Both energy access and climate change constitute sustainable development goals and are therefore high priorities. They need to be addressed in an integrated manner as they are both crucial to achieve sustainable development.

In the transition towards a near-zero emissions energy system, there might not necessarily be a trade-off between using fossil fuels and achieving those goals, if used with the correct technologies. The challenge is the way in which we use them.

93 www3.weforum.org/docs/WEF_Future_of_Electricity_2016.pdf.

Renewable energy: from energy hunter-gatherers to energy farmers

Thomas Leonard
DNV GL Energy

1. Introduction

Ten millennia ago, when the population of the world was less than 0.2% the size it is today, the human race powered itself principally on energy sources which had existed in the same form since long before prehistoric hunter-gatherers had embarked on their first resource exploitation schemes. This method had certain definite advantages. No labour was expended on the development, operation and maintenance of resources. Success could lead to extraordinary returns as, in a good year, profits could greatly exceed expended effort. However, the system was Darwinian in a literal sense, in that the penalty for failure to perform was likely to be starvation and death. Hunting and gathering was sustainable, but supported a life which was nasty, brutish and short.

However, the one consistent strand of human development has been the drive to escape from Hobbes's bleak prognosis on the condition of mankind. Central to this has been the availability of usable energy, firstly to power our own bodies, then for our livestock and finally for the machines which do our work. About 10,000 years ago, there was a remarkable development. Instead of seeking out and harvesting flora and fauna provided free by nature, humans started to more actively exercise, in the words of Genesis, "dominion over the fish of the sea, and over the fowl of the air, and over the cattle, and over all the earth, and over every creeping thing that creepeth upon the earth". In short, through the application of labour and ingenuity, we learnt to artificially and more efficiently replicate those commodities in an environment over which we had control. As the population exploded, this more efficient and sustainable method of food production allowed larger populations to be supported by relatively small areas of land.

We are now experiencing a new energy resource transition. For the greatest part of the time in which the human race has existed, the only energy consumed by humans was the food which we needed to power our own bodies. It was much later in our development that we learnt to convert biomass into heat and light through the truly momentous technological breakthrough of learning how to deliberately set things on fire. Much later, humans found that they could get other animals to do work for them, which increased the demand for food-energy. Very recently, the range of opportunities for converting chemical fuel energy into useful work has exploded. Whether generating useful electricity, heating our homes or powering our vehicles, we are converting energy resources into useful work at a much greater rate than ever before. In order to do this, biomass has not been enough. For roughly the past 250 years we have been living through our second hunter-gatherer phase, where we have been exploiting energy sources which were fortuitously laid up for us over eons through no investment on our part. Immense volumes of primary energy, in the form of coal, oil and gas, have been available to us with (relative to the reward) little exertion.

Our exploitation of these resources was a testament to human ingenuity. However, the Earth's ancient resources are finite and the potential for human growth is not. As these resources become scarcer, tension may arise between nations as they struggle to control their slice of an ever-shrinking pie.

In addition, there is a consensus that the consumption of fossil fuels is having previously unforeseen and unwanted effects on the global environment. This chapter will not address the question of anthropogenic climate change, which has been adequately covered in many other places. It is however not entirely fanciful to again draw parallels with hunter-gatherer societies, which were capable of hunting species to death and thereby causing unexpected environmental side effects. In the long term, we will need to once again take direct control of the methods by which we gather and convert the energy which is available to us.

2. The types of renewable energy

In fact, the challenge facing humans is not the lack of available energy. Energy is all around us waiting to be gathered. The difference between exploiting fossil fuels and renewable sources is the relative effort which we need to put in to get out something we can use. The Energy Return on Energy Invested (EROI) is typically much higher for fossil fuel than for renewables.[1]

Most of what we think of as renewable energy comes ultimately from the sun. We are however given a number of opportunities to turn this energy into useful work. Through the use of shaped mirrors, we can concentrate the heat of the sun and transform it into hot water or steam through what is known as concentrated solar power (CSP). This can in turn either be used to heat buildings or for other processes or can drive a turbine, creating electricity.

In recent years, we have learnt how to directly capture solar radiation by the use of photovoltaic (PV) cells. A solar PV cell is a solid state electrical device that converts sunlight directly into electricity when photons emitted by the sun meet photoactive semiconductors causing electron motion and therefore a direct current (DC). This direct current must be transformed into the more commonly used alternating current (AC) by use of an inverter.

We can also use photosynthesis to transform solar radiation into energy by growing energy crops, such as wood or grass. This biological energy source can then be transformed into useful energy via a variety of processes. The biomass can be combusted to make heat, and subsequently electricity. However, the organic material can also be transformed into other, more convenient, forms of chemical energy, such

1 JM Murphy and CAS Hall, *Year in review – EROI or energy return on (energy) invested*, New York Academy of Sciences (2010).

as gas, bio-fuel or bio-ethanol, via processes such as gasification, pyrolysis and fermentation.

The most well established form of large-scale renewable electricity generation is hydroelectricity. By this method, we harness the potential energy of water in highland rivers and lakes as it forces its way back down to the natural level of the ocean. The water was lifted up into the hills and mountains by the cycle of evaporation and precipitation: a sun-powered natural motor. The energy is captured by channelling the flow of water through a turbine, the configuration of which is dependent on the pressure and speed of the water.

We can capture the sun's energy via through other indirect routes. The unevenly distributed heat of the sun around the planet causes our atmosphere to warm at different rates. The resultant pressure difference, coupled with the Earth's rotation, creates air flows across the globe, the energy of which we can capture via wind turbines. Capturing energy from the wind is a very old idea, although using the wind to generate large quantities of electricity is quite new. A technology which is almost entirely new is the harnessing of the motion of the waves. There are various prototypical competing methods for translating the physical movement of the sea into electricity. This is still a comparatively tiny field and it will be several years before this technology is able to compete with more advanced renewables, such as wind and solar.

Other forms of renewable energy, which do not depend in any way on the sun, currently represent a much smaller part of the whole, but do have great potential. We can burrow into the earth and draw up water heated by heat emanating from the Earth's core and the decay of radioactive materials. This geothermal heat can be used for domestic heating or for other processes where heat is needed. Alternately, the steam produced can be used to drive a turbine, thus creating electricity.

Possibly our most reliable and predictable energy source is the force which our universal timekeeper, the moon, exerts upon the Earth's oceans. By causing the Earth's oceans to rise and fall, the moon is keeping literally astronomical masses of water in constant motion. By capturing a proportion of this water in tidal dams and allowing it, at our convenience, to pass through a turbine, we can generate reliable supplies of electricity. However, this is still a very marginal form of energy collection and is unlikely to provide a significant part of our needs in the near future.

3. Practical application of renewable energy

Most of the processes described above are technically quite familiar. Indeed, in some cases, the technology for doing so pre-dates agriculture. Renewable biomass, in the form of firewood, was a far more familiar energy source than fossil fuels to prehistoric humans. What has however changed is that, whereas our ancestors gathered naturally occurring biomass, we have started to deliberately and methodically generate this resource on an industrial scale.

Each of these methods of energy collection has a property which it does not share with mining or drilling for fossil fuels. As the energy available is spread across a large area, a correspondingly very large land area is needed to capture sufficient quantities to meet our needs. In addition, the effort which must be expended to even begin retrieving the energy is great when compared to the energy available. In this respect, the process has more in common with farming. Prospecting for fossil resources is more akin to hunting, in that a large proportion of the effort expended can be engaged in, often fruitless, attempts to locate the prey. As we have almost all but hunted to extinction the large, slow-moving, easy-to-kill fossil-fuel-dodos, we have turned our considerable skill and intelligence to finding more cunningly hidden, inaccessible quarry. However, notwithstanding all of our genius, we will eventually be forced out of the metaphorical fossil fuel forests and into the fertile valleys of renewable energy farming.

Solar PV is already shaping up to be one of the mainstays of the renewable energy future. The price of solar panels is continuing to fall and, in many parts of the world, the cost of electricity produced is market competitive. However, it is less viable in those places where electricity prices are held artificially low. It is a highly scalable solution and can be fitted to a single home or an immense grid-scale solar farm. However, it tends to be more cost effective at larger scales; this creates additional challenges for developers or users with capital constraints.

CSP, as we will see, has certain advantages over solar PV in terms of its ability to store and control the energy is produces. However, it is expensive and is only viable at large scale and in hot places. For this reason, it has been implemented at a much lower rate than PV, although its use is growing.

Squeezing a unit of biofuel from a patch of land takes some expenditure of effort and resources (including increasingly scarce fresh water). Such an endeavour is often likely to be, at least initially, uneconomical without some direct state manipulation of the market. This can lead to perverse situations where it can become economically sensible to expend more energy to produce a bio-fuel than is actually contained within the fuel.[2] This is also not to consider the fact that the production of energy crops from agricultural land means that that same land and water cannot be used for the old-fashioned purpose of making food to feed humans. As far as the human hierarchy of needs is concerned, the need for cheap transport, heat and power is still lower than the need for affordable food. The resultant pressure on food prices can cause a powerful public, and therefore political, reaction against such projects.[3]

Hydroelectricity is a generation method which has the controllability of fossil fuels, but without emitting the harmful carbon emissions. However, it is dependent on the presence of quite specific geographical conditions. In developed countries, most of the opportunities for large-scale generation have long been exhausted, although new hydro plants are still being built in emerging nations. These projects are often highly controversial as they can involve flooding large areas, displacing people and destroying the local environment.

Wind power is another rapidly growing form of renewable energy production. It can be installed on land or at sea. Each method has its own specific advantages and disadvantages. In general, onshore generation is cheaper; in many places it is at grid

---

2 U Chakravorty, MH Hubert, M Moreaux, and L Nøstbakken *The Long-Run Impact of Biofuels on Food Prices, Resources for the Future* (October 2015).

3 "EU caps 'bad' biofuels", Politico, 28 April 2015, accessed 23 April 2016 from www.politico.eu/article/eu-caps-bad-biofuels/.

parity. However, it tends to produce less electricity and is often subject to tortuous planning and permitting processes. Offshore wind is expensive to build and to maintain, but produces more electricity and with greater regularity. Connection of wind power to the electricity network can be problematic in all cases, as we will see in the next section.

4. Transportation and storage of energy

Since prehistoric times, the technology for capturing energy has gone hand-in-hand with methods for transporting it and for storing it in a useful form until it is needed. A large portion of the emerging renewable energy takes the form of direct electricity generation, mainly from wind and solar power. The question of how to store excess food was a problem for our ancestors as will be what to do with excess renewably generated electricity.

Electricity is an even more perishable commodity than food and must typically be produced and consumed simultaneously. Many renewable energy sources, such as wind and solar power, yield electricity gradually over an extended period and often at times which cannot be controlled or even perfectly predicted. However, electricity is not consumed evenly but varies from season to season and across the course of a day.

Wind and solar power create other problems for electricity network operators. As well as causing grid constraints, their increased use can have a negative impact on the quality of electricity on the network. Unlike large rotating generators, such as gas or steam turbines, wind and solar power does not provide the 'inertia' which helps to maintain network frequency within narrow bounds. Network operators need to work increasingly harder to avoid the potentially catastrophic consequences of sudden frequency fluctuations.

The key to the sustainable generation of renewable power is the development of methods of dealing with surplus generation and its effect on the network. Over large continent-sized areas, the variety of power sources ensures a certain minimum volume of generation should be available over the entire area. Due to the distributed nature of the energy sources, the power must be accumulated and transported to where it is to be consumed. The European Carbon Foundation[4] has projected a range of possible renewable futures for Europe. These explore the possibility of large solar projects in southern Europe and North Africa combined in a pan-European grid with huge offshore wind developments in the North and Baltic Seas. The transmission grid required to allow this will not only be an investment in infrastructure, but will make better use of the grid which we already have. The Smart Grid concept should allow a more integrated and interactive relationship between generator, consumer and grid operator.

The most common way of storing large quantities of power is to pump very large amounts of water from a lower to a higher reservoir. When required, this water is then released and allowed to pass through a turbine, generating electricity. Such pumped storage projects are expensive to build and dependent on the existence of suitable locations.

4 www.roadmap2050.eu, accessed 24 April 2016.

Electricity can also be stored effectively in relatively small quantities in batteries; this is usually worthwhile where portability is at a premium. However, storing very large volumes of battery power is expensive. Where batteries are permanently connected to the electricity network, this is done more commonly in order to regulate electricity frequency and provide other ancillary services, not to provide large-scale energy storage. This is however a situation which may undergo dramatic change in the coming years. Driven largely by the demands of the automotive industry, battery prices are falling rapidly[5] and it may, in many areas, soon become economically feasible to use batteries in to order to arbitrage between electricity time-of-use tariffs.

Other innovative power storage methods are currently under development, including fly-wheels, compressed air storage or chemical storage using improved batteries or fuel cells. An interesting future option is to use the batteries of stationary electric cars, combined with a Smart Grid, as a huge, distributed, nationwide power source, which could be used to flatten daily power consumption peaks.

Recent years have seen rapid large-scale implementation of renewable energy generation which shows many of the useful properties which one associates with fossil power. CSP (as opposed to solar PV) uses the sun's heat to directly create steam. An advantage of this is that the heat can be stored for limited periods of time, thus allowing power to be generated when there is no sun. Such installations require economies of scale as the steam cycle and turbine require a significant investment outlay.

Another solution to the problem of storing energy is to convert it into a form which can be easily stored. This chapter uses farming as a metaphor to illustrate a conceptual change in the way in which we think about where our energy comes from. However, with regard to some technologies, the idea can be taken quite literally. Increasingly we are turning over land to energy crops intended to power our vehicles, heat our homes and make our electricity. In a sense, cultivation of biomass energy crops can be seen as a kind of fossil fuel creation programme without the tedium of actual fossilisation. Like fossil fuels, such feed stocks have the happy property of being storable until we need to run our power stations and cars from them.

5. Renewable energy support

As the nascent renewable technologies move in to fill the space left by fossil fuels, we are likely to be challenged by increasing costs and reduced dependability. This transition will not be painless and will entail some sacrifice. However, the level of pain which we experience is dependent on the policies which we adopt now. Unlike the change to food-farming, which took place over thousands of years, our move into renewable energy cultivation will need to happen in a few short decades. For example, a report commissioned by the German government[6] has projected that Germany could supply its electricity needs entirely through renewable sources by 2050.

5 The Economics of Battery Energy Storage', Rocky Mountain Institute, October 2015.
6 "Energy target 2050: 100% renewable electricity supply", Umwelt Bundesamt, July 2010.

Whilst not all countries will achieve such ambitious targets within this timeline, the growth in renewable energy can be seen all around the world. However, almost nowhere has this transition happened without quite direct and aggressive intervention by state or international organisations. For example, in 1976, the Brazilian government passed laws which specified minimum proportions of biomass derived ethanol in gasoline. This effectively promoted the production of ethanol from sugarcane residues. This policy has not been without controversy and difficulties. These have often been the result of volatile oil prices, which had dramatic effects on the relative costs of ethanol and gasoline. However, the technology has recently become truly mature and ethanol derived from biomass in this way has been shown to be now cheaper than gasoline.[7]

Indeed, it is this intervention which has been the real impetus to the great energy transition. With a few notable exceptions, it is in the short to medium term still economically far more sensible to make use of non-renewable energy sources. In almost all countries where large-scale renewable energy has been adopted, it has been facilitated by some form of artificial manipulation of the market. The method by which renewables have been promoted varies from country to country, but generally has the same function: to make investment in renewable energy projects economically viable now, rather than later when shortages drive up fossil fuel costs.

These can take the form of direct incentives, such as electricity feed-in tariffs for renewable energy. These exist in various forms around the world, but in almost all cases represent a direct reward to generators who supply energy from renewable sources. Additionally, governments have implemented regulations which impose penalties on the emission of carbon dioxide (CO^2), an activity which, until recently, was entirely pain free to the emitter. Carbon trading schemes are intended to place a cost on the production of CO^2 onto power generators (as well as other processes) by requiring generators to procure tradable 'green' certificates to cover each MWh of electricity created. Since its launch in 2005, the world's largest trading scheme, the European Union Emissions Trading Scheme (EU-ETS) has however failed to deliver unto CO^2 emitters anything like the pain which is needed for a large-scale switch to non-CO^2 emitting generation. This has been due to the relatively generous allocation of free permits, as well as unexpectedly low power consumption in the economically depressed period after 2008. In response, some governments have taken direct steps to artificially support the cost of emitting CO^2. For example, the British government has implemented a Carbon Price Floor (CPF), a support mechanism in which taxes are used to 'top-up' the price to CO^2 to a minimum level.[8] The purpose of CPF is to subject fossil fuel generators to minimum costs from which renewable generators are free, thus increasing the relative viability of renewable generation.

One fact is clear; global investment in renewable energy has been rising. In 2004 the total global new investments in renewable energy was equal to \$46.6bn, rising to

7 "Sugar-Cane Fuel Wins in Brazil as Cheap Ethanol Beats Gasoline", Bloomberg, 1 March 2016, accessed 23 April 2016 from www.bloomberg.com/news/articles/2016-03-01/sugar-cane-fuel-wins-in-brazil-as-cheap-ethanol-beats-gasoline.

$285.9bn in 2015.[9] In 2015, for the first time, the majority of this investment was in developing countries. This certainly seems to suggest that investors have gained ever more confidence in the economic viability of renewable projects, in particular in those areas with the highest growth in energy demand.

6. The finances of renewable energy

As with all forms of project finance, the viability of an energy investment is measured by comparing the initial capital cost of the project with the net cash flows of its lifetime. By way of comparison we will look at the costs and income associated with an electricity generation project:

- The cost of building the generation station, including:
  - pre-construction development costs;
  - Engineering, Procurement and Construction (EPC) costs; and
  - costs associated with connecting the station to necessary infrastructure (eg, grid connection, fuel delivery);
- The costs of running the power station, including:
  - fixed and variable operating costs;
  - cost of capital (debt and equity);
  - cost of fuel;
  - cost of decommissioning the station; and
  - any applicable taxes or other payments required by government bodies.
- Income to which the power station is eligible, including:
  - revenue from sales of power;
  - any payments made by power offtakers for guaranteed capacity and availability;
  - any additional revenue for providing ancillary services (reactive power, voltage and frequency control) and energy balancing services or capacity management; and
  - any subsidies to which the station is eligible.

Any comparison of the relative economic viability is dependent on assumptions made on costs and income over the life of the plant, which can be several decades. When development of the power station commences, few of the values above can be known perfectly in advance, with some values being more uncertain than others.

Compared to many types of renewable generation, fossil fuel plants are, per installed megawatt (MW), relatively cheap to build. For example, the US Energy Information Administration (EIA) estimated the overnight specific capital cost of installed capacity for solar PV at $3,123/kW and for onshore wind at $1,850/kW. This seems to compare poorly to equivalent costs for a combined cycle gas turbine (CCGT) plant at $942/kW.[10]

---

8 "Carbon price floor: reform", Department of Energy and Climate Change, 19 March 2014, accessed 23 April 2016 from www.gov.uk/government/publications/carbon-price-floor-reform.

9 "Global Trends in Renewable Energy Investment 2016", FS-UNEP Collaborating Centre, 2016, accessed 23 April 2016 from http://fs-unep-centre.org/sites/default/files/publications/globaltrendsinrenewableenergyinvestment2016lowres_0.pdf.

10 "Cost and performance characteristics of new central station electricity generating technologies" US EIA, 25 August 2015, accessed 23 April 2016 from www.eia.gov/forecasts/aeo/assumptions/pdf/table_8.2.pdf.

However, the distribution of lifetime costs and income across these categories varies widely. The single greatest cost-uncertainty facing prospective fossil fuel generators is the price of fuel. Fossil fuel generators must therefore either risk a volatile and unpredictable market or lock themselves into long term fuel supply agreements or hedging arrangements. These necessarily add additional costs to the final megawatt-hour (MWh) delivered. For solar and wind power, the cost of fuel to the generator can be confidently estimated over the lifetime of the plant to be nothing at all.

In addition, solar PV cells are relatively small mass produced items, and dramatic improvements in cost are already being seen. On average, prices per kW for residential and commercial PV systems declined 6–12% per year between 1998 and 2014, and 9–21% between 2013 and 2014, depending on system size.[11]

With wind turbines, the story is slightly different. In some countries, onshore wind is competitive with fossil power.[12] However, the tendency with offshore wind generation is to build ever larger turbines and to move further and further offshore, where the wind blows with more regularity and there are no neighbours to object to unsightly and noisy rotating blades. Whilst the costs of turbines and their attendant equipment may come down, the shortage of suitable sites will force wind farms into deeper water, where costs increase with greater depth. A somewhat less steep learning curve has been projected for offshore wind than solar PV. However, offshore wind capital costs are expected to fall 40% between 2010 and 2030.[13]

On the other hand, solar PV and wind power produce a product which is typically less valuable than from a fossil generator. This may seem counterintuitive, as one MWh of electricity is, on the face of it, no different to any other. However, the value of electricity lies, not only in the energy value of the power delivered, but also in the optionality available to the end user. A MWh which can be guaranteed to be available from 6–7 pm on a winter's evening is far more valuable than a MWh which may be delivered on any one of 3,000 hours in a given year.

Subsidies and market manipulations of various sorts can ensure that a power project has a steady and predictable source of income which can serve to reassure investors of the low risk of that project and may tip the balance from a non-bankable to a bankable power generation project.

7. Conclusion

For a long time, the dream of generating large-scale quantities of renewable energy was, in the minds of many, associated with an idealistic fringe. Proponents of renewable energy often saw themselves as a moral alternative counterculture, defending the world against greed and self-interest. These early environmental

11 "Photovoltaic System Pricing Trends", Sun Shot, US Department of Energy, 2015 edition, 25 August 2015, accessed 23 April 2016 from https://emp.lbl.gov/sites/all/files/pv_system_pricing_trends_presentation_0.pdf.

12 "Power sector scenarios for the fifth carbon budget", Committee on Climate Change, October 2015, accessed 23 April 2016 from www.theccc.org.uk/publication/power-sector-scenarios-for-the-fifth-carbon-budget/.

13 "Review of the generation costs and deployment potential of renewable electricity technologies in the UK" ARUP Report for DECC, June 2011.

advocates played an important role in bringing the idea of sustainability into mainstream consciousness. This chapter argues that this particular narrative is not necessarily a useful way of understanding the relationship of the human race with its resources.

If one considers the complete arc of human history, the transition from fossil fuel to renewable generation is the next logical step in our development. Humans have always made immediate use of those commodities which were most readily available but, when these became scarce or reached the limit of their utility, began to synthesise substitutes under controlled conditions. The parallel which has been drawn here has been of the move from hunting and gathering to farming, but there are many other examples. We have in our history moved from flint and wood to metal and plastic, from pack animal to motor vehicle, from cave to house, and we will move from fossil fuel to renewable energy.

The main difference, however, with this transition is the speed and deliberateness with which it will need to be implemented. None of the other examples of change mentioned here were the result of deliberate government strategy or were in response to an obvious threat. They all happened because they were simply an improvement on what had gone before. Now the world is expected to change very quickly to a system which is, in many ways, initially less advantageous than what it is replacing. However, the transition away from fossil fuels is ultimately inevitable. The choice which is now open to us is how we manage the manner in which it happens. We have knowledge of the world and an understanding of the ultimate consequences of our actions of which our hunter-gatherer ancestors could have had no hope of comprehension. As a result, we are in the position to make intelligent choices about our future.

New renewable technologies

Nicholas Kelly
Kelly Legal
Dalia Majumder-Russell
Linklaters

---

1. Introduction

The diversity in energy sources for power projects propagated by the growth in renewable technologies has meant that there is now a need to consider which technologies can be characterised as established renewable technologies and which technologies are yet to reach commercial maturity. There is a confusing array of new and emerging renewable technologies under development. These range from electricity producing kites to giant solar space stations, designed to beam back unlimited quantities of solar energy to earth. But getting away from the fantastical and fanciful, there are some renewable technologies seeking to come up to par with the established renewables sectors of hydro-electric, onshore wind and photovoltaic solar energy.

Specifically, this chapter considers the following less established renewable technologies:

- wave;
- marine renewable power generation (tidal);
- geothermal;
- anaerobic digestion;
- floating offshore wind; and
- energy storage.

1.1 Why these sectors and not others?

Renewable power generation has grown as a result of many policy drivers around the world. Accordingly, solar and onshore wind, as well as existing hydropower, are close to (and some would say are at) cost parity with non-renewable power sources. Geothermal power, anaerobic digestion and marine technologies are starting to make inroads into this market. Floating technologies then take the lessons learnt from onshore solar and wind markets and apply them to new situations, so as well as representing a good overall picture of the next generation of renewable energy sources, the selected technologies illustrate some of the technical and commercial challenges faced by new renewable technologies generally. The development of these technologies is also coupled with the potential impact of the progress being made to store energy, especially through the development of battery storage technologies.

While the growth of renewable technologies is a global phenomenon and the chapter discusses these technologies in general details, some examples have been added of UK and US developments as well as examples from other countries to give a flavour of the opportunities and challenges in these sectors.

Finally, to make costs of individual technologies easier to compare, the author has used the levelised cost of electricity per kilowatt-hour (KWh) where possible. This is an estimate of the minimum power price needed for the technology to break even, taking into account:

- the capital expenditure;
- the operating and maintenance costs; and
- the cost of fuel (if relevant).

This minimum power price provides at best an approximation of the actual costs of the technology, though actual costs will of course vary widely depending on one's assumptions about the project, discount rates, taxes and cost of capital. These costs also tend to fall as technologies become more established. As a general benchmark, the cost of coal-fired generation in the United Kingdom in 2008 was around £0.041/KWh and gas-fired generation was around £0.039/KWh.[1]

1.2 What contributes to the success of emerging technologies?

Numerous factors contribute to either the success or failure of each sector and technology. However, some factors must be given more weight for an assessment of the technology to be complete. These trumping elements are:

- the technology, and how easy it is to harness the particular energy source and turn it into a useful form of power (ie, electricity, heat or chemical power);
- the costs (and their life-cycles);
- the regulatory and political support enjoyed by a particular technology, as consistent and sustained support is essential to ensure that nascent technologies can mature to a commercially viable stage; and
- the scalability of the technology, which also plays a role in the preceding considerations. Given the political ambition expressed by a number of countries to turn away from fossil-fuel generation, can the renewable technology deliver on a scale necessary to make sustained and significant change?

2. Wave energy

2.1 Resource

The promoters of marine energy make very ambitious claims:

Converted into electricity, wave energy could potentially satisfy up to one tenth of current global power demands.[2]

The wave resource around the United Kingdom and Irish waters is estimated to be approximately 840 terawatt-hour (TWh) per year, equivalent to approximately 50% of the total European wave energy resource.[3] In the longer term, between 15% and 20% of the United Kingdom's energy needs could be met by marine energy (ie,

1 House of Lords, Economic Affairs Committee, "The economics of renewable energy", November 2008, Table 2.

2 http://aw-energy.com/wave-energy-resources/resources-globally.

3 Offshore energy in the UK: renewables – marine energy (wave and tidal), the Marine Socio-Economics Project (MSEP) report published by the New Economics Foundation (NEF), June 2014, www.mseproject.net/marine-energy/doc_download/132-5-energy-wave-and-tidal.

between 6GW and 8GW).[4] However, the government's immediate targets are less demanding. The National Renewable Energy Action Plan for the United Kingdom, as submitted to the EU as part of the EU Renewables Directive, anticipates 1.3GW of marine energy capacity by 2020, although even this will be challenging.[5]

So where does wave energy come from? It is created by the action of the wind on the sea surface. The size of the waves is determined by:

- the wind's speed;
- the expanse over which the wind is blowing currents; and
- the topography of the seabed.

This energy can be captured and harnessed using a device to convert the kinetic energy of the waves into an electrical pulse.

Various devices are being developed and tested; they all take a different approach to the problem of converting the movement of the waves into electricity. So far, no particular design or approach has emerged as the dominant technology. The methods range from floating devices, such as 'attenuators' and 'point absorbers' fixed or moored to the seabed, to shore-based structures, such as 'oscillating water columns' and 'overtopping devices'.[6] In each case, developers need to grapple with the twin demands of efficiency and reliability. Efficiency is critical because wave power is highly variable in amplitude and irregular in frequency, making its energy difficult to capture in a variety of sea states. Reliability is essential, given:

- the extremely hostile environment in which wave devices have to operate; and
- the difficulties of undertaking even routine maintenance operations.

Often, the two aims can be at odds with each other – a more efficient design may be too complex to be viable at sea.

There are two further considerations for the development of wave power in the United Kingdom: permitting and grid connections. Until recently, the arrangements for the permitting of offshore installations of renewable energy were extremely confused, with permits and licences required under several different UK statutes. In late 2009, however, the Marine and Coastal Access Act came into force, creating a single body for the permitting of offshore wave farms (ie, the Marine Management Organisation). A Strategic Environmental Assessment has also been completed for the development of wave-energy devices around the UK coastline (as required under the EU Strategic Environmental Assessment Directive). The Crown Estate has granted leases for the development of up to 1.2GW of installed wave and tidal capacity in the Pentland Firth and Orkney waters by 2020, with some of this already under construction.[7] This represents the potential to power 750,000 homes with wave and tidal energy and is the world's first commercial wave and tidal leasing round. The Crown Estate has followed these awards with further invitations to bid for leases,

4 www.carbontrust.com/resources/reports/technology/accelerating-marine-energy.
5 National Renewable Energy Action Plan for the UK, 2011, p153.
6 See www.emec.org.uk/marine-energy/wave-devices.
7 www.thecrownestate.co.uk/energy-minerals-and-infrastructure/wave-and-tidal/our-portfolio/.

including for the Inner Sound near Caithness in Scotland (awarded in October 2010), and in autumn 2011, the Crown Estate prequalified four companies for wave and tidal projects of up to 30MW each, as part of the Scottish government's £10m Saltire Prize. These projects are in various stages, from planning and consenting to fully operational.[8]

The second issue is grid connection. In principle, an offshore wave farm will need to construct its own transmission line to convey the electricity onshore and connect to the grid, which will increase the cost of the project. Even where such construction is feasible, there is often no obvious connection for the transmission line when it comes onshore. For instance, the northwest coast of Scotland is considered an ideal location for a wave farm, but the local distribution network is limited and would need to be upgraded to accept the additional generation.[9] However, it is just as much an issue for offshore wind farms as for wave power projects. The UK government is looking at a number of measures to address the problem. In particular, the Department of Energy and Climate Change (the predecessor of the Department for Business, Energy and Industrial Strategy) and the Office of Gas and Electricity Markets developed a regulatory regime for licensing offshore transmission lines. This will not be of immediate relevance to the wave industry, as licensing is only required for offshore transmission lines that operate at 132 kilovolts (kV) or above while most wave farms (for the moment at least) will connect at 33kV. However, the initiative is welcome for the longer term as it will move the cost of building and connecting to the national grid away from the project developer and onto the transmission system owner.

2.2 Costs

There are over 50 different devices in development in the United Kingdom alone (with over 1,000 patents in existence worldwide for wave devices). This makes it hard to provide meaningful estimated costs as these will be device-specific. A report for the Carbon Trust, however, has given a range of £0.12/KWh to £0.44/KWh for the cost of electricity from early-stage wave farms. RenewableUK estimate a cost of energy from wave devices, once 1GW or more of capacity has been installed, to range between £0.075/KWh to £0.125/KWh.[10]

A handful of devices have become commercial operations, thus providing useful reference points. The 2.25-megawatt (MW) Pelamis wave-energy converter installed off the coast of Portugal was developed with an installation cost of £3,226/KW and enjoys a preferential electricity tariff of €0.23/KWh.[11] According to an independent report produced for RenewableUK, this puts the Pelamis project in a range similar to that of photovoltaic solar energy, but still around four times as expensive as large wind energy projects.[12] Despite the promising start and operations commencing in 2008, the project failed due to technical issues, and its backers have since gone into

---

8 www.thecrownestate.co.uk/energy-minerals-and-infrastructure/wave-and-tidal/our-portfolio/other-projects.

9 Marine Renewable Energy – State of the Industry Report, October 2009, p19.

10 "Wave and Tidal Energy in the UK", RenewableUK, March 2011, p23.

11 http://ec.europa.eu/ourcoast/index.cfm?menuID=7&articleID=92.

12 Marine Renewable Energy – State of the Industry Report, October 2009, p17.

administration. More successful projects have been launched by Ocean Power Technologies, which began installation of a 1.39MW PowerBuoy wave farm off the northern coast of Spain (in collaboration with Iberderola) in 2009, and in July 2016 announced deployment of two PB3 PowerBuoys off the coast of New Jersey, with one of them being the anticipated commercial PB3 product offering.[13]

2.3 Regulatory and political support

The UK government has committed to ensuring that 15% of the country's energy usage comes from renewable sources by 2020. Most of this target is expected to be met by increasing the share of renewable electricity production to between 30% and 40%.[14] The government reported good progress toward this goal, with renewables accounting for 15.5% of all electricity generated in Quarter 2 of 2013.[15] As the United Kingdom is recognised as having one of the best potential resources for marine energy in Europe, wave power is expected to play a part in reaching this target. The government admits, however, that the industry is still a long way from reaching commercial-scale operation.

The UK government has supported research and development in the wave industry for a number of years, primarily through capital grants administered by devolved organisations such as:

- the Carbon Trust;
- the Scottish government;
- Innovate UK;
- the Energy Technologies Institute; and
- the Marine Renewables Proving Fund.

Support has also come for wave testing centres such as:

- the European Marine Energy Centre in Orkney;
- the New and Renewable Energy Centre in Northumberland; and
- the offshore WaveHub in southwest England.

These centres are critical in allowing developers:

- to scale up their models to full-size operations; and
- to put their devices through rigorous sea trials.

The UK government has said it is committed to promoting marine energy as a key component of achieving its EU renewable energy targets. A Marine Energy Programme Board was established in early 2011, and £22.5 million has been committed to the Marine Renewables Proving Fund, administered by the Carbon Trust. Support also comes via the Renewables Obligation Scheme – that is, the obligation on electricity suppliers to source an ever-increasing proportion of their electricity from qualifying renewable sources. Renewable obligation certificates are

---

13 http://phx.corporate-ir.net/phoenix.zhtml?c=155437&p=irol-newsArticle&ID=2185508.
14 HM Government, The UK Renewable Energy Strategy, July 2009, p8.
15 HM Government, UK Renewable Energy Roadmap Update 2013, p4.

assumed to be worth approximately £0.045/KWh (but prices vary with supply and demand), which represents a significant direct subsidy for renewable generation, including wave power. Currently wave and tidal devices qualify for a range between 1.8 and 5 ROCs per MWh. Wave projects are also eligible to compete for contracts for difference in the government run CfD auctions.

Separately, the Scottish government has introduced a dedicated body for supporting the development of wave projects in Scotland. Wave Energy Scotland (WES)[16] was given a budget of £14.3m in February 2015 for awarding to technology development projects focusing on developing low cost, efficient and reliable components that can be used by various wave energy technology developers. Technology transfer and innovation are seen as key to bringing down the costs of wave technology.

However, is this enough? The government's aim is to develop a world-class wave industry in the United Kingdom. RenewableUK estimates that given the high costs of developing marine energy projects, there will be a marked divergence between government ambition and commercial reality. It notes the experience of other countries, for instance Denmark and Japan, which have spent billions to develop their wind and solar industries. With the renewables obligation scheme closing to new generation in March 2017, subsidies for renewable technologies are decreasing in the UK.

Reading between the lines, there is also a fair degree of cynicism and world-weariness about delivery of government support. Too often, good intentions run into the deep sands of bureaucracy. Money earmarked for grants rarely makes its way to developers. For instance, the Marine Renewables Deployment Fund was launched in 2004 with £50 million to spend, but was closed in March 2011 as part of the spending review without having made a single award.[17] Perhaps the most damning indictment comes from the Pelamis project. Although the project was developed by a Scottish company and tested at the European Marine Energy Centre in Orkney, the world's first commercial wave farm was not installed in UK waters. Despite taking advantage of a very favourable long term feed-in tariff offered by the Portuguese government, after launching its first full-scale commercial wave farm in Portugal, the project failed a few months into operation with its backers going into administration in 2014.

2.4 Scalability

Discussing the scalability of wave energy as a whole is difficult; instead, one should consider each device individually. Generally, one would expect each wave device to have an optimum size and scale relative to its performance. Make it too large and you lose efficiency; make it too small and you probably are not getting enough power. One thing most sea-based (rather than shore-based) wave devices have in common, however, is the ability to be deployed in arrays. Ocean Power Technology, for

---

16 www.hie.co.uk/growth-sectors/energy/wave-energy-scotland/default.html.

17 http://webarchive.nationalarchives.gov.uk/20121217150421/http://www.decc.gov.uk/en/content/cms/funding/funding_ops/innovation/historic/marine_fund/marine_fund.aspx.

example, plans to deploy its PowerBuoy device in arrays scalable to 100MW.[18] The Pelamis project, which consists of three P1-A Pelamis machines (ie, three times 750MW), was originally intended to be the forerunner of several mega wave farms, until its backer, Babcock and Brown, went into administration.

The sector had attracted quite significant inflows of private capital in 2011. Large manufacturing companies have been investing in marine energy technology companies, including Roll-Royce, Alstom and Siemens. It is estimated that approximately £230m of investment has been made worldwide.[19] Similarly, the technology giant Apple signed a memorandum of understanding with the Sustainable Energy Authority of Ireland (SEAI)[20] in November 2015 committing €1m in research and development funding to support the Galway Bay Ocean Energy test site project off the coast of Ireland.

3. Tidal energy – marine renewable power generation

3.1 Resource

Tidal power seems to be the poor, neglected cousin among renewable energy sources. Little has been done worldwide to harness tidal energy, even though:

- tidal power stations have the potential to provide large-scale, reliable and predictable sources of clean energy; and
- countries such as Canada, New Zealand and the United Kingdom have potentially significant resources.

There are still only three large tidal-barrage schemes in operation worldwide (described below) and tidal-stream devices are still at the research and development stage. However, as mentioned above, the United Kingdom is estimated to have one of the best tidal resources in the world with a potential tidal-stream resource of around 18TWh a year (50% of Europe's total tidal-energy resource) though without the political support, the UK has been lagging behind in capitalising on this potential.[21]

(a) *Tidal barrages*

The world's largest tidal power plant was constructed at La Rance in France in 1966 and has been operating continuously since then. It is rated at 240MW, which in theory is sufficient to power fully a city of around 180,000 households. The Annapolis Royal Generating Station has been in operation in Nova Scotia, Canada, since the 1980s and has a capacity of 20MW. In South Korea, a 254MW tidal scheme was completed in 2011 at Sihwa, using the ebbs and flows into an artificial lake. Other large operational plants are few and far between. The problem lies primarily in

18 www.oceanpowertechnologies.com.

19 Wave and Tidal Energy in the UK, RenewableUK, March 2011, p23.

20 www.seai.ie/News_Events/Press_Releases/2015/Minister-White-welcomes-Apple%E2%80%99s-commitment-to-ocean-energy-in-Ireland.html.

21 Energy and Climate Change Committee, Fourth Report of Session 2009–10, "Low carbon technologies in a green economy" (HC193-1), p26.

identifying suitable locations for tidal-generation plants. Tidal-stream plants need to be located where there is a significant tidal range and fast flowing current. In La Rance, for instance, the tidal range is eight metres.

Environmental concerns over damage and disruption caused by building and effectively damming a large estuary have also held back development. Not only do various organisations such as the Word Wide Fund for Nature, the Royal Society for the Protection of Birds and Friends of the Earth lobby hard against tidal projects due to the potential damage to fish and bird stocks, there is also a maze of EU and domestic legislation to navigate, including the EU Habitats Directive and the Birds Directive. A consultation on building a tidal barrage in the Severn Estuary in the United Kingdom has revealed that over 80 pieces of environmental legislation would need to be addressed.[22] The UK government's advisers have stated that "a Severn barrage project would not be possible within the current legal framework provided by the EU Habitats and Birds Directives".[23] Even though supporters of tidal systems claim that these concerns are overstated, they remain a major obstacle to the implementation of tidal-barrage systems. It is then of no surprise that in 2013, the plans for the £25bn Severn Estuary project were declared "dead in the water" as the UK government could not be persuaded that it would be good for the economy or the environment.[24]

Instead, the UK government has set its sights on a close relative of tidal barrages – tidal lagoon projects. A tidal lagoon also uses the tide to generate power but unlike a tidal barrage, a tidal lagoon does not block off a body of water but relies on the tide to fill the lagoon. One such project is the $1.6bn 320MW Swansea Bay tidal lagoon project being planned in Wales. However, as with the Severn Estuary, questions are being asked about the impact on the environment and the costs of developing the project. In addition, reports have emerged that it could be negatively impacted by the political uncertainties caused by Britain's decision to leave the European Union.[25]

(b) Tidal streams

Tidal-stream devices, like wave-energy converters, are still at an early stage of development. They work by converting the kinetic energy of the ebb and flow of tides into electricity and are generally designed as modular stand-alone units. No particular device has emerged as a clear winner in terms of technology. Devices are grouped broadly into three main categories – horizontal axis, reciprocating hydro-foil and vertical axis. Horizontal axis devices extract energy in much the same way as wind turbines extract energy from wind, although the relative density of water means that the blades in tidal systems tend to be thicker and shorter than in wind systems. Reciprocating hydro-foils work rather like the wings of an aeroplane, rising and falling with the ebb and flow of the tide, which in turn compresses and expands

22 Minutes of Evidence taken before the House of Commons Energy and Climate Change Committee, 14 October 2009.
23 Severn Barrage, Position Statement, Environment Agency, CCW, EN/NE, May 2006.
24 www.bbc.co.uk/news/uk-wales-24013575.
25 www.powerengineeringint.com/articles/2016/07/fears-for-uk-tidal-power-project-amid-brexit-fallout.html.

a piston. Vertical axis devices work in a similar fashion to horizontal axis devices, but the blades are fixed on a vertical axis. Devices can be fixed to the seabed, moored or weighted to sit on the seabed. Like wave-energy devices, tidal-stream devices face the demands of balancing efficiency with reliability. Maintenance is also a key issue.

3.2 Costs

Tidal barrages are notoriously capital-intensive. In the 1980s the Bondi Committee (led by Sir Herman Bondi) estimated that the cost of a Severn tidal barrage (the so-called 'Cardiff–Weston Scheme') would be £15 billion.[26] By late 2010 that estimate had risen to £34 billion, including the costs of mitigating the environmental and flooding impacts. In addition, the size of the project (with the potential to meet 5% of the United Kingdom's total electricity consumption) would require significant reinforcement of the local grid.[27] The grid would need to be adapted to accommodate the large surge in electricity at ebb tide (which would not coincide with a surge in electricity demand).

An investment of this size, however, is estimated to be able to provide 17TWh of electricity a year for the country and last for over 120 years. It could make the single biggest contribution towards the UK government's 2020 targets for renewable energy.[28] In October 2010, however, after a two-year feasibility study, the UK government decided not to provide any public subsidy for a Severn barrage scheme, although leaving the door open to private investors and developers coming forward with their own schemes.[29] The main reason for their decision was 'value for money'. Essentially, the scheme was deemed too expensive and too risky when compared to other forms of low-carbon generation, and it would certainly not be ready in time to meet the government's 2020 deadline for increasing renewable energy.

Although now largely academic, the power price of electricity from the Severn barrage was expected to be between £0.17/KWh and £0.2/KWh.[30] In contrast, La Rance, which has been in operation since the 1960s and has paid back its original capital costs of 620 million francs, produces electricity at around €0.02/KWh.[31] Separate sources indicate that electricity production costs for La Rance and Sihwa Dam are €0.04/kWh and €0.02/kWh, but note that these costs are very site specific.[32]

The Swansea Bay project mentioned above is one example of a project seeking state support for a tidal lagoon project. The project is designed to generate enough power for 155,000 homes from 16 underwater turbines built into a six-mile, horseshoe-shaped sea wall in Swansea Bay. Using the UK's latest form of investment enabling legal framework, the project approached the government for a contract for difference (CfD) to have a guaranteed price for its electricity of £96.50/MWh over a

---

26 Sustainable Development Commission, "Turning the Tide: Tidal Power in the UK", 2007, p7.
27 Severn Tidal Power, Conclusions and Summary Report, October 2010, Department of Energy and Climate Change, South West of England Regional Development Agency and Welsh Assembly Government.
28 www.sd-commission.org.uk/pages/tidal-power.html.
29 www.decc.gov.uk/en/content/cms/meeting energy/wave_tidal/severn_tidal_power.
30 Minutes of Evidence taken before the House of Commons Energy and Climate Change Committee, 14 October 2009.
31 www.reuk.co.uk/La-Rance-Tidal-Power-Plant.htm.
32 Tidal Energy Technology Brief, IRENA, June 2014, www.irena.org/documentdownloads/publications/tidal_energy_v4_web.pdf, p4.

term of between 35 and 90 years (depending on negotiations). At this price the project would be slightly cheaper than subsidising the cost of a new nuclear power station in the UK but still a significant cost. However, the project's future is still uncertain, as the UK government announced an independent review of tidal lagoons in February 2016, appointing former Energy Minister Charles Hendry to lead the review in May 2016.[33]

Tidal stream devices seem more promising. A number of companies around the United Kingdom are also developing tidal-stream devices. Sea Generation Ltd has been running commercial trials of its 1.2MW SeaGen tidal-energy converter in Strangford Lough since April 2008 and is developing a pipeline of over 100MW of potential tidal power. An Irish company, OpenHydro, is developing a number of tidal projects in Canada and in France, in collaboration with major European utilities. A number of these companies have also attracted significant private investment over the course of 2011, with some large-scale projects since proving these to be commercially viable.

The Paimpol-Brehat tidal demonstrator project in France, in planning since 2004, entered phase 2 with two turbines installed in May 2016.[34] The turbine manufacturer cited the project as "a global industry first, giving us key insights into the operation of our turbines at array scale".[35] This was followed by the official opening on 12 September 2016 of the 398MW MeyGen tidal stream project in Scotland, with first power expected to be exported to the grid by the end of 2016. It was hailed by RenewableUK as "a major step forward in terms of scale", marking "a significant moment in the commercial development of marine power".[36]

Information on the costs or economics of these projects is scarce. However, the Carbon Trust estimates that the cost of initial-stage tidal-stream devices ranges from £0.09/KWh to £0.18/KWh, with central estimates between £0.12/KWh and £0.15/KWh.[37] Over time, these costs are expected to fall as more devices are installed, making tidal-stream devices competitive with other forms of renewable electricity.

3.3 Regulatory and political support

For the past 50 years successive UK governments have produced reports, held consultations and conducted feasibility studies into a variety of schemes for a Severn barrage. All projects have been shelved, postponed or 'noted', but the idea never seems to be killed off conclusively. The Department of Energy and Climate Change (predecessor to the Department for Business, Enterprise and Industrial Strategy) conducted a feasibility study in 2010, concluding that it did not see a case for public investment, but did not preclude a scheme funded through private investment.[38] A second government report considered a proposal put forward by a private

33 www.gov.uk/government/news/head-of-independent-review-of-tidal-lagoons-announced.

34 www.eusew.eu/sites/default/files/programme-additional-docs/EUSEW%20160616%20Presentation%20to%20EUSEW%20by%20EDF.pdf.

35 http://tidalenergytoday.com/2016/05/30/tidal-array-at-paimpol-brehat-fully-deployed/.

36 www.renewableuk.com/news/307193/Launch-of-worlds-largest-tidal-stream-power-project-is-a-major-step-forward-for-renewables-.htm.

37 Sustainable Development Commission, "Turning the Tide: Tidal Power in the UK", 2007, p37.

38 www.gov.uk/government/collections/severn-tidal-power-feasibility-study-conclusions.

consortium, and despite the consortium's claims that the scheme would be entirely privately funded, the report noted that, "[i]n practice ... Government support would be required over a 30-year period through Contracts for Difference (CfD) or a similar mechanism".[39]

UK tidal-stream generation projects enjoy similar support to wave-energy devices – that is, through capital grants and renewables obligation certificates. Tidal energy also forms a part of the government's strategy for a transition to a low-carbon economy, although it is expected to contribute only a small proportion of the renewable energy needed. As noted above, in March 2010 the Crown Estate awarded leases to 10 companies to develop wave and tidal devices in the Pentland Firth and Orkney waters, representing up to 1.2GW of installed capacity. Of this, 600MW have been allocated to tidal-energy developers.

3.4 Scalability

Tidal-range schemes have the capacity to produce large, predictable and reliable sources of power. However, due to their high cost and the environmental concerns with which they are associated, it may be a long time before developments on any significant scale occur in this sector.

Tidal-stream devices, like wave devices:

- can be scaled both in terms of the size of the units and deployment in multiple arrays; and
- the United Kingdom offers untapped resources for development of tidal-stream projects.

In the absence of a stronger political commitment to the sector, these devices will struggle to make an impact. RenewableUK, in its 2010 state of the industry report, Marine Renewable Energy, noted:

Based on the experience of the solar and wind industries, the level of UK support for marine energy is not yet of the magnitude required to develop a world-class industry.

It may well be that other nations (eg, Canada) for the moment offer tidal-stream developers a much better return on their research and development.

4. Geothermal energy

Despite its huge ... potential, geothermal energy is often misunderstood or overlooked. It is an important and well-established source for electricity production and has an enormous variety of other uses, including school heating, district heating, fish farming, greenhouses, resorts and small power production. These applications all make geothermal energy an important, adaptable and growing energy resource for modern cities.[40]

39 www.publications.parliament.uk/pa/cm201314/cmselect/cmenergy/194/19404.htm#a1.
40 Karl Gawell, executive director of the Geothermal Energy Association, December 2009.

4.1 Resource

Geothermal energy comes from two sources:

- radioactive decay in the crust of the earth; and
- the heat that rises from the earth's core.

Geothermal energy is a potentially very large resource of clean, reliable, predicable and long term renewable energy. It has been used for centuries for heating and, since the turn of the 20th century, for power generation (the first steam plant was developed in Lardarello, Italy, in 1904). There are approximately 13.3GW of installed capacity across 24 countries.[41]

The resource was until recently limited to those areas of the earth's surface where heat is readily accessible – mainly along the tectonic plates where:

- heat and steam escape naturally; or
- it is easy to access the resource.

Certain countries enjoy prolific sources of geothermal supply. This is the case in Iceland where:

- geothermal energy provides the vast majority of the country's heating; and
- geothermal plants produce 25% of the country's electricity.

Other countries and regions, such as California, Indonesia, Japan, Mexico and the Philippines, also enjoy excellent geothermal resources. A 2006 study by the Massachusetts Institute of Technology into geothermal resources in the United States concluded that with suitable investment, enhanced geothermal systems could provide 100GW-electric or more of generation capacity in the next 50 years.[42]

There appears to be two main constraints on the further development of geothermal sources. First, identifying potential geothermal reservoirs can be extremely time-consuming and expensive, particularly if the intent is to exploit deeper sources of heat using enhanced geothermal techniques. Developers rely on seismic data and surface studies to evaluate the suitability of a particular location, but ultimately they need to drill exploratory wells to test the heat resource. Although technology and expertise are developing all the time (with transfers of experience and some technology from the oil and gas sector), significant time and cost risks remain associated with the exploration phase of a geothermal project. This in turn concentrates efforts on the most readily available resources.

Secondly, although geothermal heat does not dissipate over time, experience has shown that reservoir pressures and temperatures decline in response to production. For instance, one of the world's first geothermal projects, The Geysers in California, originally used naturally occurring steam to produce electric power. This resource peaked in the late 1980s and The Geysers plants now re-inject recycled treated water into the ground to produce steam for the power plants in operation at the site.

The use of enhanced geothermal systems (also known as 'hot dry rocks') may

---

41 Geothermal Energy Association, 2016 Annual US and Global Geothermal Power Production Report.
42 Massachusetts Institute of Technology, "The future of geothermal energy" (2006), pp1–3.

provide an alternative to more traditional geothermal projects. 'Enhanced geothermal systems' have been defined as "engineered reservoirs that have been created to extract economical amounts of heat from low-permeability and/or porosity geothermal resources".[43] Enhanced geothermal systems work by injecting a fluid into hot rocks, fracturing the rocks and then pumping the heated fluid back to the surface power plant. Enhanced geothermal systems may be simple in concept, but present numerous difficulties. One of the main constraints is the need to control (and understand) flows of heat between injection and production wells. There is also the risk that the rock fracturisation may trigger earthquakes (a $60-million geothermal project in Basel, Switzerland, was suspended in 2006 because of this potential threat[44] and a US company, AltaRock Energy, suspended drilling operations in late 2009 due to similar concerns[45]).

Mining techniques are, however, being adapted specifically for projects using enhanced geothermal systems. This could provide access to a significant new resource globally if the technical challenges can be overcome.

4.2 Costs

The costs of building a geothermal power plant are well understood and quantifiable. There are three main types of plant in operation: steam (the oldest and simplest system), flash and binary. The choice of plant is mainly dictated by:

- the temperature of the fluid (higher temperatures are used in direct steam systems and lower temperatures are used in flash and binary systems); and
- the form of the fluid (ie, water or steam).

The costs of accessing the heat source are more difficult to estimate as they are dictated mainly by the specific requirements of the location. As mentioned above, enhanced geothermal systems are likely to have a high initial capital outlay on exploration and development of the geothermal reservoir. This may make the project unviable in the absence of government support. As geothermal energy is generally predicable and it is not intermittent or variable (other than for routine plant shutdowns), it is not expected to impose additional costs on the transmission system other than the costs of connection.

Once a geothermal project is in operation, the costs of electricity production are low and availability is high. Unlike wind farms, which have a typical availability of between 30% and 40%, geothermal plants run with availabilities of over 90%.

Geothermal systems accessing lower temperatures also provide an ideal solution for local heating needs, be they industrial, municipal or residential.

Overall, the levelised cost of electricity has been estimated at US$101.7/MWh plant starting operation in 2016. This is expected to decrease over time, which will make geothermal energy production competitive with conventional forms of power generation.[46]

43 Massachusetts Institute of Technology, "The future of geothermal energy" (2006), p11.
44 www.nytimes.com/2009/12/11/science/earth/11basel.html.
45 www.altarockenergy.com.
46 Energy Information Administration, Annual Energy Outlook 2011.

4.3 Regulatory and political support

The United States leads the way in support for geothermal energy. In a volte-face from the Bush administration, the Obama government pledged approximately $400 million of federal funds to support geothermal projects under the American Recovery and Reinvestment Act 2009. In October 2009 the US Department of Energy awarded grants and support worth $338 million to 123 geothermal projects under its Geothermal Technologies Programme. The majority of these funds is going towards exploration and development activities to identify potential geothermal sources around the United States. Enhanced geothermal systems attracted approximately $131 million of funding, divided between:

- three demonstration projects; and
- research and development into geothermal reservoir evaluation techniques, drilling and reservoir simulation.

In 2013, President Obama launched the Climate Action Plan to double renewable energy generation in the United States by 2020 and geothermal is expected to make a significant contribution towards this goal.

Geothermal projects are also eligible for a $0.023/kWh production tax credit (2016) (or a 30% investment tax credit, in lieu of the production tax credit) and federal loan guarantees. Both have helped stimulate a revival of interest in the sector, even though developers point out that the sunset provisions for production tax credits can make these forms of financing inaccessible.

At state level, California and Nevada have extended their renewable energy standards. California is set to increase its renewable portfolio standard to 33% by 2020 and Nevada, to 25% by 2025. Both are strong markets for geothermal projects due to their geothermal resources. Geothermal projects in the western states have also received a boost by the completion of a wide-ranging Programmatic Environmental Impact Statement for Geothermal Leasing in 2009 by the Department of the Interior and the US Forest Service. The programme potentially opens up 190 million acres of federal land for the development of geothermal projects, with an estimated potential capacity to install 5.5GW of new electricity generation.[47] This in turn has resulted in a sale of geothermal leases by the Bureau of Land Management in California, Nevada and Utah.

Overall, nameplate capacity in the United States, supported by these federal and state incentives, increased from just over 3.0GW in 2010 to 3.7GW by the end of 2015.[48]

4.4 Scalability

Geothermal energy is clearly one of the most scalable renewable energy sources around. The potential resource is ideally suited to provide long term, predictable base-load power, as well as heating/cooling for industrial, municipal and domestic uses. The challenges remain:

47 www.blm.gov/wo/st/en/info/newsroom/2008/december/NR_12_18_2008.html.
48 Geothermal Energy Association, 2016 Annual US and Global Geothermal Power Production Report.

- the high capital cost of exploration and development; and
- the further funding and support needed for research and development in new technologies such as enhanced geothermal systems.

The international agreement reached in Paris at COP21 in 2015, however, has given an additional impetus towards development of geothermal projects internationally. A new Global Geothermal Alliance was launched at the event, with a pledge to increase geothermal generation five-fold to 65GW by 2030. A number of countries have already stated they will incorporate geothermal into their national plans to tackle climate change.

5. Anaerobic digestion

The [UK] Government has set out its commitment to an expansion of energy from waste through AD. At the heart of this commitment is the recognition that AD unites a number of Coalition Government priorities.[49]

5.1 Resource

Anaerobic digestion (AD) is a natural process which has been around for thousands of years and is commonly used throughout the world for treating and breaking down organic waste. In China in particular it has been promoted since the 1970s as a cheap and efficient way of dealing with organic waste, and it has been estimated there are now over 7 million small-scale digestors in operation in China.

The technology, however, is currently enjoying something of a renaissance in Western Europe, where it is seen as a particularly effective way helping achieve Europe-wide commitments on emissions reductions, renewable energy targets and reducing the amount of waste sent to landfill. It is already widely used for treating sewage, but in the UK alone, it has been estimated there is 16 million tonnes of organic food and drink waste a year and 90 million tonnes of manures and slurries from farms which could be treated through AD. A 2011 study by the UK Department for Climate Change has estimated that this could realistically produce 3–5 TWh of renewable electricity.[50]

AD technologies are also seen as a key buffer to intermittent renewables such as solar and wind because the electricity can be generated constantly and can be stored in the grid (in the form of gas). In addition, AD plant is relatively quicker to construct compared to some of the other waste management technologies or renewables like offshore wind.

So how does it work? Anaerobic digestion is a series of processes in which micro-organisms break down organic material in the absence of oxygen, producing 'biogas' (primarily a mixture of methane and carbon dioxide and some other contaminant gases) and digestate (a form of nitrogen rich fertiliser). There are a number of feedstocks, but the primarily sources of feedstock in the UK are food waste, farm

---

49 Anaerobic Digestion Strategy and Action Plan (2011), Department of Energy and Climate Change and DEFRA, p17.

50 *Ibid*, Ministerial Foreword, p2.

products such as slurry and manure, and, increasingly, high yielding energy crops. The main outputs, biogas and digestate, can be used for electricity/heat production and as fertiliser, respectively. With the introduction of the Renewable Heat Incentive biogas could also be injected (after treatment) into the national gas grid as 'biomethane' or used as transport fuel.

Making a profit from an AD system, however, is far more complex. There are a dizzying number of variables to take into account when planning and designing an AD system. At the heart of any operation is the management of the microbial process itself. Maximising the potential output of a system will be highly dependent on the nature of the feedstock, temperature, moisture levels, digester size and design and pH levels within the digester. AD systems have been compared to a human stomach: feeding it too quickly, not allowing enough time for digestion, loading up on fatty foods, letting acid build-up etc are just some of the problems which can lead (literally) to indigestion and a break-down of the process. This is as much an art as a science.

External factors will be just as important to the success of the venture. Designing an AD system for treatment of farm wastes, such as slurry and manure, will have very different economics and requirements to the design for a large-scale waste management plant using AD. The former is really an 'add-on' to an existing business with benefits, but also potential disadvantages. An AD plant may provide diversification of revenue streams for the farm as well as improving the quality of fertiliser, but it will also require considerable financial investment, management time and operational headaches. A small-scale operation only using 'on-farm' produced waste is also unlikely to be economic. A larger, more complex waste management plant may be far more cost effective, producing a much higher yield per tonne of feedstock, but will have correspondingly higher management, operational and regulatory challenges.

5.2 Issues

A key issue for AD technologies is ensuring adequate efficiency (heat and power generation) from the available waste sources and knowledge sharing to bring down the costs of power generation.

A key question for stakeholders in AD technologies is ensuring operational reliability, be it plant availability, maintenance or having appropriate contingency plans for when operational issues arise. Because much of the AD market, at least in the UK, is quite fragmented, this poses an additional challenge as operators cannot benefit from economies of scale or sharing of information about technological improvements as easily. To further bring down the costs of AD, issues such as those around relationships with technology and EPC providers, waste disposal arrangements and price for offtake are key.

That said in 2015, the Green Investment Bank had found that "on a like for like basis, operational performance for agricultural facilities in 2014 was 71 per cent (up from 63 per cent in 2013) whilst the corresponding figure was 72 per cent for source segregated food facilities (up from 67 per cent in 2013)."[51]

51 www.greeninvestmentbank.com/media/44758/gib-anaerobic-digestion-report-march-2015-final.pdf.

Further to the permitting and grid connection requirements that AD projects would require (the same as other power projects), the fuel source poses additional requirements on AD plants. Accordingly, the laws regulating waste and laws incentivising production of electricity from renewable sources both are likely to impact AD technologies. For example, in the UK, environmental permitting regulation has needed to be reviewed to allow for exemptions for certain AD technologies.

5.3 Costs

The two major costs of an AD system are the initial capital costs of the equipment and construction and the cost of the feedstock (depending on the feedstock and design of the system). Before considering both of these costs in more detail, it is worth reiterating that perhaps the most critical part of the process is the design and planning of the plant. The economics of the project will be highly sensitive to decisions on the size, siting and choice of the correct technology.

Turning to the capital costs, it has been estimated that the capital set-up cost will be in the region of £2,500 to £6,000 per kW of capacity. To put this in context, a small 10kWe plant using residues from 100 cows or 1,000 pigs could cost around £60,000 to £70,000 while a 1MWe plant with multiple feedstocks will cost between £3m to £4m.[52] A study by Arup for the Department of Energy and Climate Change (in 2011) estimated the median capital costs for a <1MWe plant to be closer to £4.4m. There will also be additional costs of developing the project, ranging from professional and financing fees to costs of connection to the electricity grid, gas clean-up facilities, and civil works.

The operational costs will depend on the specific design and requirements of the facility, but for a larger waste management project (1MWe–6MWe) and excluding the cost of feedstock, these have been estimated at £263,000 per year, and up to £900,000 for a smaller plant (<1MWe).[53] If the AD system uses an energy crop which has a market value, then there is an 'opportunity cost' associated with the use of the feedstock. For instance, the value of grass silage or barley diverted to the AD system would need to be charged to the 'AD' business. Transport costs may also end up becoming a significant factor if the supply of feedstock or removal of digestate (ie, for use as a fertiliser) requires transportation.

5.4 Regulatory and political support

In the UK, AD has historically received very strong government and political support. In 2010, the then coalition government made a commitment to a 'zero waste' economy, with a specific emphasis on expanding AD as one of the primary technologies to achieve this.[54] The UK also still has a number of ambitious EU commitments to reduce waste,[55] promote renewable energy[56] and reduce its carbon

52 Good Practice Guidelines, Anaerobic digestion of farm and food processing residues, p27. See also www.gov.uk/government/uploads/system/uploads/attachment_data/file/147863/3237-cons-ro-banding-arup-report.pdf.

53 *Ibid.*

54 UK Government, Structural Reform Plan, July 2010.

55 Waste Framework Directive, Directive 2008/98/EC.

56 Renewable Energy Directive, Directive 2009/28/EC.

emissions,[57] so the promotion of AD can be seen as part of the wider move to a 'low carbon' economy.

A number of forms of incentives for biogas and renewable energy produced from waste exist, although support has been cut back recently. The main ones are:[58]

- Feed-in Tariff (FiTs). From 1 July 2016, AD plants are eligible to a tariff of 6.82p/kWh for installed capacity of between 250kWe and 500kWe and 7.03p/kWh for installed capacity of greater than 500kWe. An additional 4.91p/kWh is paid for electricity exported to the grid. The government is currently (May 2016) consulting on whether the FiT tariffs should be increased, following concerns raised by industry that the current support may no longer be sufficient to attract investment.[59]
- Renewables Obligation. This provides financial support in the form of tradeable Renewable Obligation Certificates (ROCs) for renewable energy generators. Currently, each MWh of electricity from AD receives 1.8 ROCs,[60] worth approximately between £40–£50 per ROC. ROCs are for larger-scale renewable projects (> 5MW). The Renewables Obligation scheme will be phased out by 31 March 2017. Since 2014, generators of projects of >5MWe have had the option of applying for a government-backed contract-for-difference as an alternative to ROCs.
- Renewable Heat Incentive. The UK is the only country in the world to provide a financial incentive mechanism for heat. It is primarily intended to encourage the use of heat from renewable sources, but it also extends to the production of biogas from AD. The tariffs are 7.5p/kWh for biogas consumption for a scale up to 200kW and 7.5p/kWh for all injection of biomethane into the national natural gas grid.[61]
- Renewable Transport Fuel Obligation (RTFO). The RTFO requires suppliers of fossil fuels to ensure that a specified percentage of the road fuels they supply in the UK is made up of renewable fuels. Biomethane can also be used as a transport fuel and suppliers of biomethane can sell renewable transport fuel certificates to fuel suppliers to help them meet their targets.
- Landfill tax: The landfill tax is a tax on the disposal of waste to landfill. The rate of the tax increases year on year and for 2016/17 it is £84.40 per tonne of waste. Although it is not a direct subsidy for AD, it raises the level of 'gate fees' that an AD plant can charge for taking municipal waste diverted from landfill. For a waste management plant, this can be a significant source of revenue.
- Capital grants. There are also a number of capital grants and government backed loans available. However, generally, it is not possible to benefit from a grant and also be eligible for ROCs/FiTs.

---

57 Climate Change Act, 2008.

58 See www.biogas-info.co.uk for information on incentives.

59 www.gov.uk/government/uploads/system/uploads/attachment_data/file/535842/FITs_ADmCHP_consultation_document_May_2016_1_-_14_July_deadline.pdf.

60 Different allocations apply in Northern Ireland.

61 There are some additional costs in turning 'biogas' into 'biomethane', primarily the costs of removing the CO^2 and other contaminant gases from the biogas.

- AD projects also used to be eligible under the EIS, SEIS and VCT schemes, although these tax reliefs were removed by the government in March 2015.

Since 2011, the UK government has also run an Anaerobic Digestion Strategy and Action Plan to identify key barriers to the uptake of AD in the UK. Part of the action plan is improving access to key facts and figures about the AD industry and the regulatory incentives and requirements for running an AD plant.

In addition, international market mechanisms may also be available. For example, AD projects in the developing world could obtain financial support through the UN Clean Development Mechanism established as part of the Kyoto protocol.

5.5 Scalability

AD certainly has a number of advantages over other forms of emerging renewable technologies. It is a well understood technology and has been applied for over 100 years in the sewage industry. With proper management and operation, it can yield high levels of biogas and digestate at fairly predictable rates and outputs (an advantage compared to variable electricity generation from sources such as wind). Biogas also has the advantage that it can be stored (unlike wind or tidal power). The construction of AD facilities can also be swift and are relatively flexible, and can be sized to match the availability of feedstocks in the area and demand for the products of AD.

There are, however, a number of challenges in developing an AD project. Larger-scale plants require planning permission, which will be subject to a number of consultations and can take several years to obtain. Depending on the nature of the waste feedstock, the plant may also need to obtain an environmental permit. This regulates the handling and processing of waste products and it can also determine whether the digestate can or cannot be used as fertiliser. There are some exemptions from the need to hold a permit, where the AD process is treating manures and slurries at premises used for agriculture, and where the operation is small scale and low risk. An environmental permit places a number of obligations on the operations of the plant, including whether the plant uses 'best available technology'. Critically, it also regulates the categorisation of the digestate. As a rule of thumb, if the input feedstock is 'waste' under the regulations or 'non-waste' is mixed with 'waste', the resulting digestate will also be classified as waste and will be subject to waste management controls, restricting its use as fertiliser. Animal by-product regulations will also apply if the plant accepts animal by-products (such as abattoir waste, food made from animals). These were reinforced after the foot and mouth outbreak in 2001 and are not easy or cheap to comply with, so any plant planning to accept this form of feedstock will need to be configured and designed with these regulations in mind.

Since the UK government launched its Anaerobic Digestion Strategy and Action Plan in 2011, there has been a rapid expansion of the sector with installed capacity increasing from 35MWe in 2011 to 184MWe as at March 2016. However, expansion has slowed significantly in the last year, mainly due to the scaling back of subsidies and the removal of certain tax incentives for investors in AD projects, which has discouraged new investment.[62]

6. Floating offshore wind

Floating wind farms can operate in seas much deeper than ones with foundations embedded in the sea floor. As a result they can access the powerful, steady winds that blow far offshore. Over the deep seas off Japan, for instance, there's enough potential wind power to meet the country's electricity needs many times over.[63]

6.1 Resource

Development of ways to generate electricity offshore is not new, especially for nations with extensive coastlines like Japan, Norway or the UK. The concept has existed since the 1970s but has only received sufficient research interest since the late 1990s. As at 2016, there are more than 40 projects being developed and tested worldwide, seeking to have turbines that operate in depths of up to 1,000 metres.[64]

For countries like the UK where offshore wind is identified as one of the leading technology options to decarbonise the UK's energy system, floating offshore wind represents a unique opportunity to capitalise on its vast ocean resources. Thus far, in the UK, all of the installed offshore wind capacity consists of conventional fixed bottom foundation technology located in relatively shallow water depths (<40m) and near to shore (<30km) either in UK territorial waters or in the Renewable Energy Zones.[65] With the success of offshore wind development, the focus has shifted to the new frontier of taking offshore wind turbines off their fixed bases.

There are distinct benefits to doing so. Floating wind turbines build on the existing offshore wind turbine technology but instead of being mounted on foundations anchored in the seabed, these turbines are mounted on a floating structure that allows the development of wind farms in locations where seabed mounted towers are not feasible. Locations further offshore tend to have higher and steadier wind speeds as well as lower instances of turbulence, which in turn extends the wind farm life to approximately 25–30 years.[66]

Further floating offshore wind industry can benefit from lessons learnt both in the oil and gas industry (such as using platforms and vessels originally designed and proven in the offshore oil and gas industry) as well as the traditional offshore wind industry (eg, using the same proven turbine technology, or methods of laying the cabling infrastructure or choices between Sub Sea AC or HVDC cables).

According to the European Wind Energy Association, by 2013, seven experimental floating substructures were being tested: SeaTwirl, SWAY, Blue H and

---

62 www.gov.uk/government/uploads/system/uploads/attachment_data/file/535842/FITs_ADmCHP_consultation_document_May_2016_1_-_14_July_deadline.pdf.

63 Floating Wind Farms: Great Concept, Implausible Economics by Richard Martin, 18 May 2016: www.technologyreview.com/s/601481/floating-wind-farms-great-concept-implausible-economics/.

64 *Ibid.*

65 Floating Offshore Wind: Market and Technology Review prepared for the Scottish Government by the Carbon Trust, June 2015: www.carbontrust.com/media/670664/floating-offshore-wind-market-technology-review.pdf.

66 Floating Wind Turbines presentation by Paul D Sclavounos, MIT – http://web.mit.edu/windenergy/windweek/Presentations/P6%20-%20Sclavounos.pdf.

Poseidon in Europe, the Kabashima Island concept and WindLens in Japan and the DeepCwind floating turbine in the US.[67] The same report identifies that there are three main types of deep offshore foundations currently being used:

- Spar buoy: a large cylindrical buoy stabilises the wind turbine using ballast. The centre of gravity is much lower in the water than the centre of buoyancy partly because the upper parts are usually empty elements near the surface thus raising the centre of buoyancy.
- Tension leg platform: a very buoyant structure that is semi submerged with tensioned mooring lines attached to it. It is anchored on the seabed to add buoyancy and stability.
- Semi-submersible: combining the main principles of the two previous designs and with a semi submerged structure added to reach the necessary stability.

For example, Statoil's 2.3MW Hywind project was the first operational deep-water floating wind turbine. Mounted on a floating tower with a 100-metre deep draft this demonstration project has been operational since September 2009 and has been exporting electricity to the Norwegian grid ever since. The Hywind demonstration project delivered 7.3GWh in 2010, exceeding Statoil's original estimations.

Buoyed with the success of this demonstration project, Statoil is seeking to develop more floating offshore wind projects in the UK and the US. The 30MW Hywind Scotland project is expected to consist of five 6MW floating turbines operating in waters deeper than 100 metres. The project was granted a lease by the Crown Estate in March 2016[68] and is aiming to start generating electricity by the end of 2017. As noted in the energy storage section below, Statoil plans to test a 1MWh lithium-ion battery system with the Hywind Scotland project.

However, the novel locations further offshore come with their own challenges. These include not only the much higher costs of working further offshore but also the challenges of operational and maintenance activities on wind turbines located on the high seas, where the greater wind speeds and higher waves produce their own sets of health and safety hazards.

Another issue is the laying and the protection of grid cables in international waters where there are multiples users of the sea and less scope for protection of a particular type of asset. This in turn requires the development of new ways of thinking, for example in relation to insurance products to address these types of circumstances.

6.2 Costs

As with any emerging technology, a key challenge is cost. A 2014 study in the journal *Renewable Energy* estimated the cost of energy from a hypothetical floating wind farm would be between $93 and $268 per megawatt-hour.[69] The Hywind demonstration turbine mentioned above cost NOK 400m (around $62m) to build. These costs are

67 www.ewea.org/fileadmin/files/library/publications/reports/Deep_Water.pdf.
68 www.offshorewind.biz/2016/05/16/the-crown-estate-okays-hywind-scotland-seabed-lease/.

not exorbitant compared to traditional offshore wind technologies but present an obstacle partly because the costs are largely more up front (around $4.7 million per megawatt of capacity for floating, compared to $3.9 million per megawatt for fixed).[70]

The production and installation of substructures makes up to 20% of the CAPEX of offshore wind farms and so is naturally a target area for cost reduction. Floating offshore substructure costs mainly comprise the platform and the anchoring system. Accordingly, the challenge for countries such as the US and Japan, which have fewer areas of shallow waters in which to install traditional fixed offshore wind turbines, is to lower the costs of floating offshore wind to make it palatable for their consumers.[71]

6.3 Regulatory and political support

The lack of regulatory certainty outside national boundaries is a key non-technological barrier for development of floating offshore wind projects. While countries can freely legislate in their state or federal jurisdictions (including in economic zones adjacent their coast lines), the internal framework governing international waters is vague.

Further, the development of the industry depends on a stable and clear regulatory framework of incentivising renewables. For example, this is present up to 2020 through the renewable energy targets in Europe but lacks clarity after 2020.

The high cost of developing demonstration projects for floating offshore wind has already necessitated additional support subsidies above those given to fixed offshore wind projects. Several governments have provided support through grants to support research and development activities. For example, Scotland is currently the only country to offer a subsidy support mechanism for floating wind pilot projects under the Renewables Obligation (Scotland). The Scottish government offers 3.5 Renewable Obligation Certificates (ROCs) per MWh, which is 1.5 ROCs higher than that currently received by fixed offshore wind farms.[72]

Similarly, in Portugal, building on the successful 2MW demonstration WindFloat project, the Portuguese government awarded a €19m grant to support the development of a 27MW extension off the coast of Aguçadoura. This project also benefitted from European Commission funding, via the NER 300 programme, and being selected for the European Investment Bank's InnovFin programme.[73]

6.4 Scalability

Scalability is arguably floating offshore wind's trump card. Envisaged as the ultimate 'plug and play' technology, proponents argue that it can be assembled onshore and

69 Floating Wind Farms: Great Concept, Implausible Economics, Richard Martin, 18 May 2016: www.technologyreview.com/s/601481/floating-wind-farms-great-concept-implausible-economics/.

70 *Ibid.*

71 www.ewea.org/fileadmin/files/library/publications/reports/Deep_Water.pdf.

72 Floating Offshore Wind: Market and Technology Review prepared for the Scottish Government by the Carbon Trust, June 2015: www.carbontrust.com/media/670664/floating-offshore-wind-market-technology-review.pdf.

73 Portugal approves floating offshore wind, 28 November 2016, https://ijglobal.com/Articles/103556?utm_source=IJGlobal%20daily%20newsletter&utm_medium=email%20editorial&utm_content=Editorial&utm_campaign=IJ14548&N.rID=%40zaKA7sM7BSJOYp%2FtTXWUKQ%3D%3D.

then pulled out into deep waters, thus saving costs, time and safety concerns of working out on the high seas.

In addition, floating offshore wind benefits from convergence of two industries: offshore oil and gas and fixed offshore wind. This means that there are already proven supply chain systems in place and infrastructure able to support this nascent industry.

7. Energy storage

Power systems have to be flexible to allow supply and demand to be balanced at all times. As the deployment of wind and solar generation increases globally, the challenge of managing increased volatility of generation grows and hence, the need for increased system flexibility is becoming more urgent. Electricity storage is an important option to provide this additional flexibility.[74]

7.1 Resource

Energy storage, either standalone or combined with another technology like solar PV or wind, has come to the forefront in recent years. A range of energy storage technologies exist, and whilst battery storage is receiving the bulk of industry attention at present, a variety of technologies have been, and are due to be, installed.

Energy storage, although not a renewable generator technology itself, offers a range of benefits in terms of electricity grid management. For example, storage allows for price arbitrage (ie, where electricity is imported and/or stored when it is cheaper and/or abundant, and exported to the grid as needed or at times when prices are higher), peak shaving (storage devices can be called upon at peak times to reduce the imports of energy consumers, helping them to manage their electricity costs by reducing their demand charges) and variable generation integration (ie, storage co-located with renewable generation, which enables efficient use of variable generation, by storing power at times of excess generation and/or low demand, and exporting to the grid at times of peak demand and/or low generation).

Energy storage is not new – the scale of pumped hydro deployment across the globe is significant, whilst flywheel energy storage is common on oil and gas platforms. New technologies, however, are changing the renewable energy market.

Energy storage currently in the process of being more widely deployed includes:

- Compressed air energy storage (CAES) – CAES runs electric motors to compress air in under- or above-ground facilities and releases it through turbines to generate power.
- Batteries – batteries are a key storage technology; they include lead acid, copper zinc, sodium sulphur, flow and, most commonly, lithium-ion batteries.

7.2 Costs

The costs associated with energy storage vary considerably depending on the scale and type of technology deployed. Different technologies often offer a trade-off between cost and factors such as energy efficiency, durability, flexibility of use etc.

74 E-storage: Shifting from cost to value, wind and solar applications – 2016: www.worldenergy.org/wp-content/uploads/2016/03/Resources-E-storage-report-2016.02.04.pdf.

For example, CAES is relatively inexpensive but suffers large energy losses; flywheel technology also has variable efficiency but offers a longer lifecycle with low maintenance requirements; whilst pumped hydro, although a relatively mature, well priced and efficient option, is heavily reliant on topography.

Traditionally the cost of battery storage has been relatively high; this is changing, however, with technological advances making battery storage increasingly efficient and cost-effective. The cost of batteries has more than halved in the past six years.[75] Various sources expect this trajectory to continue: the costs of lithium-ion batteries have fallen by 85% since 2011, and are expected to fall by a further 45% by 2025.[76]

7.3 Regulatory and political support

At the date of writing, no jurisdiction currently has a comprehensive regulatory framework for energy storage: many jurisdictions currently allowing storage to be defined as 'generation' for the purposes of licensing and other regulatory requirements. However, many countries are increasingly aware of the need to address energy storage within the wider electricity regulatory framework and are exploring this through strategy papers, consultations and proposed draft legislation.

The majority of countries do not have a specific subsidy regime. However, there are some exceptions – Germany, for example, has a newly launched battery storage funding programme for decentralised battery storage systems, which aims to ensure that solar PV installations will be more beneficial to the overall system by smoothing their export. While some energy storage solutions are commercially viable without subsidy support, larger infrastructure-heavy projects, such as larger-scale pumped hydro, are currently struggling to attract investment due to the extent of the merchant revenue risk.

The regulatory regime also influences which industry participants are able to participate in energy storage, that is, the role that network operators should play. In Italy, for example, the transmission and distribution system operators are investing in storage facilities within their own networks, whereas the UK is allowing storage providers to bid into technology-agnostic auctions to provide services to the system operator, rather than the system operator developing energy storage projects directly.

7.4 Scalability

In the UK, battery systems and other types of storage are still in their relative infancy (particularly in comparison with the markets of Germany and the US), representing only about 30MW of capacity, a small fraction of total generating capacity.[77] The UK is, however, witnessing growing levels of investment in the sector.

Notably, UK Power Networks' commission of a 6MW/10MWh lithium-ion battery storage project in Leighton Buzzard in October 2014 served to raise industry and public awareness of storage technology. The project was pioneering in

---

75 www.moodys.com/research/Moodys-Declining-battery-prices-could-lead-to-commercial-and-industrial--PR_335274.

76 Changing the game with electricity storage – www.cornwallenergy.com/cms/data/files/pdf/160826_Chart-of-the-Week.pdf.

77 www.ft.com/content/b62b356e-2d10-11e6-bf8d-26294ad519fc.

demonstrating that grid-scale battery storage can be viable in the UK. Additionally, the Norwegian gas and oil group Statoil are currently installing what is believed to be the world's first offshore wind farm battery system at the Hywind floating turbine project off the coast of Scotland.

In a UK context, with improved technology, financing and an evolving regulatory framework, energy storage technology has the potential for great growth in the coming years. However, this is expected to occur, at least initially, in the context of many smaller-scale, decentralised projects (such as Statoil's Hywind offshore wind project) where battery storage is co-located with other energy generating technologies

8. Conclusion

Governments are advised to avoid picking winners in the renewable technology race.[78] However, in a climate of depressed carbon price and lack of access to capital, new technologies are heavily reliant on government support and stimulus. It is also unavoidable that government policy and fiscal stimulus will promote some renewable technologies over others. Public funding is limited and governments will have to prioritise investment in those low-carbon technologies which they deem are most likely to deliver their policy objectives (ie, low-carbon power generation, job creation and security of energy supply).

Picking winners in the renewable technology race, in this context, becomes a game of second-guessing policy makers' and politicians' minds and hoping that the political and regulatory wind does not change. The authors' bet is that the huge stimulus given to the geothermal industry by the Obama administration will make this source of energy the natural successor to wind and solar energy. But as the Danish physicist Neils Bohr allegedly said: "Prediction is difficult, especially about the future."

78 Energy and Climate Change Committee, Fourth Report of Session 2009–10, "Low carbon technologies in a green economy" (HC193-1), p68.

Power financing

Hugo Coetzee
CMS London

1. Introduction

Delivery of a successful power project invariably requires a substantial financial investment on the part of sponsors and developers. Following the global financial crisis, more and more sponsors and developers are not able to fund the sizeable development costs involved in constructing a major power project. Those sponsors and developers that are active in the sector are also under increasing pressure to reduce the cost of their capital. These pressures, in addition to the need to remain competitive in a changing financial environment, are steering project sponsors and developers towards the deep pockets of third party investors or debt providers. Typically the financial investment required to finance a well-structured project will consist of a combination of equity contributions and debt advances. The debt amounts will exceed the equity contributions due to the desire to optimise the cost efficiencies of the project and, of course, to take advantage of competitive debt funding terms available from financial institutions providing debt.

Those looking for debt finance from third party financial institutions will have a number of financing options available to them depending on their particular circumstances and liquidity. Sponsors or developers with a substantial balance sheet might have no concern with raising the finance by way of a corporate loan, whilst others looking for shorter term loans to finance particular assets may consider asset financing as an option. Where debt is advanced on the basis of on balance sheet lending, the focus is on full recourse to the assets of the sponsor. Due to the costs involved in the construction of large power projects this funding approach is not always viable. The most popular method of commercial debt financing of independent power projects remains project financing. Without revisiting all of the various descriptions and definitions that exist, suffice to say that project finance is essentially a financing method used to finance large infrastructure projects based on the ultimate projected revenue of the project once completed, rather than the cashflows or finance available to the sponsors or developers themselves.

The main benefit of a project financing is that it offers financing that is not on balance sheet for a sponsor or developer and in practice with very limited recourse to the sponsor or developer but rather recourse to the particular project and its cashflows. Project financing, more so than other financing mechanisms for power projects, is influenced by the particular project risks and the risks associated with the country where the project is located. This contrasts with corporate lending where the actual size of the balance sheet of the borrower and access to the assets on that balance sheet in the event of a default are of key importance. Whilst the benefits of project finance for sponsors and developers are clear, due to the fact that it is essentially all about financing a proposal (and not a completed power project), certainty for funders can be a challenge. Financial models, projected revenues and project costs as well as fixed and variable assumptions regarding revenues and costs all play a role in attempting to provide elements of certainty to the funder of a proposed power project. Project finance, notwithstanding all its benefits, is also a complex and document-heavy funding mechanism. It is a more costly way of financing compared to traditional corporate funding and it takes longer to achieve financial close in a project finance deal, due to the complexities involved, and in particular also the detailed due diligence that is required.

2. What does a power financing structure look like?

Power financing implemented through the use of a project finance mechanism is typically structured by way of long term senior debt advances to a thinly-capitalised special purpose vehicle set up for the particular project. Sponsors invest by way of joint venture structures in the special purpose vehicle which is ultimately the entity responsible for delivering the project and also the borrower of the long term debt.

Figure 1 sets out a typical contractual structure for a project financed power project where a government concession is involved.

Figure 1: Project finance contractual structure

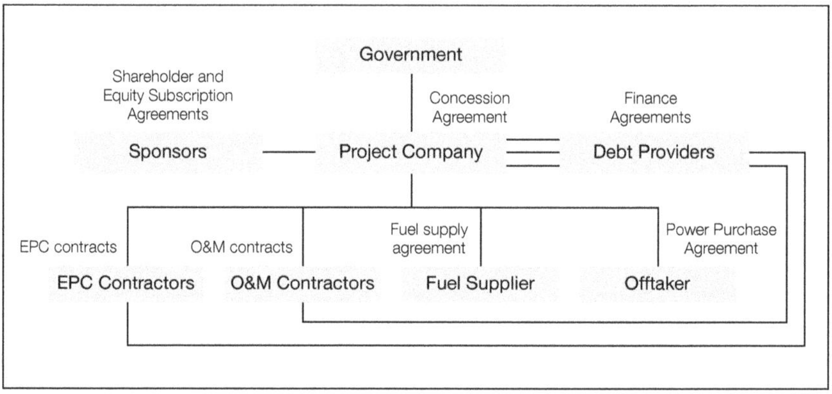

The special purpose vehicle or project company is at the core of the financing structure. It is the contractor under a concession or project agreement, the recipient of debt funding, the counterparty (employer) in respect of construction and maintenance contracts as well as the purchaser of fuel and the generator of electricity. One might think that these responsibilities are all substantive and not something you would trust a thinly-capitalised special purpose vehicle (typically taking the form of a limited company) to perform. The vehicle is however essentially just a conduit for a complex array of contractual rights and revenues and project finance as a funding mechanism brings with it established due diligence and risk management processes that analyse and assess the risks involved in contracting to deliver a power project on a project finance basis.

3. The players

We have mentioned the role of the project company but in practice, who are the key participants in this complex financing structure necessary to enable the construction and subsequent operation of a power project?

Firstly, there are the sponsors. The sponsors are entities or individuals who 'own' the project/invest equity in the project, typically expecting an ultimate return or profit from the operation of the project. The sponsors are typically privately owned entities or can be private individuals acting through incorporated ventures or indeed entities owned by the relevant government to further its political and economic policies in the power sector. The sponsors usually invest in a project using a combination of equity (share subscription) and debt (equity loans). The treatment of equity and debt returns from a tax, legal and accounting perspective in the relevant jurisdiction of the project and the treatment of equity and debt returns in the jurisdiction of the sponsor (if different) can play a major role in determining the level of equity and debt investment by sponsors.

Another key instigator of a power project is the government or quasi-governmental body of the country where the project is located. Governments are typically involved in affording concessions to sponsors for the construction and operation of projects through the use of concessions evidenced in a concession agreement or a project agreement. Their presence is however not always a requirement, for example in the case of merchant power plants where the project sells electricity directly to a stable and relatively predictable wholesale market.

The next key party is the funder. The funder provides the required substantial amount of debt funding to ensure the sponsors can commence work on the project confident that there will be sufficient funding to build and operate the project. The senior debt funding can come from a variety of sources, including multilateral financiers such as the European Investment Bank (EIB), the European Bank for Reconstruction and Development (EBRD) and the International Finance Corporation (IFC). They can also include governmental entities, or agencies set up to assist in the procurement of power projects for the relevant government. The commercial funders make up the balance. Traditionally the commercial funders consist of well capitalised banks and financial institutions, local as well as international. However, due to the financial crisis and the capital crisis experienced by banks and financial institutions generally, there has been a shake up in the market and in a number of jurisdictions we have seen the emergence of dedicated infrastructure and energy debt funds prepared to advance long term commercial debt to power projects.

The project company, as a special purpose vehicle, requires the expertise and resources of various construction, engineering, maintenance and other sub-contractors. As a result there will typically be a raft of sub-contractors, engineers and technical experts involved in a power project to enable the project company to deliver the project. The key sub-contractors are usually the construction company (operating on a turnkey contract basis or using an EPC model) and the operator who will operate and maintain the project once construction is completed, although there can be a split between the role of maintenance provider and operator.

In traditional project financed power projects, the offtaker also plays a key role. Where the project is not a merchant power plant, the project company will enter into a power purchase agreement with an offtaker in respect of the electricity generated by the project (ideally a long term offtake agreement from the perspective of the funders).

There are of course other parties involved in a power project financing, such as professional advisers, insurers, suppliers of fuel, administrative services providers and asset management services providers but the above entities are those constituting the core contracted pillars required to enable the project financing of a power project.

4. Financing agreements

Whilst sponsors typically seek financing from a variety of debt providers including financing by way of senior debt loans, subordinated equity loans and bonds, the principal financing documents involved in the project financing of a power project include:

- facility (loan) agreement;
- common terms agreement
- intercreditor agreement;
- hedging agreements;
- accounts agreements;
- security documents; and
- direct agreements.

The key financing document in a project financed power project is the facility agreement. This is the document containing the details regarding the credit facilities made available to the project company by the debt funders. The facility agreement is usually drafted on a syndicated basis allowing for more than one debt funder and for specific funder roles such as agent, arranger, security trustee and/or account bank, depending on the precise nature of the debt funding provided.

The facility agreement will contain provisions governing the mechanisms of providing credit such as drawdown conditions and mechanisms, repayment formulae and tables. It will however also contain various complex provisions based on the principle that the funding is ultimately based on a sound project generating revenues to produce a cashflow sufficient to service a long term debt facility. These provisions include detailed obligations regarding the production and maintenance of a financial model as well as detailed construction and operation budgets. Due to the nature of a project financing there are numerous financial covenants testing the performance of the project at regular intervals and considering the project cashflows compared to project costs and the project revenues compared to the debt obligations of the project company on a forward looking as well as a backward looking basis. The facility agreement will also contain extensive project specific covenants and a comprehensive 'belt and braces' events of default package to ensure maximum protection to funders.

In the event that there are different sources of credit available to a project, such as debt facilities provided by commercial banks and debt facilities provided by multilateral banks or governmental bodies, it is not unusual for funders to make use of a common terms agreement. As the name suggests the common terms agreement is a document that 'houses' provisions that are common to all of the debt advanced in respect of a project. These provisions include not only common definitions but also general representations and project covenants (including common events of default and/or trigger events) in favour of all the debt funders of the project.

The different funders to a project may have different legal interests due to the nature of their funding and as a result there will be a need to regulate the legal relationship between the various funders (including any priority of claim arrangements). The funders will enter into an intercreditor agreement for this very purpose. This document will also ensure that the claims of sponsors and equity providers are subordinated in all respects to those funders providing junior and/or senior debt finance.

Where the debt financing for a project attracts interest calculated on a floating interest rate basis which is subject to movement over the life of the loan, the funders will require that the project company enters into a hedging agreement to ensure that the risk of an adverse fluctuation in the applicable interest rate over the life of the loan is hedged against a fixed interest rate. Similarly where the debt currency is different to the currency of the project revenue and project costs, the funders will require that the project company enters into further hedging agreements to hedge against the currency risk. Depending on the precise circumstances of the project there might also be other hedging agreements (for example to address increases in pricing linked to indexation).

As mentioned earlier, the project financing of a power project is primarily concerned with the cashflows of the project. To this end the funders will usually require an array of bank accounts to be held in the name of the project company with an account bank (normally one of the senior debt funders to the project). The project company will be required to enter into an account agreement with the account bank and the funders. The funders typically require bank accounts: (i) to hold all proceeds and revenues of the project; (ii) to hold insurance proceeds; (iii) to set aside reserves required by the funders to service debt; (iv) to set aside reserves required by the funders to cover lifecycle or maintenance costs; and (v) to set aside reserves required by the funders to address particular project specific gaps or contingencies identified by the funders as part of their due diligence exercise or credit assessment of the project. Where funders are of the view that such reserves may not be sufficient on their own to cover the identified or perceived gaps, they might require the implementation of a mandatory prepayment mechanism or a so-called 'cash sweep' mechanism where, in certain pre-agreed circumstances, the cash generated by or held for the project is applied in payment of the debt should the identified or perceived gap or set of circumstances arise.

Power project finance is secured finance. The funders will require a comprehensive security package for the period that all and any funds remain due to them under the debt documents. This security consists of full asset security in respect of the assets of the project company wherever such assets are located. The funders will typically not only take security over the assets of the project company but also over the ownership in the project company by way of share security. Where the debt is syndicated or there is a club of funders the security is usually granted in favour of a security trustee who holds the benefit of the security on trust for the funders.

As the real value of the project lies in the revenue generating contracts, funders will take special care to ensure that they have unfettered access rights by way of security to the key project contracts should a default arise.

In addition to obtaining comprehensive security over the rights of the project company under its key project contracts, the funders will want to ensure that there is continuity in the event that the project company does not perform its obligations under such key project contracts. In order to avoid the termination of key project contracts by the counterparties to such contracts, the funders require that the counterparties enter into direct agreements (also known as 'step-in agreements') with the funders. The direct agreements require that the contract counterparties, prior to exercising any rights they may have to terminate the relevant contracts, grant a right to the funders or their representative to 'step into' the position of the project company under the relevant project contracts. This ensures continuity of contract and safeguards the funding and any losses that might arise due to a termination of a key contract. Direct agreements are typically required for the likes of concession contracts, construction contracts, operation and maintenance agreements, lease agreements, as well as power purchase agreements. They are however not limited to these contracts and will be required by funders in respect of any contracts regarded as key for the continuation of the project. Unlike the position in respect of traditional project financed infrastructure projects that involve public sector participants, the direct agreements in power projects do not typically follow a prescribed standard form which means there is potential for a whole raft of direct agreements, all in different forms and heavily negotiated to reflect the particular commercial circumstances of the project.

Whilst not a financing document itself, the legal due diligence report is a crucial part of the documentation required by a funder prior to committing any funding to a project. This document, issued to the funders and other key project participants is typically prepared by the legal advisers to the project company due to their proximity to the project and the sponsors, although it can also be provided by the legal advisers to the funders and sometimes the ultimate legal due diligence report can be a combination of due diligence reports from a number of legal advisers. The legal due diligence report is essentially a report on the risks contained in or identified in the transaction documentation for the project and the allocation or management of those identified risks. The legal advisers issuing the due diligence report typically issue a reliance letter in respect of the report, subject to general disclaimers and in certain instances containing limits in liability. This report is accompanied by a separate report issued by technical advisers in respect of the project and the performance of its assets. You can also expect to see reports from the insurance advisers to the funders of the project as well as the financial model auditors who in turn look at the financial model developed for the project. These reports all assist the funders in making a decision as to whether the project is 'bankable' and as such that it is a project that complies with the requirements of the internal credit approvals received by the funders to enable them to proceed towards making a financial commitment available for the project.

5. Key concerns

The project financing of a power project is a complex affair. Funders have to consider not only those risk issues which typically go hand in hand with power projects (power projects have different risk issues to oil and gas projects, water projects, transport projects or mining projects and of course there are also differences between conventional power projects and renewable power projects), but also issues that arise as a result of the implementation of the project financing mechanism.

6. Equity

In a typical project financed power project, funders will require a commitment from sponsors, not only to remain involved in the project as owner for an agreed period of time but also to provide an agreed level of equity support to the project. The debt to equity ratios vary depending on the particular market, the availability of cash and factors such as the liquidity of sponsors and project specific risk.

Funders are likely to require that the sponsors contribute the entirety of their equity up-front. Funders can also require that sponsors provide equity support to cover any cost overruns in respect of the project. Typically these arrangements are contained in an equity contribution agreement or shareholder support agreement. This agreement usually requires that sponsors inject their equity on day one of the financing of the project and, where ongoing equity support is required, the obligations of the sponsors to provide this ongoing equity are set out in detail in the agreement. Should all equity contributions not be injected on day one, due to additional support required or where the funders have agreed that sponsors can spread their equity contributions over a period of time, some element of credit support is required in respect of the obligations to subscribe for equity. This credit support or enhancement can take the form of a standby letter of credit, a parent company guarantee, a cash deposit or such other form of credit support as the funders may require taking account of the creditworthiness of the relevant sponsor.

The nature of the equity contribution can also vary from jurisdiction to jurisdiction to take account of local corporate, taxation and accounting laws. One of the most common routes for equity injection is a nominal share subscription in the project special purpose vehicle and a sizeable (subordinated) shareholder loan.

Whilst funders will usually allow sponsors to dispose of their interests in a project before all the project debt is repaid, the circumstances in which such a disposal will actually be permitted and the form such a disposal will take (for example a 'stapled' share and subordinated debt transfer) are typically the topic of substantive negotiation. In addition the precise circumstances where distributions can be paid to sponsors by the project special purpose vehicle (the so-called 'distribution lock-up provisions') will be the focus of specific attention from both the funders and the sponsors to ensure sufficient cash is retained in the borrowing vehicle to pay project costs and to service debt whilst at the same time ensuring that surplus funds are distributed to sponsors. Funders normally do not want sponsors to receive any distribution before the first repayment instalment on the loan has been made and if the project's required cash flows are not maintained.

7. Security

As discussed earlier, project financing is secured lending. Funders will require the assurance that their (comprehensive) security package is enforceable in the relevant jurisdiction where the project is based. In common law jurisdictions funders look towards a combination of fixed and floating security charges to provide complete control over the special purpose vehicle borrower and its assets and to enable them to appoint a receiver over the project special purpose vehicle and its assets to take control in the event of insolvency. Funders will specifically focus on the laws of the host jurisdiction to verify whether their rights as secured creditors are recognised, in particular how developed the laws are and how independent the judiciary are to ensure maximum protection. Different jurisdictions have different approaches to the protection of creditors which impacts legal certainty, a key requirement for a project financing.

Differing insolvency regimes and approaches with regard to the creation and registration of security are also issues which play a major role in determining the availability of financing for the relevant power project. Should project participants decide to choose a particular governing law for their project financing, funders will require specific legal advice regarding the enforceability of their security under the relevant legal system in the jurisdiction of the power project. Security over any real estate assets is another example of a complex area of law as real estate laws differ radically across various jurisdictions and in certain countries the local laws do not allow for the transfer of ownership (whether in security or other use) in real estate assets used for public services or utilised in a particular highly regulated sector.

8. Regulatory regime

The regulatory regime of the country where the project is located and the authorisations required for the construction and operation of the project are of key importance in the financing of power projects.

Power projects are subject (in the majority of jurisdictions) to detailed regulatory requirements imposing ongoing compliance with a raft of changing legislation. In order to proceed to construction and eventually commercial operation, power projects will require a broad range of authorisations and permits from different levels of the host government. These authorisations range from real estate planning consents and health and safety permits to environmental licences as well as industry specific consents. Funders of a power project will want to ensure (through a combination of legal and technical due diligence and contractual covenants) that all required authorisations are in place and there will also be an assessment of the political environment to evaluate the risk associated with any future change in regulatory regime.

9. Change in law

Project finance loans are typically long term loans. Whilst funders may get comfortable (following detailed due diligence and legal advice) with the legislation applicable to the project and the project special purpose vehicle on the date that financial close is achieved, there is no guarantee that the position will remain the same over the life of the loan.

The economic policies implemented by the various regimes that take control of the host government may change over the life of the project loan, there may be regulation or deregulation of particular aspects of energy policy, taxes may be imposed or additional environmental legislation may be imposed. All of these factors could detrimentally impact a power project and its ability to comply with relevant laws and as such to continue operating to generate revenue and to service debt. In order to protect against these risks, funders typically try to obtain direct contractual commitments from the relevant government, for example, through extensive change in law covenants in concession agreements.

10. Corporate, accounting and tax issues

Private sector sponsors typically want to ensure that the project is not included on their balance sheets, that the investment (project) vehicle is structured so as to ensure a streamlined return, that the project does not retain any serious project risk and that payments/distributions are not subject to onerous taxation regimes. In this regard they will want to ensure that the particular corporate vehicle selected as the project company is flexible with an ability to distribute surplus project revenues. Sponsors will give detailed attention to any restrictions imposed in this regard by the local jurisdiction of the project including any requirements to make use of a local investment vehicle as the project company.

The taxation regime in the local jurisdiction will play a major role in the structuring of the sponsors' investment and the terms of the project finance loans. Corporate taxes (aimed at the profits made by the project special purpose vehicle) as well as withholding taxes and real estate stamp duties may be applicable as well as sales tax or value added tax. The local investment regime may afford some concessions to investors and funders in a particular sector, but generally speaking the governing tax regime and corporate investment structuring will need to be assessed in detail in advance of any investment by sponsors and in advance of any approach to project finance debt funders.

11. Other typical key concerns

Technology risk is a key factor in project financed transactions – in particular where the technology to be used for the project is untested or complex. Funders will require comprehensive technical due diligence in power projects, usually through the use of their own independently appointed technical advisers. If the technology is new or untested (for example, in the case of certain renewable power projects) it is also not unusual for funders to ask for some form of guarantee or warranty from the technology provider.

In a power project funded on a project finance basis the offtake/power purchase arrangements are a key concern. Funder internal credit approvals for the debt financing of a project have strict requirements with regard to electricity offtake arrangements and in particular the power purchase agreements to be concluded by the project company as generator. These requirements can include:

- a long term committed power purchase agreement;
- an absolute floor level for the electricity purchase price under the power purchase agreement;
- a minimum ratings requirement for the proposed offtaker (to ensure liquidity);
- a guarantee or other credit support to provide support in respect of the performance by the offtaker of its obligations under the power purchase agreements; and
- a direct agreement between the funders, the project company as generator and the offtaker governing rights of 'step-in' afforded to the funders in respect of the power purchase agreement.

12. The future for power project financing

Project financing remains the most popular method of private debt financing of independent power projects. The onslaught of the global financial crisis has however left its mark. The days when long term debt finance was freely available for power projects are long gone. The numerous financial institutions that were prepared to commit long term facilities for power projects have all (in their own way), been affected by the financial crisis. Liquidity concerns and regulatory scrutiny affected the majority of debt providers. We have seen the emergence of equity and debt infrastructure funds as key funders of power projects in certain jurisdictions. Institutional money, whether from pension funds or insurers, is more accessible to power projects although it is still a challenge to attract funds from these institutional investors who have not traditionally had the resources to deal with long term power infrastructure projects or indeed any familiarity with the particular asset class.

For commercial financial institutions, the increased regulatory focus and the implementation of Basel III[1] will place further pressure on price and the ability to provide long term funding for power projects. Where projects benefit from government or public sector support, the economic policies of the host governments have impacted the financial support available to projects. Governments are focusing on reducing their sovereign debt exposure. These steps are leading to the abolishment or reduction of government subsidies historically available to encourage the construction and operation of power projects.

On the other hand, there is no abatement in the requirement for power infrastructure globally. Governments realise that there is a need to attract finance to assist in the development of infrastructure. Domestic development organisations continue to thrive in driving forward infrastructure investments in their local

1 Basel III is a comprehensive set of reform measures developed by the Basel Committee on Banking Supervision, to strengthen the regulation, supervision and risk management of the banking sector: quoted from www.bis.org/bcbs/basel3.htm.

markets. Multilateral financing institutions such as the World Bank, the IFC and the European Investment Bank continue to play a major role in ensuring that there is finance available for power projects, in particular in markets where perhaps access to private commercial debt is more difficult due to the particular market conditions and/or country political conditions. This is accompanied by the financing made available through export credit agencies providing financial support for the export activities of companies in the host jurisdiction of the export credit agencies.

In the Middle East, Sharia-compliant financing structures are applied hand in hand with conventional power project financing techniques. Investors are also tapping the capital markets and we have seen projects access the capital markets through the issue of project bonds. Certain jurisdictions such as the United States of America have traditionally used project bonds as a source of funding for infrastructure projects whilst in other jurisdictions the uptake has been slow. This should increase, in particular if there is a need to fund a specific aspect of a project, such as the construction period.

What is very clear from the above is that power projects are increasingly financed by way of bespoke type financings to take account of the fact that the funding for a project can come from different sources, whether from government sources, multilaterals, export credit agencies, project bonds or traditional long term debt financing from banks. We have moved towards the concept of a 'mixed grill' of financing sources that is utilised to finance the construction and operation of a power project.

Project finance as a financing method for power projects has adapted to the current financial climate and today serves as a useful financing mechanism, combining different sources of funding to deliver a long term funding package for power projects. Developers and investors originating from countries that have not traditionally used project financing as a method of financing for their power infrastructure (but rather just relied upon the size of their balance sheet) are now investing on a more global basis and as a result are obtaining exposure to the benefits of English law project financing in particular, which eases the ever increasing pressure on shrinking balance sheets. There is a sizable pipeline of power projects to be constructed globally, notwithstanding the demise or reduction in government subsidies, regulatory changes and the general pressure on capital and government budgets. Whilst there may be some new faces (such as infrastructure funds) and whilst there has been a change in the importance and role of some of the players (such as domestic agencies or organisations), the delivery of power projects through the use of limited recourse project finance as a flexible financing mechanism should (notwithstanding the availability of potentially cheaper financing options through the use of capital markets structures) remain a feature of capital project financing for the foreseeable future.

Construction

Ian Dalley
Dentons

1. Introduction

A rising global demand for electricity, ambitious climate change targets, closure of old gas and oil fired power stations and a reduction in fossil fuel reserves are contributing to a worldwide energy gap. The need to provide a reliable and consistent supply of energy, reduce carbon emissions and ensure a competitive market has resulted in many countries, particularly in the EU, adopting an approach which requires a diverse and well balanced energy mix, rather than reliance upon only a small number of energy sources. Such a fuel mix may include thermal, nuclear and renewable generation.

These demands inevitably lead to diverse and often challenging requirements in the design and construction of facilities for the generation of energy and its associated infrastructure. Whilst the construction requirement of nearly every power project is different to some degree, the same general principles apply to every construction project and the key issues of time, cost and quality, and the allocation of risk, are universal.

Take, for example, a state procured, project-financed solar power project in the United Arab Emirates. Like most project-financed power projects, lenders and sponsors will want to ensure that (as far as possible) the construction phase of the project is completed on budget, on time, and meets the relevant plant performance criteria. To the extent the project is not completed on budget, on time or does not meet the performance requirements, these project participants will want the contractor to cover the financial consequences of these shortcomings so that none of them are out of pocket.

Conversely, the contractor will want to limit these risks to levels which do not endanger its financial viability, and to exclude risks that it is not able to manage or control. The contractor will normally therefore require a series of limitations of liability for delays and performance shortfalls, as well as the right to be granted extra time and/or cost should something arise which is outside its control, such as a *force majeure* event or a change in law.

These tensions between the contractor on the one hand, and the parties procuring the construction on the other, affect nearly every aspect of a construction contract.

2. Preparing for the construction phase

2.1 External works

Typically, by the time an employer (the entity procuring the construction of the power plant) starts to look at engaging a contractor to build the power plant, the employer will already have carried out a series of studies on the suitability of the location of the site, purchased the site (or have taken steps to obtain appropriate real estate rights over the site), undertaken a series of surveys at the site itself (including geotechnical and environmental surveys) and started the process of obtaining relevant planning permissions and permits to enable the construction to go ahead.

However, the works required for a power project will seldom be limited to the footprint of the power plant itself. The employer will have considered, in conjunction with other participants in the project, the suitability of the infrastructure for the power project at the time it selects the site. Where changes outside the site boundaries are required, the employer should consider these in conjunction with the construction of the main plant. Not only will sequencing these works with the construction of the plant be critical, but the employer may be able to leverage better prices through economies of scale by using the same contractor(s). New highways access, upgrading of power management and transmission facilities and cooling water pipelines may all need to be designed and constructed, either by the employer or by another project participant. Careful coordination with statutory authorities, the grid operator and other key players is essential.

2.2 Concept design

The employer will normally already have carried out some concept design at the feasibility stage of the project. The employer (and other project participants) will need to have provided certain detailed assumptions as to the plant's cost and performance in order to create a reliable financial model, to have obtained finance in principle (if required) and to have applied for relevant permissions for the project.

Where the technology is relatively mature, preparing a reliable concept design might be just a routine activity, but for newer technologies it can require significant time and specialist expertise. Other project participants may wish to engage their own design engineers to check the design and assumptions provided by the employer at the feasibility stage of the project.

At a minimum, a concept design will typically specify, broadly, which technologies the plant will use, the required engineering and environmental standards that the plant has to meet, the available feedstock, and the required levels of performance and output of the plant.

Where the technology to be used is one that has a high safety profile in the eyes of the authorities (such as nuclear or hydro-electric), the design may need to be advanced to a considerable extent before full permission for the project can even be applied for.

A myriad of other different factors will need to be considered at concept design stage, depending on the nature of the project. When deciding where to locate an offshore wind farm in the United Kingdom, for example, designers will need to take into account the geological conditions of the seabed, the effect on local wildlife and the overall visual impact. Detailed environmental impact assessments would be required before planning permission is granted.

2.3 The procurement process

Given the large sums of money involved in most power projects, a competitive tender process is by far the most common procurement process used today. Typically, an employer will advertise for potential bidders to apply for pre-qualification, and will draw up a shortlist of bidders who meet its minimum requirements, which normally relate to the bidders' track record in similar projects, their technical expertise and their financial capability.

The pre-qualified bidders are then asked to submit their bids based on the technical, commercial and legal requirements of the employer. The bids will include pricing as well as comments on the legal and commercial terms of the project, and it is not uncommon for bidders to be permitted to submit one 'compliant' bid and one or more 'non-compliant' proposals, so that the employer can consider the bidders' alternative ideas. The next steps often vary, with some employers accepting the lowest compliant bid (which may be mandatory for some government entities), and others selecting a 'preferred bidder' in an attempt to drive the price down further by negotiating key issues.

However, procurement of power projects may be subject to certain regulatory requirements. For example, European Union law sets out minimum harmonised public procurement rules to create a level playing field for all businesses across the European Union, and these rules are transposed into national legislation and apply to tenders by public entities whose monetary value exceeds a certain amount. A public entity such as a utility which is subject to these rules may face challenges from unsuccessful bidders if the rules are not properly followed – remedies may include a suspension of the project whilst the national courts deal with the challenge, and claims for damages. It is also illegal for European Union governments to give financial help (state aid) to some companies and not others in a way which would distort fair competition.

3. Methods of procurement

At some stage a decision needs to be made on the contract structure for the construction of the power project, often known as the 'method of procurement', distinct from the procurement process referred to above. There are a number of different methods of procurement that can be used. These include:

- a 'turnkey' contract, where a single contractor is responsible for the whole project from design through to 'turning a key' to start up the finished plant; and
- multi-contracting, where the employer engages a number of separate contractors for different tasks, either all at the same time, or in some cases, one after the other.

A further variable is the extent to which the contractor(s) carry out, or assume responsibility for, the design of the project.

Deciding how the construction of a power project is going to be procured is a critical early decision. Making the wrong decision can have a major impact on the likelihood of success of the project.

The key factors involved in any construction project are the inter-dependent variables of time, cost and quality. How risk is allocated between the contractor and the employer needs to be carefully assessed, and this will feed into the choice of procurement method. Issues to consider include:

- the scale of the project;
- the availability of experienced contractors in the location of the project in the relevant specialisms;
- whether the project is externally financed;
- the risk appetite of the lenders and sponsors (some of whom will prefer a higher original contract price in exchange for the contractor taking on more risk, and hence absorbing more potential cost over-runs);
- the risk associated with any new or immature technology used in the project;
- whether any individual items of plant used in the project constitute a very large proportion of the overall price or complexity of the project;
- the extent to which the design of the project is already available, and the extent to which the employer is prepared to pay a premium for the contractor to adopt responsibility for that design;
- the aggressiveness of the timetable for completion of the project;
- the experience of the employer in managing power projects of a similar nature; and
- whether any relevant local public procurement laws put constraints on the available options.

3.1 Turnkey

Turnkey contracts are a form of design and build contract. Under the usual arrangements for turnkey projects, the contractor carries out all the engineering, procurement and construction (EPC), providing a fully equipped facility ready for operation 'at the turn of the key'.

The turnkey method of procurement is suitable for use where certainty of price and completion date is a high priority for the employer, where the project is to be delivered so that it is capable of meeting its designed production and output costs and, for project-financed deals, where lenders require greater certainty over final costs.

There are a number of advantages of a turnkey contract, including:

- the contractor is the single point of responsibility for the design, construction and delivery of the plant, so in the event of a problem with the plant, the employer knows that (generally) the contractor cannot argue that someone else was at fault;
- since the contractor absorbs more risks under a turnkey contract, it is more likely that the price paid by the employer will not exceed the original contract price; and
- the contractor is responsible for any subcontractors and suppliers, so the employer does not need to get involved in their management.

These advantages will need to be weighed against:

- only limited control can be exercised over the contractor whilst it is performing its obligations, particularly on issues of design;
- the original contract price for the works is likely to be higher to reflect the additional risks the contractor is assuming responsibility for;
- the cost of any changes which the employer instructs during the course of the project are likely to be higher than for other kinds of contract; and
- sometimes, the advantages of a single point of responsibility will be diluted where the contractor refuses to accept any greater liability for a major item of plant (such as a turbine) than the supplier gives to the contractor.

A turnkey contractor will often have its own in-house design engineers, and so the engagement of an external engineering design team to complete the employer's concept design may not be necessary.

3.2 Multi-contracting (non-EPC)

Under a multi-contracting method, the employer enters into separate agreements for different elements of the works, such as civil works, the design and installation of plant, supply of relevant equipment and other related infrastructure works. There may also be separate contracts for specialist elements of design and engineering.

There are a number of advantages of a multi-contracting method, including:

- the opportunity to have greater control over design;
- the commencement of a contract can be delayed until an appropriate point in time, which could assist if an earlier contract package is subject to delay; and
- the sum of the original contract prices for all the packages is potentially lower compared to a turnkey contract.

The disadvantages of the multi-contracting method include:

- no single point of responsibility. In the event of a complex defect in the plant, the works contractors may simply blame each other, leaving the employer with the difficult and costly task of working out who is at fault;
- a relatively long overall programme if the separate contracts are to be carried out as sequential processes; and
- the employer is likely to have to engage, or provide, additional experienced project managers to run the different works packages.

Typically, the employer will use the same engineering design team (whether in-house or external) to progress the concept design to the level that it can be completed by the package contractors.

3.3 Peripheral contracts

Whichever method of procurement is chosen, if the timetable is tight, it is also common for a separate 'early works' contract to be let (in the case of turnkey contracting, often to the potential turnkey contractor) so that certain site preparation and groundworks can be carried out whilst the employer finalises negotiations with the turnkey or package contractors. Typical activities may include site clearance, demolition of structures, removal of contaminated soil, shoring works, the connection of utilities necessary for the carrying out of the works and the levelling of the site.

In multi-contracting, where there is a major item of plant which constitutes a substantial proportion of the overall construction value of the project, it is common for there to be two large contracts, one for the installation of the major item of plant and its associated elements, and a 'balance of plant' to cover the remainder of the works.

In multi-contracting, an employer sometimes requires each package contractor to enter into cooperation agreements with each other, so that each package contractor interfaces smoothly with each other.

3.4 Contract structures

The exact contract structure of the project will depend on many factors, such as the type of project and who is carrying out the design. Examples of contract structures used for turnkey and multi-contracting are shown in Figures 1 and 2 below:

Figure 1: Example contract structure for a turnkey or EPC contract in a power project

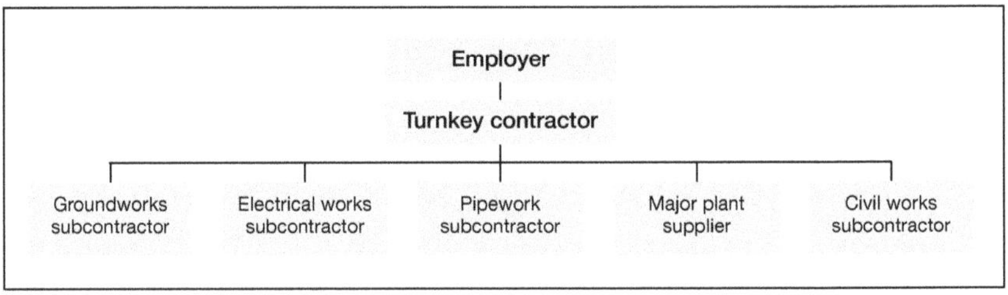

Figure 2: Example contract structure for multi-contracting in a power project

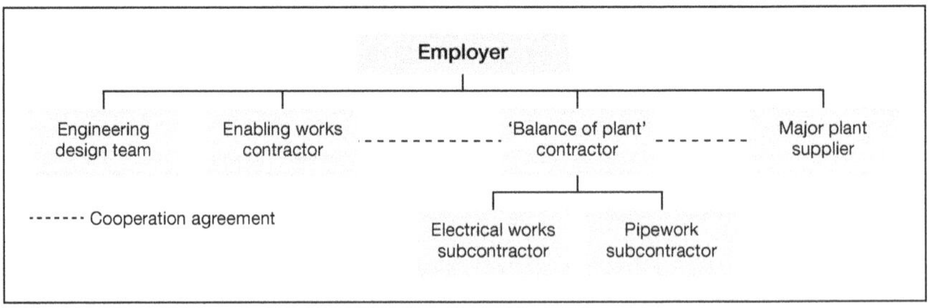

4. Forms of contract: the options available

4.1 Published standard forms of contract

Published standard forms are used to form the basis of contracts in a number of large-scale power projects, as they are widely accepted in most jurisdictions and may result in shorter contract negotiations. Another advantage is that their conditions are usually well tested on other projects.

The most frequently used suites of contracts are those published by, for example:

- the International Federation of Consulting Engineers (FIDIC), such as the 'silver book' for turnkey projects;
- the Institution of Engineering and Technology (IET) and the Institution of Mechanical Engineers (IMechE), such as the model form MF/1; and
- the Institution of Civil Engineers (ICE), such as the New Engineering Contracts (NEC).

It would however be unusual for a standard form to be used on a power project without significant amendment. Amendments arise due to the need to reflect project specific requirements and to change the risk profile.

In considering whether a standard form is appropriate, it is necessary to consider:

- the nature, type and value of the power project and complexity of the contractual structure;
- the country in which the project is being carried out, and which standard form contracts are typically used there;
- how risk should be apportioned;
- what control the employer intends to have over design;
- the likelihood of changes to the design and/or construction;
- how the contractor will be paid; and
- whether the negotiating strength of one of the parties enables it to stipulate that bespoke contractual terms should be used.

(a) Bespoke forms

Use of a standard form as a basis for a contract on a power project may not be appropriate where a contract is required to be consistent with financing documents or other project documents. This is often the case in a concession based project, where the provisions of the concession agreement between the relevant public authority and the employer need to be passed down by the employer to the contractor. In such a case, a bespoke contract may be more appropriate.

4.2 Ancillary documents

The purpose of putting ancillary documents in place for a power project is to provide security against the covenant strength of the contractor, to incentivise proper performance, to mitigate insolvency risk and to assist with cash flow issues. Typically, in project-financed structures, lenders will insist on a more robust and comprehensive package than on a balance sheet financed project.

The types of ancillary documents commonly seen are:

- *Cost overrun guarantees:* Cost overruns are a concern on any project. Larger projects, for example nuclear power projects, are particularly sensitive to cost overruns, due to the significant capital costs involved, which reduce the returns over the life of a project. The debt financiers on these types of projects are likely to request that a third party, potentially a government entity, provides a guarantee that it will meet the shortfall.

- *Parent company guarantee:* Parent company guarantees are commonly required. The parent company of a contractor, with its greater credit worthiness and resources will often be asked to enter into a guarantee, particularly where a local subsidiary is undertaking the works.
- *Bonds:* The types of bonds which may feature in a project include advance payment bonds, performance bonds and retention bonds. Bonds can also be required in other circumstances, including to back up liquidated and ascertained damages and bonds in respect of snagging items, or defects liability. A bond will be provided by a bank or other financial institution and will typically be for between 10% and 20% of the contract value.
- *Direct agreements:* These contracts will provide privity of contract between certain interested third parties and key contractors and subcontractors. Direct agreements are of particular value to the procuring authority and/or the funders to a project. Their aim is to protect the integrity of a defaulting project and to enable the funders/authority a period of time to rectify the project by stepping into the role of the employer before the termination rights of the contractor crystallise.
- *Product warranties:* As we have seen, on many power projects there will be a substantial item of plant which constitutes a major element (in terms of cost and/or complexity of technology) of the project. Sometimes, the supplier of this plant will be a larger concern than the turnkey contractor it is supplying to. As a result, the employer will look to receive product warranties from the supplier, warranting that the plant is free of defects, and in certain cases also warranting the performance of the plant.

5. Key provisions in construction contracts for power projects

Construction contracts in the power sector bear substantial similarities to those used on other large scale infrastructure projects. Typically, such contracts (whether a standard form or bespoke) will incorporate all the common provisions that one would expect to find in a complex, multi-party, high value project.

In this section, we focus on:

- the key provisions for all power projects; and
- specific issues applicable for plants in a number of main sectors.

During negotiation of these provisions and issues, the tensions between the employer and the contractor over the allocation of risk noted in the introduction of this chapter are ever-present.

In some markets (which we could define as a certain type of power project in a certain geographic region) there will be a 'market standard' position on many of these issues which is based on the positions agreed on previous projects, and these are usually the starting point for negotiations.

One hot negotiation topic will often be the extent to which the contractor is required to assume the 'back-to-back' risk passed down under a head agreement.

Take, for example, a gas fired power station in Malaysia which is being procured by a government entity, which will enter into a concession agreement with a developer. The developer will want the contractor to assume every risk and obligation that relates to construction which is contained in the concession agreement, and will seek to limit the contractor's right to make any claims under the construction contract to the extent that the developer cannot make such a claim under the concession agreement. Generally, a market will need to be relatively mature with some track record of successfully completed projects before a prudent contractor will contemplate adopting this risk.

5.1 Design

Responsibility for design needs to be clearly allocated in the contract. There should be an obligation on the contractor to complete the design. Where applicable, there should also be an obligation on the contractor to adopt responsibility for any design carried out by the employer.

The contractor is, however, unlikely to accept responsibility for the fundamentals of the concept design to the extent these are essentially the employer's commercial decisions (eg, to build an oil fired plant rather than a coal fired plant).

5.2 Price

Although it is common to talk about 'fixed price lump sum' contracts, or 'guaranteed maximum price' contracts, conceptually these are misnomers. A contractor will nearly always be entitled to make a claim against an employer for additional money if certain circumstances arise, regardless of what the contract says (for example, if he is prevented from building the plant due to an act of prevention of the employer).

In addition, in practice, the contractor will always look to price into the contract any risks the contractor is required to take on, and there may be some risks (eg, environmental risks) that may be prohibitively expensive for the employer to try to offload to the contractor.

The issue is really where the allocation lies between risks which entitle the contractor to extra cost and time, and risks which the contractor must absorb. The contractor's appetite for absorbing risks at an economical price changes depending on how competitive the contracting market is in terms of geographical location and the stage of the economic cycle.

5.3 Environmental risks

Due to the potential costs of environmental hazards, the allocation of environmental risks will nearly always be a major concern to both the employer and the contractor. Many contractors will simply refuse to accept any risk for pre-existing conditions at the site, regardless of any environmental surveys. It will, however, be more normal for the contractor to accept responsibility for the plant complying with all current environmental legislation.

5.4 Intellectual property

The protection of a plant supplier's intellectual property rights will normally be central to its ability to continue as a successful business. The suppliers of major items of plant are therefore unlikely to compromise on the need to retain control and ownership of their intellectual property.

The use by a contractor of plant which infringes another person's intellectual property may result in a court action with a court order injuncting use of such equipment and ordering the infringing item to be replaced.

The effect on an employer can be significant. For example, the plant may need to be shut down, alternative parts ordered and, potentially, sections of the plant redesigned to cope with the new parts. Meanwhile the plant is not operating and the employer is losing profits. It is common therefore to include an indemnity from the contractor in the construction contract in respect of costs incurred for intellectual property right infringement. The employer may well seek to exclude such costs from the general cap on liability.

5.5 Performance security

The type of performance security will typically depend on the procurement route chosen for the plant, that is, whether the plant is being built through a turnkey method or multi-contracting.

Wrapped parent company guarantees are commonly sought in multi-contracting projects where the employer contracts with two different entities – for example, one for the supply of turbines and the other for the balance of plant.

Other performance security includes performance bonds, which can be 'on-demand' bonds in some jurisdictions (ie, the employer can liquidate the bond without having to demonstrate that the contractor is at fault).

5.6 Limitation of liability

Commercially, it is common to see an overall cap on liability, sub-caps and a number of exclusions to these caps.

The contractor might, for example, accept a cap on delay damages of 20% of the main contract sum (see 5.12 below). This may not be a risk which the contractor can pass down fully to its subcontractors – a subcontractor might only accept a cap of 20% of its own contract price, and if that subcontractor is the cause of all of the delay, then the contractor will carry the risk in the difference between 20% of the main contract price and 20% of the subcontractor's (much smaller) contract price.

5.7 Consents

The construction contract should identify all permits which both the employer and contractor must obtain, and the contractor should be required to adhere to the conditions attaching to any licence, permit or approval. For instance, in relation to onshore wind farms, planning obligations may impose restrictions including in relation to working hours, access, noise and frequency of deliveries to site during the construction phase.

5.8 Testing and commissioning

This is one of the most sensitive stages for any power plant, as such provisions impact on handover and performance. Testing regimes will often need to align with those required under other project documents, such as power purchase agreements.

Tests are often used to define completion and the entitlement to performance damages in the event of the plant not running to specification. All or some of the following tests may apply for a power plant:

- *factory tests:* where the equipment manufacturer demonstrates the design and quality of the equipment and, if possible, its design life, prior to the equipment leaving the factory;
- *mechanical completion:* where the plant has been physically constructed on site and is ready to commence its performance tests; and
- *full commercial operation tests:* these may include a reliability run test – requiring the plant to operate at, say, 100% capacity for an extended period; a full load rejection test – which demonstrates the plant's ability to withstand full load rejection; and environmental performance tests – perhaps monitoring emissions and noise.

5.9 Despatch

At some stage, the power plant will need to be connected to the offtaker. The process of allocating output of the plant to a load is known as despatch. Where the offtaker is an electricity grid, this involves the technically complex process of sychronising the electrical output of the plant with that of the grid, and the grid operator will have detailed regulations on how this is to be done.

5.10 Feedstock and output generated

One detail that should not be overlooked in a construction contract is who pays for any feedstock, and who is entitled to the benefit of the plant's electrical output during the test and commissioning phase. In large plants, such costs can be significant.

5.11 Completion

The construction contract will set out a time for completion and a procedure for acceptance of the power plant. If there is a power purchase agreement in place, consideration of the applicable remedies in the power purchase agreement will be required so as to ensure that the provisions dovetail adequately. The same certification regime should apply for the works under the construction contract and the power purchase agreement.

5.12 Delay damages

A construction contract will have a completion date, or series of completion dates for different stages of the project or different physical sections of the project.

Where the contractor is delayed in the performance of the contract, and this delay is due to a risk attributable to the contractor, the employer will be entitled to levy delay damages on the contractor. Delay damages are typically a pre-agreed sum that the contractor must pay to the employer for each day that the contractor is late, where the late completion is due to a risk attributable to the contractor. Such pre-determined damages are 'liquidated' damages.

5.13 Phased completion

Phases of a power project may be commissioned sequentially, for example, turbines in a wind project are likely to be tested and commissioned in batches. In such an instance the parties will need to cater for this by ensuring that handover of part of the plant does not prejudice the contractor's obligations to develop the whole plant. Consideration will need to be given to how taking over of a batch relates to the operation of any delay or performance damages provisions. These may either operate at final taking over or will apply on a batched basis.

Further, the logistical aspects of ensuring that the contractor has access to the operating plant in order to complete any snagging items or remedy any defects need to be accommodated, and the contractor must not be prevented from carrying out its obligations to complete the installation and commission of the remainder of the units.

5.14 Performance

The performance of the power plant is crucial as its value is based on attaining a guaranteed performance level in order to deliver power and earn the expected revenue. A power plant will typically need to meet a minimum performance guarantee in terms of efficiency, electrical output and reliability.

In the event that a power plant fails to meet guaranteed performance levels during testing, the employer will be entitled to pre-agreed performance damages in order to compensate the employer for the lower revenue the plant will generate.

In addition to the guaranteed performance level, there may be a provision for a minimum performance level. This provides that, in the event the plant fails to reach a minimum performance level by a certain date, the employer has the right to reject the plant, terminate the contract and recover all sums paid to the contractor.

The procedures for testing must set out what is to be done if the plant fails the performance test, how many times the test is to be performed and how long the contractor has to rectify it before performance liquidated damages are applied.

A unique feature of some solar projects is the lengthy testing period which follows such completion, typically lasting two years.

5.15 Dispute resolution

Most large power projects have a tiered dispute resolution procedure under which a party can refer a dispute of a technical nature to a third party engineer if no resolution is obtained after negotiations between the parties at a senior level. Often, the third party engineer's decision will be binding until finally determined by arbitration or court proceedings.

Arbitration is common as the residual mode of dispute resolution, in part because it may be seen as more impartial than the courts of a country associated with any one of the parties, and also because the parties can select arbitrators who have knowledge and experience of the particular issue in dispute. For major projects, arbitrations under the rules and administration of the International Chamber of Commerce, the Stockholm Chamber of Commerce and the London Court of International Arbitration are common, with a seat in a well established arbitration hub such as New York, Hong Kong, London or Singapore.

The contractor will also be keen to include provisions in its subcontracts allowing it to join subcontractors to any proceedings initiated by the employer.

Dispute resolution under cooperation agreements in multi-contracting structures need particular consideration. Supposing, for example, that contractor A wrongfully causes a delay to contractor B. Contractor B may then have a claim for additional expense against the employer under its subcontract, and the employer will normally have to try to recover any additional sums it has to pay to contractor B for any such claim from contractor A. In any cooperation agreement between contractors A and B, the employer will often try to make contractor A directly responsible to contractor B, thus allowing the employer to avoid any direct involvement in their dispute.

6. Conclusion

Construction contracts in the power sector have a lot in common with construction contracts for large scale infrastructure projects in general. However, such contracts will have their own specific issues including those arising due to the method of power generation testing and commissioning regimes, completion procedures, performance requirements and methods of financing.

Construction contracts for new and developing technologies will generally be complex, adopt a multi-contracting approach, be both costly and risky, and will rely on government subsidies for funding. As technology and infrastructure for a particular type of power generation becomes more standardised and established, the method of procurement will eventually shift to turnkey as the risks decrease.

O&M contracts and long-term service agreements

Nicholas Hilder
Ashurst LLP

1. Introduction

Long before a power station is complete and has achieved commercial operation, thoughts will have turned (or should have) to the arrangements pursuant to which that power station is to be operated and maintained. Power stations are built to generate electricity and, in the context of a power station that is developed by an independent power producer, to provide a return on investment. In project financed transactions the income to be earned from that electricity generation is essential to service the debt borrowed to finance the power station's design and construction.

Operation and maintenance contracts (O&M Contracts) and long-term service agreements (LTSAs) are therefore a means by which a project's sponsors and, where applicable, lenders seek to manage the realisation of their base case assumptions on the performance of the power station during the commercial operations phase. The engineering, procurement and construction contract (EPC Contract) may have been a strong document, with an owner friendly allocation of risk; the power station may have achieved completion on time, or even early, and be meeting or exceeding all the relevant guaranteed performance levels; but without a competent operator (Operator) to run the power station, and a competent LTSA contractor (LTSA Contractor) to perform the necessary major maintenance there is a real risk that the forecasted returns will never materialise and that the owner of the power station (Owner) will find itself in breach of its obligations under related project agreements such as power purchase agreements and finance agreements.

This chapter examines the issues that are likely to be encountered when preparing O&M Contracts and LTSAs and the different ways of addressing those issues in the context of the financing of the power station (ie, project finance using a thinly capitalised special purpose vehicle or on balance sheet financing using internal reserves or retained profit).

The O&M Contract between the Owner and its Operator focuses primarily on the means by which the completed power station facilities are operated and managed after the construction phase has been completed. The LTSA on the other hand governs the maintenance and necessary replacement of equipment not covered by the scope of the O&M Contract, which is more focused on routine maintenance. The LTSA can be between the Owner and the LTSA Contractor, who will usually be the original equipment manufacturer or affiliate or it can be a sub-contract between the Operator and the LTSA Contractor. As would be expected, there are many variations on the same theme and section one covers the different approaches to O&M

contracting, with section two adopting the same approach for the LTSA. Finally, in section three we look at issues that are common to both O&M Contracts and LTSAs from the perspective of UK law.

2. The O&M Contract

2.1 O&M strategy

There are two main ways in which an Owner may procure the operation and maintenance of its power station. At opposite ends of the spectrum in terms of risk transfer and control are:

(a) In-house option

The Owner can carry out the operation and maintenance function using its own in-house resource. If this approach is adopted the Owner would need to convince lenders that the Owner has the relevant expertise and sufficiently skilled and experienced employees in-house.

(b) Arm's length contract with a true third party

The owner can contract out the operation and maintenance function to a true third party (a true third party being an entity with which the Owner has no corporate link). Sometimes where the EPC contractor (EPC Contractor) has the resource to fulfil the role it will perform the operation and maintenance function.

Keeping the O&M function in-house should mean closer control and a flatter management structure but does not result in the same level of risk transfer as that which can be achieved by contracting with true third parties. The trade-off being, of course, that those third parties will not necessarily share the aims and objectives of the Owner will be more difficult to control and will charge a premium in return for their assumption of risk. To bridge the gap between those two different strategies some Owners favour hybrid approaches whereby:

- instead of using in-house employees the Owner may staff itself with experts from another source – these could be drawn from various specialist agencies but more likely is that they would come on secondment from one of the project sponsors; or
- instead of contracting with a true third party the Owner may contract with a project related party – most commonly a sponsor whose primary interest in the project is the chance to award itself or a member of its group an O&M Contract.

As highlighted in 2.1(b), in some projects it is the EPC Contractor who assumes the role of operator. Such a structure brings a number of advantages. A key benefit for the Owner arising from having a single point of responsibility will be that there is reduced scope for disputes as to who is responsible for defects in the work. For example, has the defect arisen as a result of the EPC Contractor's defective workmanship or the Operator's failure to properly operate and maintain the power station. Otherwise, Owners may want to consider entering into an interface agreement between the EPC Contractor, Operator and LTSA Contractor where one member of the supply chain agrees to assume prima facie liability for a particular issue with rights of recovery against the supply chain counterparties to the interface agreement. In addition, in theory, there should be less conflict between the operator and the EPC Contractor during the start-up, commissioning and testing of the power station. Notwithstanding these benefits there may be doubts as to the EPC Contractor's ability to, for example, run the power station as a commercial venture with responsibility for dispatch.

2.2 Key considerations – what, how long for and how much will it cost?

Once the choice of contracting structure has been made the Owner can move forward and begin to consider the key commercial terms that will figure within the O&M Contract. The three primary commercial questions will be: (a) what is the scope of the Operator's services; (b) for how long will the Operator perform these services; and (c) what will the Operator charge the Owner to perform these services. Each of these questions is considered below.

(a) What is the scope of the Operator's services?

The scope of the services to be performed will vary from project to project and depend in part upon the power generation technology involved. Nonetheless, across all technologies it is possible to identify certain patterns. For example, it is common to group the services by reference to the times when the Operator will perform those services, and so we see development services, mobilisation services and operations phase services. Dealing with each in turn:

Development services: the development services largely comprise desktop activities such as review and approval of the EPC Contractor's detailed design. Where the Operator has been involved in the development of the project since its inception and prior to signature of contracts, it is common for the Operator's requirements as to power station design to find their way into the Owner's technical requirements and power station specification which will form part of the EPC Contract and with which the EPC Contractor will need to comply.

Mobilisation services: during the mobilisation phase the Operator will become a more visible project participant and may be required to liaise closely with the Owner and EPC Contractor on the development, testing and commissioning procedures in general and in some areas provide resource for the commissioning process so as to gain valuable 'on the job' experience of the power station and its operating characteristics, or at the very least a right to attend such tests. The Operator is also likely to assist, or at least comment on any list prepared as part of the process for taking over and testing the power station under the EPC Contract (such a list will identify parts of the works which are not 100% in conformity with the EPC Contract but are substantially compliant and will not prevent the taking-over certificate being issued).

Operations phase services: after the commercial operations date (ie, the date upon which the power station will begin operation, which is triggered by the issuing of the taking-over certificate under the EPC Contract), the power station and the Operator will move into the operations phase. This accounts for the majority of the Operator's work and is likely to cover the routine and planned maintenance of the power station as well as the day-to-day operation of the power station and dispatch of electrical energy to the grid or local offtaker. Other common tasks include inventory management, preparing budgets and metering of fuel consumption and electricity and (in cogeneration power stations) steam production. It is worth bearing in mind that it will often be the case that in the early part of the operations phase there will be a degree of overlap between the activities of the Operator and the EPC Contractor. A good example of this overlap is in the context of defects rectification. The EPC Contract will likely oblige the EPC Contractor to return and remedy defects during the defects rectification period. This defects rectification period will overlap with the operations phase and so careful consideration will need to be given to the EPC Contractor's access requirements, care of the site provisions and the impacts that any such defect or defect rectification activities could have on the plant's performance and availability and associated Operator's guarantees.

(b) ***For how long will the Operator perform the services?***

Properly maintained, a power station can be expected to have a long and productive life. For example, the average lifetime of a typical gas turbine can be expected to be between 100,000 and 150,000 equivalent operating hours (EOH). EOHs are explained at 3.1 below. Operators are however unlikely to be able to offer fixed prices for the full useful life of a power station and any price so proposed is likely to be so heavily caveated and qualified with assumptions and swollen by excessive risk premia as not to offer the Owner or its lenders value for money. Indeed, traditionally it has been a challenge to align a borrower's and its lenders' need for price certainty across the assumed debt repayment period with the Operator's willingness to commit to a term that is co-terminus with a borrower's repayment obligations under its finance documents.

The most common means of striking a balance between the Operator's desire to retain a degree of pricing flexibility and the desire of the Owner and its lenders for long-term cost certainty is to accept a fixed term at the outset but to provide the Owner with an option to extend the term having given the Operator an opportunity to reprice after the expiry of the initial term. In terms of the points of reference against which the term of the O&M Contract is measured it is common for the fixed term of the O&M Contract to start either on the date of the O&M Contract itself or by reference to the date on which the EPC Contractor commences works activities under the EPC Contract. The expiry date of the fixed term O&M Contract will commonly be set as a number of years after the commercial operations date.

(c) ***What will the Operator charge the Owner to perform these services?***

Once the Operator's scope of services has been settled it will be possible to set the terms by which the Operator is to be paid. There are two broad types of payment structure that can be adopted, being:

Fixed contract price: as its name suggests, under this pricing structure the Operator agrees to perform the services for a fixed price. Whilst such a pricing structure provides the Owner with the highest degree of risk transfer (given the long term nature of the Operator's obligations), a well advised Operator will begin by resisting this form of pricing structure as any additional cost incurred in performing the services in excess of the agreed fixed contract price will be borne by the Operator, and in the unlikely event the Operator accepts such a structure the Operator will almost certainly insist on an indexation mechanism to take account of inflation. Even though an indexation mechanism will afford the Operator a degree of protection in respect of inflation linked price rises, it will not provide protection in respect of a non-inflation linked price rise and as a result an Operator offering a fixed price can be expected to include a risk premium (which may be considerable) in its contract price.

Cost pass-through: here the Owner reimburses the Operator the costs incurred by the Operator in the operation and maintenance of the power station. In addition to those costs the Operator will charge a management fee. This can either be a fixed fee or a premium on all costs incurred by the Operator. A fixed fee is preferable for an Owner as it gives increased certainty of price. In contrast to the fixed price structure detailed above, with the cost pass-through formula the Owner has a greater exposure to price increases. Conversely, since the Operator is being reimbursed all of his costs on a pass-through basis, it does not need to include as big a risk premium. Therefore, if properly managed, a cost pass-through approach can result in lower O&M costs for the Owner.

2.3 O&M Contracts – common features

Having examined the key drivers that will frame the commercial agreement between the parties, this section takes a look at the some of the contractual provisions one would expect to find in a typical O&M Contract.

(a) Standard of performance

Once the scope of the services to be performed by the Operator has been agreed, the parties will need to set the level at which the Operator is required to perform those services. This can be achieved by imposing on the Operator obligations to meet specific performance guarantees and/or to comply with more open-ended generic performance standards.

Performance guarantees: often the Operator will be required to ensure that the power station is operated within specified performance parameters with a failure to comply with such specified performance parameters being treated as a breach of the Operator's performance obligation. This breach will entitle the Owner to a claim in damages (general or liquidated) and in extreme or prolonged cases a right to terminate the O&M Contract. Parties will normally agree 'liquidated damages' (typically based on an estimate of the loss that will result from the breach of contract, which the Owner can recover from the Operator at a pre-agreed daily rate whilst the breach subsists) as opposed to relying on a claim for general damages at law. Whilst liquidated damages are unlikely to protect the Owner 100% from the loss suffered as a result of Operator breach of contract, they are likely to appeal to the Owner on the basis that the Owner will not need to prove its loss flowing from such a breach and that by allowing the Owner to claim liquidated damages immediately on breach they provide a source of liquidity.

The Operator will therefore need to exercise care in agreeing what effectively amounts to guarantees of the power station's performance capabilities at a time when the power station has yet to achieve commercial operation. A properly advised Operator will seek to ensure that there is a degree of flexibility in all guarantees as to operational performance as a result of the EPC Contractor's construction of the power station or some other external event (such as *force majeure*) which makes it impossible for the power station to achieve the operational performance guarantee. By way of illustration, clauses detailing the apportionment of responsibility as between Owner, Operator and EPC Contractor in circumstances where, notwithstanding the Operator's performance of the services in accordance with its obligations in the O&M Contract, a defect in works carried out by the EPC Contractor affects the performance characteristics of a power station are often heavily negotiated and may be hived off into the interface agreement previously discussed at 2.1.

Generic performance standards: where the Operator does not expressly guarantee the operational performance of the power station, the Owner will expect the Operator to perform the services in accordance with a series of more generic operating principles. These will include obligations to perform the services in accordance with:

- good industry practice;
- in compliance with all applicable laws and regulations; and
- the requirements set out in related project documents such as tolling agreements or fuel supply and power purchase agreements and consents and permits.

For example, many independent power station projects in regions such as the Gulf and Africa impose minimum requirements on the local labour content of the project company's and its Operator's workforce. Where these requirements do filter down to the Operator, they should either be expressly written into the O&M Contract or incorporated by reference back to the relevant project document.

The generic warranty option is clearly less onerous for the Operator and allows him the opportunity to apportion blame to other project participants more easily than an Operator who has warranted guaranteed operational performance levels and this should be reflected in the price of the Operator's services.

Moreover, the two approaches to setting the Operator's standard of performance should not be seen as mutually exclusive. Not all aspects of the operation of a power station easily translate into a guaranteed performance level and so for this residual category (for example, health and safety) a generic obligation to operate the power station in accordance with good industry practice and in accordance with applicable laws and consents is appropriate. A good example is with respect to noise levels. Almost all operational and environmental consents will impose strict maximum noise levels for different areas within the project site. Failure to comply with these noise levels may result in fines or ultimately revocation of the consent.

(b) ***Cost control and budget oversight***

On the assumption that a large part of the Owner's O&M spend will be accounted for by pass-through costs items, it is important that the Owner can control and monitor how those pass-through costs are incurred.

Such control can be achieved by requiring the Owner's approval before certain large orders are placed, but the most useful tools at the Owner's disposal are the budgets prepared by the Operator. Each budget should be accompanied by a plan setting out how the Operator intends to operate the power station during the period to which the budget relates and both the budget operating plan should be prepared in advance of the period to which they relate and allow good time for the Owner and Operator to resolve any dispute relating thereto. In particular, permitted expenditure under the finance documents will restrict expenditure to budgeted items subject to a limited degree of flexibility. In project finance transactions, the lenders' technical advisor is likely to be heavily involved in agreeing the budget and operating plan, and the lenders will control the project company Owner's rights to agree the budget and operating plans and any updates thereto. Therefore any material budget overruns may result in waiver requests being required from lenders.

Once the content of the budget and operating plan have been agreed, the Owner will be able to monitor the Operator's performance against budget. Whilst it is very rare for the budget to act as a cap on the amount the Owner needs to pay in respect of the covered items, with the Operator bearing the risk of cost overruns, the consequences of a budget overrun remain serious for the Operator.

Budget overruns are likely to trigger increased Operator reporting obligations, and increase Owner monitoring and Owner approval rights. Harsher sanctions will include liquidated damages mechanisms linked to budget overspend and where the budget is exceeded on a regular basis or by a large amount the Owner may be entitled to terminate the O&M Contract.

(c) ***Incentives and remedies***

Whatever pricing structure is ultimately adopted it is likely to be supplemented by a series of remedies and bonus payments that can either increase or decrease the Operator's overall level of remuneration to reflect the risk allocation on the project. These are examined below:

Structural incentives – equity participation: before exploring the various price linked incentives and liquidated damages mechanisms, it should not be forgotten that an ownership interest in the project as a whole can be an effective mechanism to incentivise the Operator.

Equity participation in the Owner project company by the Operator or an affiliate should result in an incentivised Operator who will not only earn a fee under the O&M Contract but may, where the project is a success, generate dividends and capital growth. Where the project is not a success, the Operator will see the value of its investment suffer, distributions dry up and may be faced with the prospect of having to make further capital injections in order to sustain the project with a view to making a return at some time in the future.

If such an approach to incentivisation is adopted and the benefits thereof are to be maintained, there will need to be restrictions on the transfer of shares in the Owner special purpose vehicle in order to ensure that all parties retain control of when and how the Operator investor is allowed to alter its interest (and, therefore, its incentivation levels) in the project.

O&M Contract incentives: some basic incentive mechanisms operate by way of comparison of the actual revenue produced by the power station against forecast revenue, with the Operator receiving bonuses where the power station exceeds base case revenue assumptions. Whilst the simplicity offered by this structure has its appeal, it takes no account of the overall financial health of the project and assumes that just because the power station is generating more revenue than forecast, there will be funds with which to reward the Operator. This may not be the case – construction programme delay and construction overspends may have placed the Owner perilously close to breaching the terms of its financing arrangements and mean that any additional revenue generated would be better used shoring up the Owner's financial position. Unsurprisingly, the Operator's reaction to such an argument will be that that is an issue for the Owner and the EPC Contractor to resolve, and that having operated the power station beyond the threshold levels written into the O&M Contract it is entitled to its reward.

A more sophisticated way of upside sharing is to link the Owner's ability to make incentive payments to the Operator to the Owner's ability to make distributions to the project sponsors. This structure will be attractive to lenders as it removes the risk that the Operator may become entitled to bonus payments at a time when the project can ill afford to be releasing funds. Such a structure will not however address the underlying problem that the Operator may be performing admirably but is prevented from receiving a reward for such performance as a result of an event over which it has no control and with which there is no link to the Operator's performance of its obligations – such as EPC Contract cost overruns.

Alternatively, where an Operator has provided specific performance guarantees, as discussed above, the incentives and liquidated damages can be triggered by exceeding or falling short of these guarantees. Guarantees of availability, power curve and heat rate are commonplace. For example, if the Operator guarantees a certain heat rate and in fact operates the plant more efficiently so less fuel is consumed in generating a certain amount of power, the Operator could share in the cost saving in relation to fuel and carbon emissions. Conversely, if more fuel is used in generating a certain amount of power, liquidated damages could be imposed on the Operator to compensate the Owner for an increase in its fuel and carbon emissions costs.

However, depending on the Operator's scope of work, availability, heat rate and power curve guarantees may also be included in the O&M contract, or in the alternative, may be covered in the LTSA. Owners will also need to ensure that any incentives payable to the Operator are covered by increased revenues and lenders will closely scrutinise the income streams which support any bonus payment to the Operator.

O&M Contract remedies – liquidated damages and availability damages: where the Operator cannot demonstrate that the power station is achieving the guaranteed values set out for the power station in the O&M Contract, contractual remedies are likely to be in the form of performance liquidated damages and availability liquidated damages payable by the Operator to the Owner. The rates of liquidated damages payable will be informed by any corresponding liability the Owner assumes under its power purchase arrangements and/or offtake arrangements, or lost revenue for failing to generate or otherwise be available. Such liquidated damages are likely to be subject to an appropriately sized sub-cap sitting within the Operator's annual aggregate cap on liability.

As is the case with the incentive payments, a well advised Operator will have to draw a distinction at the contract negotiation stage between those performance shortfalls that have been caused by the EPC Contractor's or LTSA Contractor's sub-standard performance of their respective obligations, and the Operator's own act, error or omission, with the Operator only assuming liquidated damages liability for the latter.

These liquidated damages will include an element of indirect and consequential loss and so any general exclusion on the recoverability of these heads of loss will need to include a carve-out for the performance liquidated damages that are payable.

(d) Termination for poor performance and transitional arrangements

The caps on the Operator's liability effectively preclude the Owner from transferring the entire risk of the power station's poor performance to the Operator. The Owner is then faced with a choice of continuing to allow the Operator to operate the power station, albeit at a level below the Operator's contractual obligation, or terminating the Operator's employment under the O&M Contract (once the Operator has reached its liability cap in relation to performance) and engaging a replacement operator.

Notwithstanding the restrictions placed on Owner termination by lenders (the financing documents are likely to require lender consent for the termination of the O&M Contract), this may be a difficult decision for the Owner to make as even a poorly performing incumbent Operator should have amassed a detailed specialist knowledge of the power station and the Owner will be concerned that whilst any replacement operator is 'learning the ropes' the project will continue to under-perform. Properly drafted clauses dealing with the transitional period following the Operator's termination should go some way to making the Owner's decision easier. These should include Operator obligations to:

- cooperate with the replacement operator, which may extend to providing a phased handover with on-the-job training to the replacement operator;
- to the extent possible, assign any remaining warranties to the Owner or its

nominee and grant licences to use any intellectual property required for operation and maintenance of the power station.

Such transitional arrangements should also apply where the O&M Contract terminates on the expiry of the term.

3. Long-term Service Agreements (LTSAs)

3.1 The LTSA distinguished from the O&M Contract

The LTSA is in many respects similar to the O&M Contract in that it is also a contract for the provision of services. What is different however is the scope of services to be performed. Under the O&M Contract the services will focus on operating the power station and routine maintenance. The LTSA on the other hand is primarily concerned with large scale planned maintenance and, if agreed as part of the scope, unplanned maintenance.

The focus on unplanned maintenance and planned maintenance can be explained by the fact that in power station projects the turbine supplier will be expected to warrant under the LTSA the availability of its gas or steam turbines. In other words, if the turbines are operated and maintained in accordance with the turbine supplier's instructions, the supplier should be able to guarantee that the turbines will operate at a certain level which will produce a particular number of EOHs per year. In order to protect itself against the risk of turbine unavailability (howsoever defined) and associated unavailability liquidated damages, the turbine supplier will want to be involved in and perform the ongoing maintenance of those turbines. The LTSA is the agreement pursuant to which the LTSA Contractor (who is likely to be the original equipment manufacturer or an affiliate thereof) assumes the obligation to perform this major maintenance. The parties to the LTSA will be the Owner and the LTSA Contractor or, where the Operator takes responsibility for major maintenance under the O&M Contract, the LTSA may be a sub-contract to the O&M Contract, in which case the parties will be the Operator and the LTSA Contractor. Equipment covered by the LTSA will vary from project to project, but equipment commonly covered includes the turbines (gas and steam), the generators and the distributed control systems.

Risk of liability under the availability warranty should therefore motivate the LTSA Contractor to perform planned maintenance within the clearly scheduled periods of time for maintenance (as an allowance for these periods will have been factored into the calculation of the availability warranty) and to respond to events requiring unscheduled maintenance (for which there will be only limited tolerances within the availability warranty) promptly so as to minimise any period of unavailability. Whilst the liquidated damages should provide the Owner with a degree of recourse against any non-performing LTSA Contractor, it is also common to include an Owner self-help remedy to allow the Owner to perform the maintenance work itself or to instruct third parties to do so in the event the LTSA Contractor is not performing its obligations. The Owner should also reserve the right to recover as a debt due from the LTSA Contractor the Owner's costs reasonably and properly incurred in exercising such rights, or to set off such amounts against sums the Owner owes to the LTSA Contractor.

3.2 LTSA strategy

Whilst the LTSA Contractor has no obligation to operate any of the equipment covered by the LTSA, the O&M Contract and LTSA can be relatively similar in terms of scope in relation to maintenance arrangements. There is likely to be at least some degree of overlap and interface between the two and in some cases with the EPC Contract. The Owner will need to plot a course through these issues to ensure that the liabilities of the various project participants dovetail and that it is not paying twice for the same service.

The Owner will need to be aware that the LTSA Contractor will seek to escape liability for a failure to meet the availability warranty if it can show that such failure was caused by the Operator's failure to perform routine maintenance pursuant to the O&M Contract. Similarly where the unavailability is caused by a defect for which the EPC Contractor is responsible, the LTSA Contractor will look to avoid liability under the availability warranty.

In order to remove these interface issues, it is sometimes the case that the Operator will wrap the LTSA Contractor's obligations in the O&M Contract and manage the LTSA Contractor as a sub-contractor, effectively providing a single point of responsibility for the Owner.

3.3 Key considerations – what, how long for and how much will it cost?

Once the choice of contracting structure has been made the Owner can move forward and begin to consider the key commercial terms that will figure within the LTSA Contract. Again, the three primary commercial questions will be: (a) what is the scope of the LTSA Contractor's services; (b) for how long will the LTSA Contractor perform these services; and (c) what will the LTSA Contractor charge the Owner to perform these services.

Each of these questions is considered below. Whilst the questions are similar to those for the O&M Contract, the issues are different.

(a) What is the scope of the LTSA Contractor's services?

It is usual for the LTSA Contractor to perform scheduled maintenance and unplanned maintenance on the equipment covered by the scope of the LTSA Contract and certain 'extra work' as may be requested by the Owner. Given that the pricing methodologies for the different types of service (ie, planned, unplanned and extra) may be different, it will be important for the Owner to clearly define the LTSA Contractor's scope with regard to each element of the services.

The service scope should include a complete list of all component parts of the equipment that are subject to the LTSA Contractor's maintenance obligations. Once the extent of the covered equipment has been established the LTSA Contract should go on to specify the general nature of the LTSA Contractor's obligations with respect to each component included within the covered equipment (eg, inspect, repair, refurbish and/or replace). Finally, the LTSA should include a description of the activities to be performed by the LTSA Contractor during each scheduled maintenance outage.

(b) ***For how long will the LTSA Contractor perform the service?***

Start of term: given that the LTSA Contractor's maintenance obligations cannot begin until the power station is complete, there should be a mechanism for adjusting the commencement date under the LTSA. The LTSA Contractor will insist on payment during the period of delay to cover the cost of having mobilised and placed its workforce on standby from day one after completion in case a piece of equipment is damaged on such day and unplanned maintenance is subsequently required. Whilst in the case of culpable delay by the EPC Contractor the Owner will have recourse to the EPC Contractor's delay liquidated damages (which should be sized to include an element sufficient to cover the LTSA Contractor's costs), there will be no liquidated damages payable from the EPC Contractor to the Owner in respect of delay events for which the EPC Contractor receives an extension of time – in which case the LTSA Contractor's costs will need to be met by either contingencies or equity, unless covered by insurance.

End of term: unlike the O&M Contract, which is likely to be for a set number of years, the LTSA's term will be fixed by reference to the performance by the LTSA Contractor of a specified set of inspections or planned outages (ie, the periods during which planned maintenance takes place) which are themselves usually set by reference to the number of equivalent operating hours of power station operation. Equivalent operating hours (or sometimes factored fired hours) are used to reflect the fact that a power station that is being run as a peaking plant, and whose generating output is ramped up and down, is likely to encounter more wear and tear and need servicing sooner than a power station operating as a steady state base load plant. As a result a cold start (ie, firing a turbine after a period of inactivity) will attract more equivalent operating hours than a warm start or hot start.

Whilst the concept of equivalent operating hours takes into account the way a power station is operated the Owner will need to be careful as to the treatment of hours of operation prior to taking-over under the EPC Contract. For instance, in reaching the prerequisites for the issue of a taking-over certificate and the Owner's acceptance of the power station under the EPC Contract, the EPC Contractor may have spent considerable time retesting the power station and trouble-shooting equipment commissioning issues. During this period, the power station may have undergone repeated cycles of being started up, run for several hours and then shut down. In many LTSAs no distinction is made between hours and/or starts occurring before or after taking over. This will be a commercial point for negotiation but in the absence of clarification to the contrary, pre-takeover equivalent operating hours will count towards the thresholds for planned outages under the LTSA. A well advised Owner will therefore press for the LTSA Contractor to assume the risk on all pre-takeover equivalent operating hours so that commissioning defects do not count towards the LTSA thresholds.

(c) *What will the LTSA Contractor charge the Owner to perform these services?*

The fee payable should reflect the services performed and whilst the Owner and the LTSA Contractor will be able to fix a fee by reference to assumptions as to how the power station is to be operated and by identifying the best times to perform scheduled outages (ie, outside periods of high electrical demand) and how much unplanned maintenance is likely to be needed – these will be assumptions. In the event those assumptions do not reflect the reality there should be a price adjustment calculated in line with LTSA service variation mechanism.

In terms of the fees payable for planned maintenance the parties will need to agree whether the costs of planned maintenance, which may be performed on a relatively irregular basis, will be spread evenly across the term of the LTSA or track the likely cost of performing the planning maintenance. Each approach has its pros and cons for the Owner and LTSA Contractor but an amortisation type approach (ie, prorating the cost over a period of years) is likely to be favoured by the Owner on the grounds of certainty of cashflow. The Owner will however need to bear in mind that where payments are evenly spread in this manner there is a risk that in a termination scenario, the Owner may have paid in advance for service/maintenance that it will no longer receive. In these circumstances the LTSA Contractor should be obliged to make a balancing payment to the Owner to take into account payments received for work that has not been done.

The payment profile under the LTSA will also impact the need for a maintenance reserve account under any finance documents where money is put aside to cover a project's maintenance and repair costs. If payments are spread evenly, then the Owner should be able to argue that no such maintenance reserve account is needed.

Where the LTSA Contractor also takes responsibility for unplanned maintenance, the overall payment profile is likely to become more variable to reflect the fact that the LTSA Contractor will want to avoid assuming an open-ended maintenance obligation within what is effectively a fixed annual fee. Equally unlikely is the Owner accepting the LTSA Contractor's risk margin to accept these risks within a fixed annual fee. The most widely accepted commercial compromise is to include a fixed set of fees for certain unplanned maintenance activities with the Owner accepting that this brings the risk of a variable component to the Owner's annual outgoings.

To cover against this risk the Owner should and the lenders will require that project revenues be credited to an unplanned maintenance reserve account.

3.4 LTSAs – common features

Having examined the key drivers that will frame the commercial agreement between the parties, this section takes a look at some of the contractual provisions one would expect to find in a typical LTSA

(a) *Spares and upgrades*

The Owner will also need to give consideration to the issue of spare parts. In the exercise of its maintenance obligations the LTSA Contractor will be replacing equipment. The spares will either be provided from the Owner's own stock of spares (sometimes an initial inventory of key spare parts is included as an 'option' under the EPC Contract) or will be provided at a cost by the LTSA Contractor. The same principle applies to the Operator under the O&M Contract, albeit different equipment will be covered by the LTSA and O&M Contract respectively, as previously discussed. The LTSA Contractor will often offer spare parts at a discount to encourage the Owner to enter the LTSA. Where the LTSA Contractor is the original equipment manufacturer it is sensible for the Owner to seek an undertaking from the LTSA Contractor not to discontinue the manufacture of certain key components or, if this is not achievable, to at least provide for an advance notification that the part will no longer be available so that, if the Owner so chooses, it can stockpile.

Where upgrades of spare parts become available, the LTSA Contractor should be required to notify the Owner and, where the Owner agrees, shall be permitted to incorporate such parts in the power station. The incorporation of upgraded parts should not be used to justify any detrimental adjustment to the availability warranty.

(b) Post term warranty

Given that the term of the LTSA is likely to expire by reference to one of the final planned outages it will be important for the Owner to ensure that any warranties and warranty period relating to the maintenance works performed as part of that outage are not extinguished on termination of the LTSA.

4. United Kingdom law issues

4.1 Payment and dispute resolution

For power station projects in England, Wales and Scotland, both the O&M Contract and the LTSA will need to comply with the requirements of the Housing Grants Construction and Regeneration Act 1996, as amended by the Local Community Economic Development and Construction Act 2009 (the 'Act'). Failure to include payment provisions and adjudication mechanisms which comply with the Act will mean that the Scheme for Construction Contracts will be deemed to apply to the O&M Contract and the LTSA.

The deemed incorporation of the scheme for construction contracts into these contracts will import a series of provisions which are likely to upset the finely balanced cash flows upon which the project is based and jeopardise any carefully crafted dispute resolution joinder provisions that ensure a harmonised procedure for the resolution of connected disputes across the associated project documents.

O&M Contracts and LTSAs are caught by the Act on account of the Act's wide definition of 'construction contracts'. Section 104 of the Act provides that a construction contract is a contract for the carrying out of 'construction operations' as defined in the Act. Section 105 of the Act provides a wide definition of what constitutes 'construction operations' and includes maintenance and repair works.

The Act does provide an exemption for contracts that relate to the assembly, installation or demolition of plant or machinery on a site where the primary activity is power generation. However, this exemption is only of any real use for contracts that solely comprise these activities (for example, perhaps a turbine supply agreement for a wind farm), because the Act also provides that where the contract in question relates to some activities which fall within the Act's definition of 'construction operations' and some activities which do not, the Act will only apply to those activities which are 'construction operations'.

It is the author's view that it is unlikely that an Owner would be minded to incorporate two parallel sets of payment provisions and dispute resolution provisions, in each case one complying with the Act for those activities which constitute construction operations as defined by the Act and another for those activities that do not. Instead the simplest and safest approach would be to incorporate one set of Act-compliant payment and dispute resolution provisions which will apply to all contract activities.

Environmental and planning issues

Angus Evers
Shoosmiths

1. Introduction

Irrespective of the type of technology used, the environmental and planning implications of developing a power project must be considered at an early stage in the development process. A failure to obtain the correct permits and authorisations for a project in a timely manner can have major implications for the development and commissioning of a project. Environmental issues associated with power projects also pose the risk of attracting local opposition and legal challenges.

Most countries operate regulatory systems requiring power plants to obtain various regulatory approvals for their construction and operation. The precise nature of these approvals will depend on the nature of the project (for example, a nuclear project will present very different issues to a solar photovoltaic project), but they can be divided into two broad categories: first, approvals required for planning and/or construction purposes (which may also involve some form of environmental assessment) and, secondly, pollution control and environmental protection approvals.

The legal frameworks governing environmental regulation are different in each jurisdiction and it would be impossible to summarise them all in a single chapter. This chapter therefore focuses on the framework currently in place in England (with reference to the underlying EU legal framework where appropriate), as an example of a well-developed and robust framework. It starts with an overview of the English planning regime as it applies to both large-scale and smaller-scale power projects, and the various environmental assessment processes that may be required as part of the planning process. The second section deals with the main environmental permits that may be required to regulate pollution from a thermal power plant and how other environmental impacts such as land contamination and nuisance are regulated.

Although much English environmental legislation currently derives from EU legislation, following the UK's referendum decision on 23 June 2016 to leave the EU, this may well change. This chapter reflects the law as at 1 November 2016, but those involved in power projects in the UK should be aware that the legislative framework governing those projects may be affected by the terms of the UK's exit from the EU.

2. Planning and development control

The construction of a power plant and associated infrastructure in England will inevitably constitute 'development'[1] and therefore require planning permission. The procedure that the applicant must follow to obtain planning permission depends on the generating capacity of the proposed plant, its location and the technology used. As a general rule, however, smaller plants require planning permission from the local planning authority (usually the Borough or District Council) and larger plants require consent from central government.

2.1 Consenting regimes

(a) Infrastructure planning

The Planning Act 2008 introduced a consenting regime for 'Nationally Significant Infrastructure Projects' (NSIPs), purportedly to address concerns about the length of time taken to determine applications for major infrastructure.

Section 31 of the Planning Act 2008 requires developers to obtain 'development consent' for development to the extent that the development is or forms part of a NSIP. 'Development' is defined in the same way as in the Town and Country Planning Act 1990 (TCPA 1990).[2] Onshore generating stations with a capacity of more than 50 MW (except onshore wind farms)[3] and offshore generating stations with a capacity of more than 100 MW are designated as NSIPs.[4] If a project does not qualify as a NSIP because of its generating capacity, there is nonetheless scope for it to be designated as being of national significance.[5] Applications for offshore generating stations with a capacity of between 1 MW and 100 MW (which fall below the threshold for NSIPs) are determined by the Marine Management Organisation under a similar procedure contained in Section 36 of the Electricity Act 1989.[6]

An order granting development consent (known as a 'development consent order' or 'DCO') can also provide for ancillary development.[7] This means that the DCO for a new power plant can include ancillary development such as the construction of overhead power lines and pipelines. A DCO can also authorise the compulsory acquisition of land[8] and confer statutory authority for the purpose of providing a defence in civil or criminal proceedings for nuisance.[9]

The final decision-maker on an application for a DCO for a power plant is the Secretary of State for Business, Energy and Industrial Strategy, but applications are processed by the Planning Inspectorate, which makes a recommendation to the Secretary of State. There is no right of appeal for the applicant against a refusal to

---

1 Section 55 of the Town and Country Planning Act 1990 defines 'development' as "the carrying out of building, engineering, mining or other operations in, on, over or under land, or the making of any material change in the use of any buildings or other land".
2 Planning Act 2008, Section 32(1); see fn 1.
3 All onshore wind farms fall under the town and country planning regime – see the Infrastructure Planning (Onshore Wind Generating Stations) Order 2016.
4 Planning Act 2008, Section 15.
5 Section 35(1) of the Planning Act 2008 enables the Secretary of State to make such a direction if an application for a consent or authorisation such as an application for planning permission is submitted to the relevant authority and the Secretary of State considers the project is of national significance.
6 Marine and Coastal Access Act 2009, Section 12.
7 Planning Act 2008, Section 120(3).
8 Planning Act 2008, Section 122.
9 Planning Act 2008, Section 158.

grant a DCO or against any conditions imposed on it. The only remedy open to the applicant is to apply for judicial review of the decision within six weeks.[10] A third party can also challenge the decision within six weeks.[11]

(b) *Town and country planning*

Onshore power plants with a generating capacity of less than 50 MW (and all onshore wind farms) require planning permission from the relevant local planning authority under the TCPA 1990. Most onshore renewable energy projects will therefore be determined under this regime rather than under the infrastructure planning regime in the Planning Act 2008.

The English planning system is a plan-led system. In determining a planning application the local planning authority must have regard to the provisions of the development plan, so far as that is material to the application, and to any other material considerations.[12] The development plan system comprises the National Planning Policy Framework,[13] the Planning Practice Guidance[14] and local plans adopted by local planning authorities.

The Secretary of State for Communities and Local Government has the power to 'call in' any planning application to determine it himself.[15] This automatically transfers jurisdiction over the application from the local planning authority to central government, although in practice the application will be administered by the Planning Inspectorate. This power is generally only used for applications of national or regional importance, or for controversial applications, so there is a reasonable chance that an application for a power project could be called in.

Unlike with infrastructure planning decisions made by central government, the applicant has an automatic right of appeal on the merits to the Secretary of State against a decision by a local planning authority to refuse planning permission. If the application is not determined within eight weeks (or 16 weeks in the case of an application requiring environmental impact assessment), then the applicant has the right to appeal against a deemed refusal.[16] There is also a right of appeal for applicants who are refused planning permission by the Secretary of State (either on appeal or following a call in of the application) to challenge that refusal,[17] although the challenge must be made within six weeks of the date of the decision and the only permitted grounds of challenge are that the decision is not within the Secretary of State's powers or that one of the relevant requirements of the TCPA 1990 has not been complied with. Third parties can use that same right to challenge the grant of planning permission by the Secretary of State. In practice, the Secretary of State's powers are usually delegated to Planning Inspectors appointed by the Planning Inspectorate.

10 Planning Act 2008, Section 118(2).
11 Planning Act 2008, Section 118(1).
12 Town and Country Planning Act 1990, Section 70(2).
13 Available at www.gov.uk/government/publications/national-planning-policy-framework--2.
14 Available at: http://planningguidance.communities.gov.uk/.
15 Town and Country Planning Act 1990, Section 77.
16 Town and Country Planning (General Development Procedure) Order 1995, Article 20.
17 Town and Country Planning Act 1990, Section 288.

(c) Planning obligations

Planning permission for the construction and operation of a power project may be accompanied by a planning obligation: either a unilateral undertaking entered into by a developer/landowner or, more commonly, an agreement between a developer/landowner and the relevant local planning authority, under Section 106 of the TCPA 1990. Planning obligations are therefore usually referred to as 'Section 106 Agreements' and are used to attempt to rectify issues with a development that may result in planning permission not being granted.

Government guidance is clear that planning obligations should only be used where a planning condition would not adequately address the effect that the obligation is designed to mitigate. However, they are often used because they have a wider remit than planning conditions. In particular, planning obligations can apply to areas outside of the development site (whereas planning conditions are restricted to the planning permission) and can require actions on the part of the local planning authority.

Only those with an interest in the land may enter into a planning obligation with a local planning authority. Where a developer who is not the freeholder of the land enters into a planning obligation, the landowner will often try to protect itself from any liabilities under the planning obligation through appropriate indemnities.

The most common issues that planning obligations are designed to address are:

- the provision of physical infrastructure;
- facilities or financial support for local communities;
- the provision of additional utilities to service the development;
- restrictions on the use of the development site;
- financial payments to the local planning authority to enable it to regulate the development (eg, through the support of noise surveys or odour monitoring); and
- the mitigation of any of the negative impacts of the development (eg, landscaping, increasing the capacity of local sewerage systems).

(d) Non-planning consents

Many power projects will require one or more non-planning consents (in addition to environmental permits, which are addressed later in this chapter). Developers ignore these consents at their peril, as they can take a considerable amount of time and resources to obtain and can cause significant delays to projects. They are too numerous to list here, but examples include orders for stopping up or diverting highways,[18] bridleways and footpaths.[19] A developer can also be required to construct new highways or carry out improvements to existing highways as a pre-condition to being granted planning permission or development consent, which will require it to enter into an agreement with the relevant highways authority.[20]

---

18 Town and Country Planning Act 1990, Section 247/Highways Act 1980, Section 116.
19 Town and Country Planning Act 1990, Section 257/Highways Act 1980, Sections 118 and 119.
20 Highways Act 1980, Sections 38 and 278.

2.2 Environmental assessment

English environmental assessment legislation closely mirrors requirements in other EU Member States and is based on a number of EU Directives which have been implemented in national law. Power projects are often required to be subject to some form of environmental assessment before they can be allowed to proceed: first, strategic environmental assessment may be required for a plan or programme set by government under Directive 2001/42/EC on the assessment of the effects of certain plans and programmes on the environment (more commonly known as the Strategic Environmental Assessment (SEA) Directive); second, environmental impact assessment (EIA) may be required for an individual project under Directive 2011/92/EU on the assessment of the effects of certain public and private projects on the environment (EIA Directive);[21] and third, 'appropriate assessment' may be required under Council Directive 92/43/EEC on the conservation of natural habitats and of wild fauna and flora (Habitats Directive) if a project is likely to have a significant effect on a protected species or habitat.

(a) *Strategic Environmental Assessment (SEA)*

The SEA Directive seeks "to provide for a high level of protection of the environment and to contribute to the integration of environmental considerations into the preparation and adoption of plans with a view to promoting sustainable development".[22] It requires a SEA to be carried out for certain plans or programmes that are likely to have significant environmental effects and is implemented in England by the Environmental Assessment of Plans and Programmes Regulations 2004[23] (SEA Regulations).

If a SEA is required, an environmental report must be prepared which identifies, describes and evaluates the likely significant effects on the environment of implementing the plan or programme, and reasonable alternatives, taking into account the objectives and the geographical scope of the plan or programme.[24] The report must be made available with the draft plan or programme for consultation to interested parties (including other EU Member States if relevant) and relevant consultation bodies.

(b) *Environmental Impact Assessment (EIA)*

The construction of a power project and related infrastructure such as power lines and gas pipelines is likely to require EIA. EIA is the process of collecting environmental information for a proposed project and publicising that information. The information must then be taken into account by the body granting consent for the construction and operation of the project. By requiring developers to comprehensively and transparently consider any potential environmental impacts arising from developments, the EIA process is designed to ensure that these impacts

---

21 Directive 2011/92/EU has been amended by Directive 2014/52/EU and Member States are required to implement the amendments by 16 May 2017.
22 Article 1.
23 SI 2004/1633.
24 SEA Directive, Article 5; SEA Regulations, Article 12.

are considered from the start of the project, thereby ensuring that mitigation measures can be introduced into the design of the development.

The EIA Directive is primarily implemented in England by the Town and Country Planning (Environmental Impact Assessment) Regulations 2011.[25] There are two additional sets of regulations which are relevant to power projects: the Electricity Works (Environmental Impact Assessment) (England and Wales) Regulations 2000[26] and the Infrastructure Planning (Environmental Impact Assessment) Regulations 2009.[27]

Whether an EIA is required for a particular project depends on whether the type of project is listed in Annex 1 or Annex 2 to the EIA Directive. EIA is mandatory for types of project listed in Annex 1. For types of projects listed in Annex 2, whether an EIA is required depends on whether the project is likely to have a significant effect on the environment by virtue of its nature, size or location. This determination must be based on a case by case examination and/or thresholds or criteria set by the Member State. Annexes 1 and 2 include the types of projects listed in Table 1 below.

In England, in order to determine whether a project falls within Annex 2 to the EIA Directive it is possible to apply to the relevant local planning authority for a 'screening opinion' (for projects requiring planning permission) or the Secretary of State for a 'screening direction' (for projects requiring other types of development consent such as a DCO). In spite of the time and cost of doing this, a negative screening opinion or direction (ie, that EIA is not required) is a useful protection against third party legal challenges brought on the grounds that EIA should have been carried out, but was not.

In preparing an EIA, the developer will need to include: a description of the project; an outline of the main alternatives studied by the developer; a description of the aspects of the environment likely to be significantly affected by the proposed project; a description of the measures envisaged to prevent, reduce and where possible offset any significant adverse effects on the environment; and a non-technical summary of the information provided. There are strict requirements relating to the publicity and public availability of EIA information; accordingly consultation is a major part of the EIA preparation process.

It is not permissible to 'salami slice' projects into sections which individually fall under the thresholds for EIA. For example, a power project comprising the construction of a gas-fired power plant, the construction of a pipeline connecting the power plant to a gas supply and the construction of overhead power lines to transport electricity to the grid is likely to be viewed as a single project for EIA purposes and the environmental effects of the component parts will have to be assessed cumulatively.

(c) *Nature conservation issues and appropriate assessment*

Developers of power projects need to be aware of the impact that nature conservation laws can have on projects and the additional environmental constraints they may impose.

---

25 SI 2011/1824.
26 SI 2000/1927.
27 SI 2009/2263.

Table 1: Examples of power projects and related infrastructure included in Annexes 1 and 2 to the EIA Directive

Annex 1	Annex 2
• Thermal power stations and other combustion installations with a heat output of 300 MW or more. • Nuclear power stations and other nuclear reactors including the dismantling or decommissioning of such power stations or reactors (except for research installations for the production and conversion of fissionable and fertile materials, whose maximum power does not exceed 1 kW continuous thermal load). • Waste disposal installations for the incineration of hazardous waste. • Waste disposal installations for the incineration of non-hazardous waste with a capacity exceeding 100 tonnes per day. • Pipelines with a diameter of more than 800 mm and a length of more than 40 km for the transport of gas, oil or chemicals, or for the transport of carbon dioxide streams for the purposes of geological storage, including associated booster stations. • Construction of overhead electrical power lines with a voltage of 220 kV or more and a length of more than 15 km. • Storage sites for the geological storage of carbon dioxide. • Installations for the capture of CO^2 streams for the purposes of geological storage from installations covered by Annex 1 where the total unit capture of CO^2 is 1.5 megatonnes or more. • Any change to or extension of projects listed in Annex 1 where such a change or extension in itself meets the thresholds, if any, set out in Annex 1.	• Industrial installations for the kW of electricity, steam and hot water (projects not included in Annex 1). • Industrial installations for carrying gas, steam and hot water; transmission of electrical energy by overhead cables (projects not included in Annex 1). • Installations for hydroelectric energy production. • Installations for the harnessing of wind power for energy production (wind farms). • Installations for the capture of CO^2 streams for the purposes of geological storage from installations not covered by Annex 1. • Oil and gas pipeline installations and pipelines for the transport of CO^2 streams for the purposes of geological storage (projects not included in Annex 1). • Installations for the disposal of waste (projects not included in Annex 1). • Any change or extension of projects listed in Annex 1 or Annex 2, already authorised, executed or in the process of being executed, which may have significant adverse effects on the environment (change or extension not included in Annex 1).

In the EU, the principal pieces of legislation that developers of power projects need to be aware of are Directive 2009/147/EC on the conservation of wild birds (Wild Birds Directive) and the Habitats Directive. In England they are implemented by the Wildlife and Countryside Act 1981, the Conservation of Habitats and Species Regulations 2010[28] and the Offshore Marine Conservation (Natural Habitats, &c.) Regulations 2007.[29]

The Wild Birds Directive requires EU Member States to take the requisite measures to maintain the population of all wild bird species in their territories "at a level which corresponds in particular to ecological, scientific and cultural requirements, while taking account of economic and recreational requirements, or to adapt the population of these species to that level"[30] and to "take the requisite measures to preserve, maintain or re-establish a sufficient diversity and area of habitats" for all species of wild birds in their territories.[31] It also requires Member States to classify the most suitable territories in number and size as special protection areas (SPAs) for the conservation of certain species of birds. The Habitats Directive requires Member States to take measures to maintain or restore, at favourable conservation status, natural habitats and species of wild fora and flora through setting up an ecological network of special areas of conservation (SACs) known as 'Natura 2000'. Member States cannot refuse to consider sites as potential SACs on the grounds that the species or habitats they contain may be affected by a proposed development on them.

The key provision within the Habitats Directive that affects developers is the requirement for Member States to "take appropriate steps to avoid, in the [SACs], the deterioration of natural habitats and the habitats of species as well as disturbance of the species for which the areas have been designated" and for any plan or project which is likely to have a significant effect on a SPA or SAC to be subject to an "appropriate assessment". Any plan or project that has a negative assessment may be consented only if there are no alternative solutions and the plan or project must be carried out for "imperative reasons of overriding public interest" (including social or economic reasons) and if the Member State takes "all compensatory measures necessary to ensure that the overall coherence of Natura 2000 is protected". These "compensatory measures" entail taking measures such as creating new habitats, rather than financial compensation.

3. Pollution control

3.1 Environmental permitting

Most power projects except onshore wind and solar photovoltaic projects will typically require some form of environmental permit from a government agency or regulator. For a thermal power plant these permits will principally regulate emissions to air, but may also cover matters such as discharges to water, waste production and

---

28 SI 2010/490.
29 SI 2007/1842.
30 Wild Birds Directive, Article 2.
31 Wild Birds Directive, Article 3.

the abstraction of water. Additional requirements may apply to plants using waste as a fuel.

There is a degree of overlap between the development control and pollution control regimes: most projects requiring both development consent and environmental permits will be likely to require EIA (and possibly appropriate assessment), but it is still possible that a project could obtain development consent but be refused an environmental permit (or vice versa).

(a) *EU Industrial Emissions Directive*

In the EU, the legislative framework governing emissions from thermal power plants has now been consolidated into Directive 2010/75/EU on industrial emissions (integrated pollution prevention and control) (Industrial Emissions Directive). The Industrial Emissions Directive has applied to all new plants with effect from 7 January 2013.

The Industrial Emissions Directive requires EU Member States to prevent and control pollution arising from specified activities. It lays down measures designed to prevent or, where that is not practicable, to reduce emissions to the air, water and land in order to achieve a high level of protection of the environment taken as a whole. Combustion installations with a rated thermal input exceeding 50 MW which emit sulphur dioxide (SO^2) and oxides of nitrogen (NOx) fall within the ambit of the Industrial Emissions Directive and must therefore comply with its requirements.

Member States are required to take all necessary measures to ensure that installations are operated in such a way to ensure that all appropriate preventative measures are taken against pollution, in particular through application of 'best available techniques' (BAT). Installations which are subject to the Industrial Emissions Directive can only be operated if they hold a permit issued in accordance with the Directive. Permits are required to include conditions which deal with emission limit values for polluting substances, in particular for SO2 and NOx. Where appropriate, limit values may be supplemented or replaced by equivalent parameters or technical measures. The emission limit values and the equivalent parameters and technical measures must be based on BAT, which takes into account the technical characteristics of the installation concerned, its geographical location and the local environmental conditions. Guidance on what constitutes BAT is contained in BAT reference documents published by the EU IPPC Bureau.[32]

Permits are also required to contain suitable release monitoring specifications, outlining measurement methodology and frequency, evaluation procedures and an obligation to supply the regulator with data required for checking compliance with the permit. The permit must also contain measures relating to conditions other than normal operating conditions. Therefore, where there is a risk that the environment may be affected, appropriate provision must be made for start-up, leaks, malfunctions, momentary stoppages and definitive cessation of operations.

Essentially, the Industrial Emissions Directive requires EU Member States to

32 There is a BAT reference document for large combustion plants, available at http://eippcb.jrc.ec.europa.eu/reference/BREF/lcp_bref_0706.pdf.

regulate emissions to air, water and land by issuing a single permit. Therefore, the release of SO2, NOx and particulates from a combustion plant will require a permit to be issued to the operator by the relevant Member State. In England the Industrial Emissions Directive is implemented by the Environmental Permitting (England and Wales) Regulations 2010[33] (Environmental Permitting Regulations).

(b) ***EU Medium Combustion Plant Directive***

Directive 2015/2193/EU on the limitation of emissions of certain pollutants into the air from medium combustion plants (Medium Combustion Plant (MCP) Directive) regulates pollutant emissions from the combustion of fuels in plants with a rated thermal input between 1 MW and 50 MW across the EU. It is therefore likely to catch smaller combustion plants. It regulates emissions to air of SO2, NOx and particulates, with the aim of reducing those emissions and the risks to human health and the environment they may cause. It also lays down rules for monitoring carbon monoxide (CO) emissions.

The MCP Directive has to be transposed by Member States by 19 December 2017 and the emission limit values it sets will have to be applied from 20 December 2018 for new plants. Given the UK's intended exit from the EU, it is possible that the MCP Directive may not be formally implemented in England. However, combustion plants with a rated thermal input of less than 50 MW are already regulated in England through the Environmental Permitting Regulations.

(c) ***EU ETS and greenhouse gas emissions permits***

Any thermal power plant in the EU that uses fossil fuels will be subject to the EU's greenhouse gas emissions trading scheme (EU ETS). The EU ETS is designed to provide a mechanism for the EU to meet its obligations under the 1997 Kyoto Protocol to the 1992 UN Framework Convention on Climate Change. Waste to energy plants are not subject to the ETS Directive; however, developers and operators of power plants using biomass as a fuel should note that the EU ETS exempts only installations 'exclusively' using biomass from its scope.[34]

The workings of the EU ETS and the trading issues that the operator of such a power plant will face during the operating life of the plant are outside the scope of this chapter, but in a project development context it should be noted the ETS Directive prohibits an installation from undertaking any controlled activity without a permit granting authorisation to emit greenhouse gases from all or part of the installation.[35] These requirements are implemented in England by the Greenhouse Gas Emissions Trading Scheme Regulations 2012.[36]

(d) ***Carbon capture and storage***

In 2009 the EU adopted Directive 2009/31/EC on the geological storage of carbon

33 SI 2010/675.
34 ETS Directive, Annex I, paragraph 1.
35 Articles 5 and 6 of the ETS Directive lay down requirements for applications for permits, the conditions of their grant, and their contents.
36 SI 2012/3038.

dioxide (CCS Directive) in order to create a legislative framework for carbon capture and storage (CCS) in the EU. Article 36 of the Industrial Emissions Directive implements the requirements of Article 33 of the CCS Directive in respect of combustion plants with a rated electrical output of 300 MW or more. The operator of any such plant for which the original construction licence (or in the absence of such a licence, the original operating licence) was granted after 25 June 2009 must assess whether the following conditions are met:

- suitable carbon dioxide storage sites are available;
- transport facilities are technically and economically feasible; and
- it is technically and economically feasible to retrofit the plant for carbon dioxide capture.

If these conditions are met, the competent authority granting the construction/operating licence must ensure that suitable space on the installation site for the equipment necessary to capture and compress carbon dioxide is set aside. In England this requirement is usually implemented through a planning condition attached to the DCO or planning permission for the plant.

(e) ***Water issues***

For certain types of power project, water may be a key issue. Most obviously, a hydro-electric power plant will require the impounding of sufficient quantities of water to achieve the intended generation capacity. However, most thermal power plants will require water for the generation of steam and/or for cooling purposes.

In the EU the principal piece of legislation governing water resources is Directive 2000/60/EC establishing a framework for Community action in the field of water policy (Water Framework Directive). It covers inland surface waters, coastal waters, transitional waters[37] and groundwater, and has a broad range of aims, including preventing the further deterioration, protecting and enhancing the status of aquatic ecosystems,[38] and promoting sustainable water use.[39] Member States are required to implement a range of 'basic measures' as part of a programme of measures in each river basin district within their jurisdictions, including:

- controls over the abstraction of fresh surface water and groundwater, and impoundment of fresh surface water, including a register or registers of water abstractions and a requirement of prior authorisation for abstraction and impoundment;[40] and
- for point source discharges liable to cause pollution, a requirement for prior regulation, such as a prohibition on the entry of pollutants into water, or for prior authorisation, or registration based on general binding rules, laying down emission controls for the pollutants concerned.[41]

---

37 Bodies of surface water in the vicinity of river mouths which are partly saline in character as a result of their proximity to coastal waters, but which are substantially influenced by freshwater flows.
38 Article 1(a).
39 Article 1(b).
40 Article 11(3)(e).
41 Article 11(3)(g).

In England, the abstraction and impounding of water are regulated by Chapter II of Part II of the Water Resources Act 1991, although it is anticipated that this regime will be incorporated into the Environmental Permitting Regulations in the future.[42]

Water pollution in England is regulated by Part III of the Water Resources Act 1991 and by the Environmental Permitting Regulations. A power plant that discharges its cooling water or other trade effluent into another body of water will therefore require its environmental permit to cover that activity, as well as any combustion activities.

If a power plant discharges its cooling water or other trade effluent into sewers it will require a trade effluent discharge consent from the relevant sewerage undertaker.[43]

Power plants that store large quantities of water on site and hydro-electric plants need to consider the implications of the Reservoirs Act 1975 and the amendments made to that Act by Schedule 4 of the Flood and Water Management Act 2010. The legislation regulates the safety of 'large raised reservoirs'.

3.2 Other environmental issues

(a) EU Environmental Liability Directive

If their activities (whether related to construction or operation) cause environmental damage, developers and operators of power plants may face liabilities under Directive 2004/35/EC on environmental liability with regard to the prevention and remedying of environmental damage (Environmental Liability Directive). The Environmental Liability Directive establishes an EU-wide framework for environmental liability based on the 'polluter pays' principle. 'Environmental damage' is defined as direct or indirect damage to the aquatic environment covered by EU water management legislation, direct or indirect damage to species and natural habitats protected at EU level by the Wild Birds Directive or by the Habitats Directive, or direct or indirect contamination of the land which creates a significant risk to human health. The liability regime covers not only actual environmental damage, but also the imminent threat of damage, in each case resulting from certain occupational activities listed in Annex III to the Environmental Liability Directive, which include any activity covered by the Industrial Emissions Directive (and therefore most power projects). In order to establish liability a causal link between the damage and the activity in question must be established, but this is subject to individual Member States' rules on evidence.

The Environmental Liability Directive is implemented in England by the Environmental Damage (Prevention and Remediation) (England) Regulations 2015.[44]

(b) Waste

Certain types of power plant, notably those burning solid fuels, will produce solid waste which needs to be managed. Coal-fired power plants produce pulverised fuel ash (PFA) and furnace bottom ash (FBA), and those fitted with flue gas desulphurisation plants will also produce gypsum. Biomass plants will produce

---

42 See the Water Act 2014 and www.gov.uk/government/uploads/system/uploads/attachment_data/file/492411/abstraction-reform-govt-response.pdf.

43 Water Industry Act 1991, Sections 118 and 119.

44 Si 2015/810.

bottom ash and waste to energy plants will produce both incinerator bottom ash (IBA) and air pollution control residues (also known as 'fly ash'). Although some of these materials are useful products in their own right (for example, gypsum is used to make plasterboard, PFA is used as a secondary aggregate in the construction industry and bottom ash from biomass plants can be composted), careful consideration needs to be given to whether they are subject to controls under Directive 2008/98/EC on waste (Waste Framework Directive). Fly ash from waste to energy plants is classified as hazardous waste and, under Directive 1999/31/EC on the landfill of waste, may only be disposed of at a landfill site authorised to accept hazardous waste.

In England the Environment Agency and the Waste and Resources Action Programme have, in a joint collaboration with industry, sought to develop a number of 'Quality Protocols' which are intended to provide guidance on how to recover waste and remove it from regulatory controls, in order to take advantage of the end-of-waste provisions of Article 6 of the Waste Framework Directive. Schedules 9 and 10 of the Environmental Permitting Regulations contain specific provisions relating to the permitting of waste operations and landfill respectively.

(c) Land contamination

Land contamination may impact on a power project in two ways. First, a project may be developed on previously-used land which may require some degree of clean-up before it can be redeveloped. Secondly, during the operating life of a plant, contamination may occur. Most jurisdictions will have some form of legal regime dealing with land contamination. In England it is normally dealt with through the planning system, by way of conditions attached to planning consents for the redevelopment of previously-used land requiring site investigations and, if contamination is found, remediation. England adopts a risk-based 'suitable for use' approach to land contamination and remediation, so that land is only required to be suitable for its existing or proposed use. In practice this means that it is unlikely that a planning authority would require a site intended for use as a power plant to be significantly remediated, if at all.

When applying for an environmental permit for any type of industrial installation, the application will normally have to include a baseline assessment of the site conditions. On closure of the site, it will have to be remediated to that baseline condition before the regulator will accept a surrender of the permit.

More serious cases of land contamination in England are dealt with under the contaminated land regime contained in Part 2A of the Environmental Protection Act 1990. The threshold for land to be designated as contaminated land is relatively high. Primary liability falls on any person who has caused or knowingly permitted the contamination, but if no such person can be found then liability falls on the current owner or occupier of the land. Further details of the regime are contained in regulations and statutory guidance.[45]

---

45 In England, the Contaminated Land (England) Regulations 2006 (SI 2006/1380) and the Contaminated Land Statutory Guidance issued by the Department for Environment, Food and Rural Affairs – available at www.gov.uk/government/uploads/system/uploads/attachment_data/file/223705/pb13735cont-land-guidance.pdf.

(d) *Nuisance and noise*

Both the construction and operation of a power plant have the potential to attract opposition from third parties such as local residents and NGOs. All the legal controls described so far in this chapter are essentially regulatory regimes and although private citizens and organisations often participate in these regimes in different ways, such as by responding to public consultations, the regimes generally govern the relationship between the regulator and the developer/operator, rather than the relationship between the developer/operator and the rest of society. However, legal regimes also exist that govern this latter relationship.

In England the common law remains a useful legal tool for third parties to seek redress in respect of harm they have suffered to their health or property. Developers and operators of power plants would be well-advised to take note of the risks they face. The tort of private nuisance is the main cause of action raised against industrial activities causing environmental harm and originated in the Industrial Revolution, when it developed to protect landowners' interests in land from largely unregulated industrial development. Although developers of NSIPs can apply for statutory immunity from nuisance claims,[46] such immunity is only available if the nuisance is not the result of negligence. Developers/operators of power plants should also note that it is no defence to a nuisance claim that the plant is fully compliant with all regulatory requirements and has not committed any breaches of its environmental permit.[47]

Bringing private proceedings for nuisance in England can be expensive for claimants, so a number of frequently-occurring nuisances have been designated as 'statutory nuisances' and are regulated under Part III of the Environmental Protection Act 1990. These include nuisances which may occur during the construction and operation of a power plant, such as noise, dust, smoke and steam. Local authorities have a duty to inspect their areas for statutory nuisances and when they find them they have a further duty to serve an 'abatement notice' on the person(s) responsible, requiring the abatement of the nuisance and/or prohibiting its recurrence. Breaching an abatement notice is an offence. Where a nuisance occurs on industrial, trade or business premises (which will be the case for a power plant), it is a defence to any prosecution that the best practicable means were used to prevent, or to counteract the effects of, the nuisance. It is also relevant for power plants that a local authority cannot prosecute for a breach of an abatement notice without the Secretary of State's consent if proceedings could be brought under the Environmental Permitting Regulations.

Where a local authority will not take action in respect of a statutory nuisance, any person aggrieved by the nuisance can apply to the Magistrates' Court for an 'abatement order', which has the same effect as an abatement notice.

4. Conclusion

Although both the planning process (through the infrastructure planning regime in

---

46 Planning Act 2008, Section 158.
47 *Barr and others v Biffa Waste Services Limited* [2012] EWCA Civ 312.

the Planning Act 2008) and the pollution control regime (through the Environmental Permitting Regulations) have been improved and streamlined in England in recent years, obtaining the necessary planning and environmental consents and permits for a power project can still be a time-consuming and costly process. The planning process is often high on the political agenda, meaning that changes and proposals for reform now occur frequently. The pollution control regime is less prone to political interference, but with many of England's pollution control laws emanating from the EU, there is likely to be a period of uncertainty for the next few years.

Independent power projects and offtake arrangements

Rajan Phakey
Dentons

1. Introduction

This chapter considers legal and contractual issues in private power generation, from the perspective of the main contract in an independent power project (IPP[1]): the power purchase agreement, or PPA. In keeping with the aim of this book, this chapter is an introductory guide, and aims to inform the reader of basic principles that underpin how the key parties approach a power project. These basic principles will inform the approaches that may be taken on more complex matters that arise on projects.[2]

The chapter is split into three parts. First we will look at the basic structure of a private power project. We will then consider the relationship between the two key players (the power station owner and the electricity offtaker[3]). Finally we will discuss how this relationship is affected by external factors and the relationships with other parties involved in the project.

Before looking at these issues, it is useful to clarify some points of terminology and context.

We will consider the term 'IPP' in the broad sense, to mean any arrangement under which a power station owned by one party supplies power to another party. The model case is where a power station is owned in the private sector and supplies power to a public sector utility. There are many other variations, but the common feature is the separate private sector ownership of the generating plant. The consequence of this arrangement is that there will need to be a contract in place to allocate risks between the parties. This can be contrasted with an 'all public sector' arrangement, where there will typically be no risk allocation.[4]

We will consider IPPs in general terms, since the basic issues are similar to all projects.[5]

1 As matter of terminology, IPP is now used interchangeably in the power sector to mean 'independent power producer' and 'independent power project'. In this chapter, we will use 'generator' to refer to the former, and 'IPP' to refer to the latter.

2 If more detail is sought, the reader may wish to refer to the sister title to this publication, *Renewables: A Practical Handbook*, which considers project structuring and risk allocation in more depth.

3 In energy projects, 'offtaker' is used to describe the entity that purchases the electricity from the generator.

4 In some cases, there is an allocation of price risk, through a bulk supply tariff.

5 Note that the use of a particular technology (for example, CCGT, cogeneration or renewables technologies) can give rise to some legal or contractual implications depending on the legal regime of the country in which of the project is located. From an operational point of view, the details of the despatch regime may also vary depending on the technology.

We will consider what the participants of an IPP are looking for, in contractual terms. However, it is important not to overlook the question of why an IPP should be undertaken. This is important, because the project will only succeed if the objectives of all parties can be reconciled. For example, where the government is the offtaker of power, its objective may be to avoid the need to find capital to fund power station construction, or to achieve efficiency by placing risks with the private sector. The private sector's objectives will be to make money out of the project and to be rewarded for taking risks. In practice, many projects fail to reach fruition because the sponsoring parties (both the government and private sector) make unrealistic assumptions.

2. The basic structure of an IPP

2.1 The key players

The key players in a project are the generator (the owner of the power station or other generating plant) and the offtaker (the company that buys electricity from the generator). The offtaker may be a utility in the public or private sector or a large user or group of large users buying direct. The PPA is often the main contract between these key players. In simple terms, it is an agreement for the generator to sell electricity to the offtaker.

For the purposes of this chapter, we will make the following assumptions:

- the generating plant is a thermal power station;[6]
- the power station is not built when the project begins;
- the offtaker is a public sector utility; and
- the PPA will provide for the sale of electricity at a contracted price.[7]

We will later examine some variations on these assumptions.

We will also assume that the project is financed on a limited recourse basis, by one or more banks or financial institutions.[8] This will mean, amongst other things, that the generator is a project company[9] established for the sole purpose of the project. This is almost always the case. Usually there are several investors (sponsors/developers) in an IPP; no one company is willing to take the whole risk of the project, and the project often needs promoters with a range of different skills and objectives.

---

6 A thermal power station is one in which steam is used to drive a turbine. Examples would include a coal or gas-fired power station. It can also include renewables technology, such as a concentrated solar thermal power system, where light is converted to heat that subsequently drives a steam turbine.

7 One alternative is to structure the project as a 'merchant' power plant, where the electricity is sold into a market (such as a power pool). The concept of a power pool is discussed further in the chapter on Market liberalisation and organisation: an economic perspective.

8 'Limited recourse' means the lenders to the project look primarily, but not necessarily exclusively, to the property, assets and revenues of the project as the primary source of repayment of their loans. The shareholders of such project will expect their liability for those loans will be limited to their equity in the project and other support or guarantees they have given to the lenders. The chapter on Power financing addresses finance issues in more detail.

9 This is also referred to as a special purpose company (SPC) or special purpose vehicle (SPV).

2.2 Other players

IPPs are typically very complex. While the generator and the offtaker are the key players, in most IPPs there are a large number of other players that have an impact on the project. It is the large number of players, and the need to keep them happy enough to go ahead with the project, that creates this complexity. The lawyer's role is to try to limit the complexity by producing documents that explain in plain language the relationships between all the players and how they are intended to be kept happy.

Where the offtaker is a utility with a public supply duty, its principal relationship will be with the state (the government or an independent regulator). It will also have relationships with its customers.

As far as the generator is concerned, it is likely to have both contractual relationships with private sector third parties and relationships with the government (and/or an independent regulator). Its relationships with the private sector may include contracts:

- for the construction of the power station, often including design, engineering and procurement;[10]
- for the supply of fuel, with one or more fuel suppliers;[11, 12]
- for the operation and maintenance of the power station (once built) with an 'O&M contractor';[13] and
- with its financiers and with insurers.[14]

The generator's relationship with the government (or a regulator or other electricity industry participants) will usually include:

- a specific licence or concession to build and own the power station, granted by the government or an independent regulatory body; and
- the general consents and permits for any major industrial project.

Later in this chapter, we will describe the implications of these relationships, and the risks they reflect or create, for the PPA itself.

2.3 Variations

The above description reflects a fairly typical project, although there are various ways in which a project's structure may differ. Some examples include.

(a) *The ownership of the power station*

Under a project that is financed under a BOT (Build-Operate-Transfer) model, the ownership will eventually be transferred to the offtaker. This will have significant implications for the PPA.

---

10 See the chapter on Construction for a discussion of construction issues.
11 See the chapter on Trading electricity for a discussion of fuel supply issues.
12 Sometimes the fuel supplier will be a state owned company, in which case this contract may be treated as a relationship with the government.
13 See the chapter on O&M contracts and long-term service arrangements for a discussion of operation and maintenance issues.
14 See the chapter on Power financing for a discussion of finance issues.

(b) ***Construction***

In some projects there is an existing power station to be transferred to the private sector. The main obvious consequence is that a construction contract will not form part of the project. The terms of sale of the power station, and the condition of the plant (as measured against the generator's obligations under the PPA) can be areas of particular difficulty in such a case.

(c) ***The fuel purchase arrangements***

The generator may purchase fuel in a spot or short-term market, rather than under a long-term contract. In this case the terms of the individual contracts by which fuel is bought will be less significant for the project.

(d) ***Single or multiple units***

Whether the power station is to be viewed by the offtaker as a single station or as separate generating units will have significant implications for the PPA. It ultimately determines whether the generator determines which units to run or whether the offtaker has the right to despatch[15] each generating unit separately in order to meet its offtake requirements.

(e) ***Operation and maintenance***

Whereas there might typically be a contract for operation and maintenance of the power station, these roles may alternatively be carried out by separate contractors, or the generator may employ its own operations staff so that no contract for operation is needed.

(f) ***The physical delivery of power under the PPA***

There may be a separate company that owns and operates the electricity transmission network, in which case the offtaker or the generator (or possibly both) will need arrangements for connection and use of system with that company.

At the end of Section 3 below, we also briefly cover another variation, renewables.

3. The Power Purchase Agreement (PPA)

3.1 PPA objectives

The PPA is the core document of an IPP. Under the PPA the generator will make the power station available for despatch by, and supply electricity to, the offtaker, and the offtaker will, in exchange, make payments to the generator. As we will see during this chapter, the PPA is more complicated than a typical sale and purchase agreement.[16]

The offtaker's main obligation is one of payment. However, the principal

---

15 Despatch (or dispatch) refers to the generation of electricity in accordance with instructions given to it by the offtaker. The PPA will contain a process involving the exchange of information between the buyer and the generator, normally consisting of forecasts on a periodic basis stating when the generator anticipates being capable of generating electricity and how much electricity the offtaker is likely to require.

obligations of the generator are basically non-financial in nature: to design, build, maintain and operate the power station.

The objectives of each party reflects the opposite position. The generator's fundamental objectives are financial: it will want to make profit out of the project. In order to do this, it must maintain the projected relationship between costs and revenues. The offtaker's fundamental objectives are not only substantially non-financial, but are also more complex. This asymmetry between financial and non-financial objectives and obligations has strong implications for the structure of the PPA.[17]

In Section 4 of this chapter, we will look at the generator's objectives in more detail. In general terms, the generator's objectives are to limit or even exclude the circumstances in which:

- it incurs a cost that it cannot pass on to the offtaker under the PPA; or
- its revenues under the PPA may be delayed (or reduced or interrupted) without having recourse to a third party for compensation.

The offtaker's objective is to obtain a reliable source of generation at the originally projected costs.

Where an offtaker commits to a power project, that power station will form part of the offtaker's generation planning. The stated capacity of that power station will displace possible alternatives, and so the offtaker must be able to place reliance on it.

In practice, the offtaker will need to be confident that the power station will be built on time and to specification, available for despatch when required (at least to the agreed capacity) and will operate in accordance with the operational criteria originally specified by the offtaker.

In order to meet these requirements, the PPA will place various obligations on the generator, and create incentives in order for the generator to comply with those obligations. A well-structured and negotiated PPA will be drafted so that it is directly in the generator's interest to perform, rather than having to enforce the contract in court. The key incentive that we will cover will be the pricing arrangements, as that is essentially what makes the project viable. Before doing so, we will look at the typical term and structure of a PPA, and then some of the main obligations it will contain.

3.2 PPA term and structure

A typical term for a PPA on a large IPP is between 15 and 20 years, although there are many projects with shorter and longer terms. The usual structure of a PPA is to have all the substantive, legal provisions (principally, the rights and obligations) included in the body of the agreement, with details of various procedures, milestones, technical requirements, standards, tests, insurance requirements and so on in schedules.

---

16 In addition to the complexity, the variety of PPAs should not be underestimated. These differences are a consequence of various factors, such as the size of the project, jurisdiction specific differences in legal and regulatory frameworks, renewables technologies, government support schemes and different risk profiles of the key players. As a rule of thumb, the larger the size of the project, the greater will be the complexity of the PPA.

17 The asymmetry is common to all contracts involving payment for goods/services.

3.3 PPA obligations

The PPA will impose obligations on the generator to:

- build the power station in line with the agreed timetable and specification;
- make the power station available and submit it to despatch by the offtaker;
- operate the power station consistent with the offtaker's instructions; and
- repair and maintain the power station so as to maintain its operational specification.

The specification of the power station will be a key part of the generator's PPA obligations and it is worth saying a few more words about this. A PPA will typically contain either a functional specification or a full design and engineering specification.

A functional specification sets out the basic specifications, such as the intended net generation capacity, technology type and perhaps some details about the operational criteria. If operational criteria are specified, then this might typically include the start-up times, loading and de-loading rates, reactive power capability, dynamic and minimal sustainable load.

A full design and engineering specification is significantly more detailed than a functional specification. It will always be contained in the construction contract, but in some cases it is also included within the PPA. This is typically a matter of negotiation, and relevant factors include market practice for the country in which the project is located, size of the power station and the technology type.

A generator might argue that the offtaker's interests under the PPA should stop at the point of delivery where electrical power transfers from the generator to the offtaker. Thus, provided the power station is performing to the standard which was agreed, the offtaker should not impose the full design and engineering specification or operating practices. However, the offtaker will often counter-argue that it has a crucial interest in ensuring that the plant is engineered for sustained performance for the PPA life, and other interests in areas such as safety and protection.

A further consideration in this argument is that, as mentioned above, a key benefit of an IPP is to obtain competitive pricing. The less flexibility over design and engineering the generator has, the more constrained its ability will be to offer competitive pricing.

3.4 PPA pricing

Having discussed the types of obligations imposed on the generator, we will now look at pricing. Arguably pricing is the most important part of the PPA. As mentioned earlier, the offtaker will want the pricing arrangements to create incentives for the generator to perform.

However incentives are only useful where the generator can respond economically to them. Most PPA pricing structures start by recognising that it is not sensible for a generator to accept demand (or despatch) risk. For this reason, the pricing mechanism will typically be structured in two separate parts: energy and capacity charges.[18] The purpose of the capacity charge is to pay for the generator's fixed costs. The offtaker must pay the capacity charge whether or not it chooses to despatch the power station. The purpose of the energy charge is to pay for the generator's costs to run the power station (its variable costs).

3.5 Energy charge: general concept

The energy charge (sometimes referred to as the commodity charge or variable charge) is simpler than the capacity charge. It is based on the principle that whenever the offtaker chooses to despatch the power station, the offtaker will meet the generator's variable costs.

For the purposes of the assumptions we made earlier, the most significant variable costs will be the generator's fuel costs. In practice the energy charge may be comprised of various other components, so as to more accurately reflect the variable costs incurred. For example, these can include charges for incremental heat (in $/MWh), fixed heat (in $/hour) and specific events such as start-ups; in some PPAs such supplemental charges are categorised as a separate (ie, third) part of the tariff rather than within the energy charge.

3.6 Energy charge: fuel risks and implications for the PPA

The relationship between fuel supply arrangements and the PPA is particularly important. Key risks are fuel price, quality and availability. Typically, under a PPA, fuel price risk will sit with the offtaker and other fuel risks will sit with the generator. This has direct implications as to how the energy charge is calculated, and so we will discuss these issues here (rather than in the discussion on risk in Section 4 of this chapter).

Since fuel is the most significant part of the energy charge, one may ask whether it is easier to just have the offtaker pay the generator's fuel bills. However, this approach would effectively place the 'thermal efficiency' risk with the offtaker. There are certain risks associated with operating a power station that an offtaker will expect to be placed on the generator, and one of these is the thermal efficiency of the power station. In a PPA, the energy charge will typically be calculated by reference to the generator's electrical output, as this is effectively what the offtaker is paying for. The calculation will be based on an agreed heat rate, rather than the actual heat rate of the plant.[19] If the plant's actual efficiency is lower than the agreed heat rate in the energy charge, the generator will make a loss. Likewise, if the generator is able to operate the plant at a higher efficiency than that stated in the PPA, the generator will make a gain from the energy payments it receives from the offtaker. Under this structure, the offtaker is insulated from the thermal efficiency risk.

If the generator can purchase fuel in the spot market, the PPA energy charge will typically be indexed to a published market price, so that the offtaker bears the risk of fuel price movements in the market. As with the position on thermal efficiency,

---

18 The two-part pricing arrangement does have some disadvantages. For example, its relative complexity, difficulty of administration and, in particular, the need to determine availability. Many PPAs (particularly in the renewables sector) provide for fixed prices.

19 In the power sector, the thermal efficiency of a power station is typically measured as a 'heat rate'. This is the amount of energy used to generate power: the lower the heat rate, the higher the thermal efficiency.

depending whether the fuel price actually paid by the generator is below or above the index, the generator will either make a gain or a loss.

However, where the generator purchases fuel under a medium or long-term fuel supply contract, the pricing basis in that contract may be by reference to competing fuel prices (for example, gas prices may be set by reference to the price of crude oil). Alternatively, the parties may decide to establish a suitable index as a proxy for a market price. The basis for energy price indexation under the PPA will have to mirror the fuel supply contract price formula.

We can turn now to some other fuel-related risks. Unless a tolling arrangement applies, the offtaker will not want to accept the risk of changes in quality of the fuel used at the plant.[20] The PPA energy charge will therefore assume not only a given thermal efficiency but also a particular gross calorific value (also known as heating value) for each unit of fuel. Having accepted this risk under the PPA, the generator will look to pass this risk down to the fuel supplier, in the shape of the contract specification for the fuel.

The arrangements can get rather complicated where the generator commits to purchasing fixed quantities of fuel over a given period of time (for example, under a take-or-pay commitment for pipeline gas). The PPA energy charge is designed to recover the generator's variable costs. However, a take-or-pay commitment for fuel will effectively represent a fixed cost for the generator. The concern here is that (as with other fixed costs) the generator will not want to accept any despatch risk. There are various ways to address this issue, such as rebalancing the capacity and energy payments; alternatively, the offtaker may be willing to commit to a minimum despatch (ie, a corresponding take-or-pay commitment). Another option would be for the offtaker to become a party to the fuel supply contract and accept the fuel take or pay risk; in this case the generator has arguably become a toll processor of fuel for the offtaker.

3.7 Capacity charge

The capacity charge is sometimes also referred to as an availability charge or a fixed charge. The purpose is to cover the generator's fixed costs. These will typically include costs of financing the power project, construction costs, fixed operating and maintenance costs, fixed transmission/use of system charges, insurance costs, taxes and profit.[21]

The principle that underpins the capacity charge is that provided the generator makes the power station available to the offtaker for despatch, the generator should be entitled to recover his fixed costs (regardless of whether the power station is despatched by the offtaker, ie, the generator is insulated from demand risk). The

20 Sometimes a power project may be structured around a tolling arrangement, whereby the generator enters into a tolling agreement (sometimes referred to as an energy conversion agreement) rather than a PPA. The main difference is that under a tolling agreement the offtaker (toller) is responsible for procuring fuel supply and assumes fuel availability and price risk. Instead of buying electrical energy, the toller is in effect paying the generator to perform the service of converting fuel into electric energy.

21 It can also include any fixed component of the fuel supply and transport charges, for example, those charges that the generator is required to pay pursuant to take-or-pay obligations under its fuel supply agreement (see the previous paragraph).

crucial part of this principle is that the power station is made available. The capacity charge can also be structured to include operating variables other than availability.

As mentioned earlier, the PPA pricing incentives will be key. One way of structuring the capacity charge is to provide both short and long-term incentives to the generator, so that it complies with its obligation to make the power station available. For example, a short-term incentive is that the generator will not normally start earning capacity payments until it has demonstrated that the power station (or perhaps an individual unit) has been built and commissioned.

Typically, the capacity charge will be a unit charge for available capacity, expressed in $/MW for a given period of time, that is, the generator will earn capacity payments for a particular period, depending on the availability of the station during that period. Availability can be determined by reference to periods as short as half an hour to something much longer. The determining factors will usually be the amount of complexity in the incentives and also how availability is defined.

3.8 Availability

The concept of availability is quite simple: it is the capability of the power station to generate power if despatched. However, one of the trickiest parts of structuring and negotiating a PPA is how to define 'availability'. This is because availability is hypothetical (capability to run if despatched) and so cannot be measured. In practice, an offtaker will only despatch the power station if the power station has (in advance) been declared available.

To take an example, the PPA may require the generator to make daily declarations of availability, covering each hour of the following day. Since availability is linked to capacity payments, the offtaker will want some reassurance that the generator is not tempted to make false (or falsely inflated) declarations of availability, such as declaring availability at a time when the generator knows the offtaker is unlikely to despatch the power station. This will take the form of a right under the PPA to challenge availability declarations by despatching the power station to the level declared by the generator. The offtaker may also seek a right to test the capacity of the power station (or units).

As stated earlier, the PPA should be structured so that it is directly in the generator's interest to perform: these arrangements have to be workable in practice. Therefore the consequences of a successful challenge should be structured so as to discourage false declarations of availability. An example of such an approach would be to recalculate the capacity payments on the basis of the lowest tested availability in a given period of time (rather than on the basis of zero availability). The details will depend on various considerations, such as the size of the power station relative to the offtaker's overall needs.

3.9 Operating incentives

The basic capacity charge described above incentivises the generator to maximise availability, and aims to ensure that the offtaker does not have to pay for capacity that is not available. It is possible to refine the basic arrangement so that the generator is given more structured incentives. These include:

(a) ***Time-based weighting***

The principle here is that the value of available capacity, and the amount of the capacity charge, will be higher at times of high demand. A typical way to achieve this is for each hour of the day (or other time frame, such as each season) to be attributed a weighting that reflects the offtaker's daily (or seasonal) demand profile.

(b) ***Performance specification***

The offtaker will not obtain the full value of the available capacity when the power station is not capable of meeting operational performance levels. For example, if the start-up time of a unit is temporarily increased, the offtaker will lose despatch flexibility. It is possible to structure a capacity charge to reflect the impact of the generator's failure to comply with key operational criteria.

3.10 Long-term aspects of the capacity charge

The pricing arrangements will be efficient if they provide the correct incentive to the generator, or (if the overall cost is less) compensate the offtaker for replacing the generator's deficient performance.

The performance specification arrangement described above deals with short-term failure by the generator to comply with the power station's operational criteria. In the long term, the structure of the capacity charge is also very important. It is in the offtaker's interest (as well as the generator's interest) to ensure the value of its payments is maintained over time. Erosion of value due to inflation needs to be addressed, and as a minimum, the component of the capacity charge which represents fixed operating costs should be indexed to an appropriate measure of inflation.

Beyond that, however, there is no uniform answer to the question of the long-term incentives to be created by the capacity charge; these issues are influenced by many factors – principally, the level of debt and the structure of the financing arrangements offered by lenders.

The basic problem is that over time, the cost of the maintenance and repair of the power station will increase. This gives rise to a fundamental issue, which is how to ensure that the generator's capacity earnings are always sufficient to cover those increasing costs, as well as allowing the generator to keep earning a profit.

From the offtaker's perspective, the risk is that the generator may be tempted to cut costs and increase its profits in the early years, at the expense of later reliability, if it can earn a sufficient return on investment before the PPA has expired. If in later years the operation of the power station becomes uneconomic, but the generator's lenders have been paid and the generator's shareholders adequately rewarded, then the generator may choose not to perform its PPA obligations. In these circumstances, the offtaker has little comfort. If the generator becomes bankrupt, the only asset to meet the offtaker's claim for damages is a power station that is uneconomic to operate.

One approach would be to maintain (or even increase) the value of the capacity charge in real terms over time. However, this approach conflicts sharply with the requirements of financing the construction of the power station, in view of the normal debt repayment profiles and periods (which are substantially shorter than PPA terms). This problem is somewhat resolved because the loan will be paid off during the early years of operation, meaning over time more of the capacity charge will represent profit to the generator. Also of relevance to this issue is the offtaker's desired tariff profile, as it may not want the tariff to be front-loaded, that is, higher in the initial years.

3.11 Other aspects of PPAs

The PPA should also deal with a number of other important matters. We will touch upon three examples:

(a) The despatch regime

At a basic level, the offtaker may not normally call for the power station to operate outside the functional specification. However, there does need to be sufficient detail as to what despatch instructions may be given, how and when they may be given, and how they will be complied with and recorded. This should cover not only operational capability (such as reactive power capability or minimum generation), but also notice periods for changes in operation (such as times for hot and cold starts and notice periods to synchronise) and limitations on such changes (such as maximum numbers of starts or load cycles in a 24-hour period).

(b) Metering

The PPA energy charges will be determined by reference to metered quantities of delivered electrical energy. It is therefore important that the PPA clearly sets out the arrangements for meter installation, testing, operation and maintenance. Provisions are also needed to address what happens if there is a meter failure or if a party disputes the meter readings. Related issues can also require careful attention, such as the treatment of the internal load of individual units and of the power station, and of imports of electricity to the power station.

(c) Plant outages

In the longer term, the planning of maintenance outages of all generating plant on the system must be coordinated. The offtaker can reasonably expect to have some control over when the generator schedules maintenance. The treatment of outages does however give rise to some difficulties in the short term. As discussed earlier, one of the generator's core obligations is to make the power station available. Defining this obligation is not straightforward, and can form a significant part of PPA negotiations. Since a power station will suffer forced outages from time to time, the generator cannot commit to 100% availability at all times and it should not be treated as being in breach of contract if there is a forced outage. However, the offtaker will still want an effective availability obligation that can be enforced, particularly if the pricing incentives are not working as effectively as intended.

3.12 Renewables PPAs

Given the increasing prevalence of large-scale renewables IPPs being developed across the globe, we will briefly cover some issues relevant to PPAs on those projects.[22] Renewable projects are those where the generation technology is based around a 'renewable source of energy'. This is a somewhat imprecise term. It traditionally refers to energy from natural resources such as sunlight, wind, tides and waves, but the definition can often include energy from a variety of other resources, including fuels such as biomass, biogas and waste. For present purposes, we will assume the narrower definition. Where the generation technology type is not fuelled, then one obvious difference is that the PPA will not need to impose any fuel supply commitments on the generator.

(a) ***Intermittent generation***

The absence of fuel supply obligations (and risk) may suggest that a renewable PPA is simpler than a conventional PPA, but this is not necessarily the case. Non-fuelled generation is often referred to as intermittent generation.[23] The electricity cannot be generated on demand but will depend on external factors relevant to the particular technology type, such as when the wind is blowing or the level of solar radiation.

The plant cannot be despatched by the offtaker to meet its demand (for this reason renewable generation typically forms only a small part of a public utility's overall portfolio of energy procurement). Therefore instead of the generator making availability declarations, the plant will typically perform on a 'must run' basis such that the generator commits to generate when the external factors permit, and the offtaker must accept delivery of the corresponding electrical output. The generator will provide its forecast for what the plant will generate (for example, hourly, daily or weekly) but it will insist those forecasts are not contractually binding.

(b) ***Tariff***

For intermittent generation, the tariff will be structured differently, in recognition that the generator cannot commit to unconditional availability and the offtaker cannot despatch the plant. There are various models, but the most common is to remove the capacity charge and instead structure the energy charge (in $/MWh) such that it is sufficient to cover the generator's costs and return on investment. Another model used in some countries is a regulated feed-in tariff.

(c) ***Incentive schemes/tradable certificates***

Some renewables projects may qualify for financial support, such as subsidies, credits (such as tax credits or energy net metering credits) and tradable certificates. This is dependent on the specific rules for the relevant scheme, which may be international in nature (such as the Clean Development Mechanism under the Kyoto Protocol) or country-specific. A typical feature is the issuance of electronic certificates or credits to the generator, recognising each unit of qualifying metered output it produces. In

---

22 As with conventional IPPs, the actual generation technology on a renewable IPP will have various technology-specific implications for the PPA. The sister title to this publication, *Renewables: A Practical Handbook*, contains chapters on legal, technical and commercial issues relevant to various renewables technologies.

23 A notable exception is geothermal renewable energy.

some cases these credits attract a financial value and can be traded. An offtaker may seek to purchase those credits from the generator or perhaps argue that it should be entitled to some of the revenue from any sale by the generator to a third party. The renewables PPA will contain provisions detailing these arrangements.

4. External factors and their implications for the PPA

4.1 Introduction

We have covered the basic obligations and pricing arrangements under a PPA. This part of the chapter now addresses how the key relationships in a power project can affect the PPA. From the project participants' viewpoint, this issue is really about project risks and how they should be allocated. What follows is a brief overview of the type of issues and considerations involved. A lot has been written about this topic, and there are many good resources available that contain further information.[24]

It is important to set the context when we talk about risk allocation. A risk will usually be defined by reference to an event or circumstance – for example, the risk of breakdown of equipment at the power station. An event will typically affect one party, but have consequences for more than one party. In the above example, the equipment breakdown affects the generator directly, but consequences can affect both the generator (such as increased costs and lost revenue) and the offtaker (interruption of supply).

Where an IPP is financed by a lender, the project will need to be 'bankable' (financeable); a core aspect of this is that the project's risk allocation must be appropriate both in terms of generally accepted principles of bankability for a power project and the specific project itself. The essence of limited recourse financing of a project is that the risks are allocated to the party that is best able to manage and mitigate these risks, with a view to leaving very little risk with the project company. This provides the greatest opportunity for effectively managing and reducing these risks.

As the central party in a power project, the generator has most of the third party relationships and most of the project risks are ones that directly affect the generator. Before considering those risks, we will look at some risks from the point of view of the offtaker.

4.2 Risks affecting the offtaker

(a) Power station performance risk

In circumstances where there is a delay, interruption or reduction of electricity supply (not caused by the offtaker), the offtaker will expect the PPA to relieve it from its payment obligations or reduce the payment. The offtaker might also be able to claim damages under the PPA. For example, if there is a delay in construction of the

24 The sister title to this publication, *Renewables: A Practical Handbook*, contains detailed chapters on project structuring and risk allocation. Another very useful guide on project risk in energy and infrastructure projects is available for download at www.dentons.com/en/insights/guides-reports-and-whitepapers/2015/november/30/global-project-finance-risk-guide.

power station that results in the generator missing the agreed date for scheduled commercial operations under the PPA, the offtaker may be entitled to liquidated damages from the generator.

(b) ***Generator creditworthiness***

Since there are circumstances under the PPA where the generator is liable to pay damages to the offtaker, this raises a risk of whether the generator is financially robust and able to deliver such commitments.

If the problem is serious enough, the offtaker faces the risk of the generator becoming insolvent (whether as a result of increased costs or reduced revenues or otherwise). If the generator becomes insolvent, the only asset to meet the offtaker's claim for damages is a power station that may not have been built yet or might be uneconomic to operate. The offtaker's right to damages may therefore not be of much value at all.

The offtaker must assure itself at the outset that the project is technically and financially viable, and that the risk of the generator's insolvency is very remote. The project's lenders will share the same concerns.

The offtaker may look for the generator to provide credit support (such as payment guarantees from its shareholders or a bank) as a precondition to the PPA becoming effective. The offtaker may also seek a last resort protection – the right to take over the power station from the generator. Here, the offtaker's rights may conflict with those of the lenders, who will want to be able to exercise their rights prior to the offtaker. The respective rights of the offtaker and lenders in such circumstances must be clearly defined in a separate agreement. The lenders will also enter into such agreements (known as direct agreements) with other third parties that the project is reliant upon, such as the construction contractor and the O&M contractor.

(c) ***Political and regulatory risk***

Outside the PPA, the offtaker's main relationships are with the government (and/or an independent regulator) and with its customers (such as industrial, commercial and residential users of electricity). A typical starting assumption is that a government or regulator will not interfere in a private contract such as a PPA. Many of the concerns are therefore with extreme actions such as expropriation, and must be viewed (and if possible dealt with) as political risks.

4.3 Risks affecting generator

As discussed earlier, the generator's key contractual relationships are with a contractor for construction of the power station, with a supplier of fuel to the power station, and with an O&M contractor for operation and maintenance of the power station.[25]

---

25 Note that two other key risks (despatch risk and fuel risk) were already discussed earlier, in the section on PPA pricing. In terms of fuel supply risk, an additional point is that the parties will also need to carefully consider the risks of non-availability or interruption of fuel supplies. In some cases, this might be treated as a particular category of *force majeure* and the generator may have no effective remedy against the fuel supplier. Non-availability and interruption will be of great concern to the offtaker, and it may seek to impose on the generator certain minimum requirements under the PPA to purchase fuel and maintain fuel stocks on site, to limit the risk of power supply interruption.

In discussing the risks affecting the generator, we will concentrate on the consequences of these risks for the generator. These may be either to reduce, interrupt or delay the generator's revenues, or to increase his costs. The means by which the generator can be protected from cost increases are either to require a third party to bear the cost increase, or to pass the cost increase to the offtaker by increasing the PPA price. Risks that affect revenue will be those that prevent its performance under the PPA, and here the generator's approach will be to ensure that these risks do not occur or that a third party compensates the generator for the relevant loss of revenue, unless the generator can persuade the offtaker to continue to pay under the PPA.

(a) *Construction*[26]

Construction is the time when a power project faces its most significant risks. The main risks for the generator here are cost overrun, project delay, and failure to perform.

The impact of construction cost overruns is self-evident. In terms of construction delay, if the power station is completed late, the generator's revenue stream under the PPA will also be delayed. The interest due on the generator's loans will either have to be met or capitalised, thereby increasing subsequent debt service.

Where the power station does not comply with the contracted specification, there are two types of consequence. If it affects the generator's ability to meet the performance obligations under the PPA (for example, the capacity of the plant is less than what was promised), the generator will not be entitled to the full capacity charges and it will therefore lose revenue. If the non-compliance relates to the plant's internal requirements, such as target thermal efficiency, the generator's costs of supplying power will increase (even though its ability to perform the PPA is not affected).

The offtaker will generally not agree to assume construction risk through an increase in the PPA price; there will be specific exceptions, for example, where the offtaker has requested a change in power station specification. However, the starting position for the generator's approach to construction risk is to pass construction risks down to the contractor.

The generator will look to procure the construction works on a fixed price turnkey basis, so that the risk of cost overruns will be for the contractor's account. Where construction is delayed beyond the contractually scheduled completion milestone(s), the generator will require the contractor to pay liquidated damages (ie, pre-determined damages). These will at least need to be sufficient to cover the generator's interest costs for the period of delay. Where there is underperformance, the contractor will be required to remedy performance defects or pay further liquidated damages as compensation.

Whilst this may sound straightforward, it should be emphasised that the arrangements are not simple. The construction contract will contain exceptions to these general rules (such as a price re-opener where there is a change in the

26 See the chapter on Construction for a fuller discussion of construction issues.

contractor's scope of the work) and these types of issues can be a significant part of the contract negotiations with the contractor. In practice, the relevant risks and rewards to the contractor mean that the generator is unlikely to obtain a full indemnity for all of the consequences of construction risk. The generator will therefore bear some residual risk.

(b) ***Operation and maintenance***[27]

The main risks for the generator here are increased costs of operating or maintaining the power station, and deficient performance of the power station.

The operating and maintenance costs will be treated as fixed costs covered by the capacity charge. However, any increases to those costs beyond inflation will not normally be reflected in an increase to the capacity charge.

To mitigate the risk of cost increases, the generator will therefore expect the O&M contractor to commit to a fixed price for providing its service to the generator. Inflation indexation should match the capacity charge indexation under the PPA.

Where the O&M contractor does not perform its services to the expected standard, this can result in a loss of revenue for the generator. For example, where there are overruns in the scheduled maintenance windows, the power station remains unavailable to be despatched and the generator cannot earn expected capacity charges under the PPA. Deficient performance can also result in increased costs. Some of these costs may fall to the generator, for example if the O&M contractor allows the plant's thermal efficiency to degrade, the generator risks having to incur increased fuel costs to meet the agreed heat rate under the PPA.

The O&M contract will contain obligations to meet the required performance standards and service levels, and provide for compensation for its failure to do so. However, it is unlikely that the O&M contractor will agree to protect the generator with a full indemnity, and the generator will therefore bear some residual risk. As with the above position for construction contractors, this position essentially comes down to the risks and rewards for the contractor.

(c) ***The offtaker***

Provided the offtaker continues to makes payment, the generator is largely indifferent to other risks affecting the offtaker.[28] Therefore, from the generator's viewpoint of the offtaker, the risks that are of most concern are those that affect the creditworthiness of the offtaker, since the PPA is the sole source of the generator's revenue in a power project. This is a vital consideration for the generator, and where the offtaker is a public utility, the generator may expect some form of credit support from the government.

A related issue in this context is regulatory risk. A basic risk is that the offtaker is prevented from passing costs incurred under the PPA (or other generation costs) on

27 See the chapter on O&M contracts and long-term service arrangements for a fuller discussion of operation and maintenance issues.

28 The generator is also concerned with demand (despatch) risk but, as discussed earlier, a well structured PPA will already insulate the generator from this risk, for example through the imposition of a capacity charge. This obviously highlights the importance of looking at the creditworthiness of the offtaker.

to consumers. This is usually a question of the price restrictions under the offtaker's licence (or other such concession instrument) and how it is regulated. On the other hand, if the country has competition in its electricity supply market, there is the risk that (irrespective of price regulation) the offtaker's costs may be too high for it to be competitive; in this case, its customer base will be eroded. In many countries the offtaker will have some kind of monopoly, often in the form of a 'franchise' or exclusive right to supply customers, but the possibility exists that the franchise will be withdrawn or narrowed in scope.

Regulatory issues of this kind cannot be resolved by arrangements between the generator and the offtaker. The generator will need to satisfy itself that the offtaker operates within a regime which will not expose it to these risks and that the regime will not be changed (or obtain a government guarantee of the offtaker's credit).

(d) *Other risks*

It is worth briefly covering some other significant external risks, such as *force majeure*, changes in law and actions taken by a government or regulator.

The legal concept of *force majeure* is that a party should not be held responsible for performing its obligations under a contract where that performance is prevented by circumstances beyond that party's control.[29] Construction, operation or maintenance of the power station, or the supply of fuel, may be prevented or delayed by events that are outside the control of the affected contractor or supplier, and this might mean the generator is unable to perform its PPA obligations to the offtaker. The relevant contract will normally relieve the contractor or supplier of liability to the generator. It is therefore important for the generator to ensure that the PPA contains equivalent protection so that it is not liable to the offtaker (likewise, the offtaker will not normally agree to continue to pay the capacity charge where the power station is not available). The exact definition of events of *force majeure* is usually negotiated at some length. Mitigation of *force majeure* risks is also possible for certain risks through commercial insurance (for example, floods, storms and earthquakes).

As a general theme, we have seen that project risks will leave the financial consequences with the generator and that the generator will seek to pass them down to its contractor or suppliers. We have covered some exceptions, such as fuel price risk and inflation. Another important risk is where there is a change in legal requirements or other government action that increases costs. For example, introducing a new environmental standard for power stations after the power station has already been built. The generator will expect to pass this cost increase to the offtaker and, in turn, the offtaker will expect to pass the increase to consumers. The actual PPA mechanism for charging the increased costs will need consideration, for example, the offtaker will likely prefer an adjustment to the energy or capacity charge, rather than paying for the costs as they arise. This will mean the recovery of

29 Despite the prevalence of *force majeure* clauses in commercial agreements, the term 'force majeure' has no recognised legal meaning under English law, and will generally only be enforceable to the degree expressly set out in the contract.

such costs will be linked to the generator's performance of its obligations under the PPA.

Note that blanket protection for the generator against all changes in law that have a material impact on the project or the project's economics would be rare. It is typical is to share these risks and for the government to provide relief only against 'discriminatory' changes in law, that is changes in law that only directly impact the generator or companies undertaking similar projects in the relevant country. For example, new (or increased) tax on all companies operating in a particular country will not be viewed as discriminatory but a tax only on IPPs would be treated as discriminatory.

The generator's relationship with the government can give rise to a number of other project risks, which are not necessarily changes in law. The generator will need to satisfy itself that it is not exposed to the possibility of not obtaining or losing its power station concession or licence, or any other licences and consents, or being subjected to legal requirements with which it is unable to comply, in circumstances that it cannot control. These are issues of regulatory and political risk and they are of crucial importance to the generator and comprise a major aspect of any IPP.

4.4 Finance and insurance

Finally, we will look at the relationship of the generator with its insurers and financiers.[30]

We have already seen that residual risks can often remain with the generator. In many cases these will be insured, as a comprehensive insurance package will be mandatory for any energy or infrastructure project. Insurance arrangements are essentially additional means of mitigating or passing risk down to someone else. Risks may include fire, storms, earthquakes, floods, typhoons and other extreme weather conditions. The capacity charge will factor in the cost of these insurance premiums.

The most important insurance cover is for the costs of rectifying any loss or damage to the power station. This is usually covered by a construction 'all risks' policy. Further cover will usually be taken out to cover any delay in commissioning, 'delay in start up' and any interruption in a project's revenues flowing from loss or damage to the power station, 'advance loss of profits' or 'business interruption' cover. There will also be 'third party liability insurance' to cover the project against third party claims for which the project is responsible.

Moving on to the generator's financing arrangements, this will be a major aspect of the project and such issues can often dominate an IPP. At a basic level, the lenders' interests are essentially the same as those of the generator and the generator's relationships with its lenders do not of themselves create risk for the project. Nevertheless, when assessing the project risks, the lenders will be more risk adverse than the generator; essentially they will be more willing to sacrifice upside profit potential to limit downside risk. The lenders may require the generator to make

30 Although we only briefly touch on financing issues, the chapter on Power financing explores this topic in more detail.

contingent funding arrangements to cover the residual risks we looked at earlier in the context of construction, operating and fuel supply contracts if they cannot be insured.

From the offtaker's view, the arrangements with lenders do create an additional risk. The offtaker's concern here is that in a PPA default scenario (for example, due to the generator's insolvency), the lenders might take over the power station, turn off the lights and invite the offtaker to re-discuss price. This type of issue should be addressed in advance in the direct agreement between the offtaker and the lenders.

One area where the generator's relationship with the lenders does create risk for the project is the cost of finance. Some are risks for the lenders and the investors (ie, the generator's shareholders) rather than the generator itself. One example is floating interest rates. The project loan (and many of the project costs) may be in a different currency to the currency of the PPA price, and this creates exchange rate risk. Other risks include risks of taxes or withholdings, and can reduce the value of payments to lenders or investors.

The investors will therefore seek a financing structure that minimises these risks; in many jurisdictions, this can involve seeking some form of support from the government, for example through the concession contract or a project implementation agreement. Sometimes, the PPA allows these risks to be passed to the offtaker, such as structuring the capacity charge indexation to address interest rate risk (although this can be fairly complex in practice).

Trading electricity

Rajan Phakey
Dentons
Neil Schofield
Financial Markets Training Ltd

As is common with many concepts in finance, terms such as 'trading' do not have any accepted definition. One popular approach defines trading as the buying and selling of a commodity where the primary motivation is profit. This would differ from hedging, where the aim is to mitigate the risk associated with some underlying exposure. However, there is often a grey area between the two extremes where it is difficult to determine the exact nature of the trader's motivation.

In this chapter, we will consider the nature of trading and the main trading products used in the wholesale power market. We will then go on to look at how electricity trading can be contractually documented, focusing in particular on the most popular contract used in Great Britain (GB).

1. What is trading?

Within this chapter we will consider two categories of trading. Operational trading strategies involve the buying or selling of electricity to balance the demand for and supply of power as part of an entity's physical operations. Within this category we may choose to include derivatives that help manage the market participant's price risk. The second category will relate to so-called 'view driven' trading strategies which typically involve the use of derivatives to express views on expected market movements. These definitions suggest that the main trading participants are likely to be:

- participants in the physical market for power;
- investment banks;
- hedge funds; and
- commodity trading houses.

Within the context of the GB power markets, operational trading strategies may loosely break down into three elements:

- longer dated forward contracts;
- shorter term bilateral markets; and
- the balancing markets.

View driven strategies may be initiated for a variety of reasons:

- To express views on how prices are expected to move relative to the forward price. This type of strategy will be based on expected changes in the balance of demand and supply for power.

- How forward prices at different maturities move relative to each other. Within this category it would be possible to include views based on seasonal factors.
- How power prices in different countries will move relative to each other (eg, price movements in Germany relative to price movements in France).
- How power prices move relative to the other components of the energy complex (eg, the price of power relative to coal and natural gas).

2. Risk management fundamentals

'Risk' is a meaningless word; to understand the context to which it relates, the term needs to be further qualified. Within financial markets there are arguably five key risks:

- *Market risk* – sometimes referred to as price risk. This is the risk that something that you own (or monies that are owed) will change in value as a result of a change in price.
- *Credit risk* – the willingness or ability to repay a debt.
- *Operational risk* – the risk that a company could lose money as a result of a failure of processes or procedures.
- *Business risk* – the risk that a company enters into a business that they do not fully understand.
- *Legal and documentary risk* – the risk of loss that arises from inadequate documentation or as a result of legal action.

However, only two of these risks are tradeable; market risk and credit risk. This means that there is a suite of products that could be used to manage a particular risk profile. But even the phrase 'risk management' is ambiguous. Arguably, participants can choose to:

- avoid risk;
- retain risk;
- transfer risk;
- reduce risk; or
- increase risk.

Each market participant will usually develop their own internal mandate that will outline their philosophy and operational guidelines as to how price risk is managed. At the two extremes the approaches to risk management would be:

- *Risk aversion* – this type of entity requires an extremely stable cost/revenue structure and is willing to forgo any opportunity to benefit from favourable market movements.
- *Risk taking* – this participant is willing to absorb price risk and tends only to hedge on an opportunistic basis when market conditions are very favourable.

In some respects, the price risk faced by electricity market participants is relatively straight forward. Producers of electricity to the market (ie, generators) have exposure to falling prices, whereas suppliers and consumers will have exposure to rising prices. It would seem that a logical state for the market would be for participants to agree fixed price contracts for all their transactions. Generators would know how much they would receive and suppliers and consumers would not be faced with unexpected price increases. However, this idealised state is unlikely to occur in a traded market for a number of reasons:

- Market participants may be publicly-owned entities whose shareholders expect to benefit from rising share prices and dividends. Fixed price contracts would cap the revenues of producers and would not allow consumers or suppliers to benefit from periods of low prices.
- The energy inputs needed to generate electricity are themselves procured in traded markets where prices are determined by fundamental demand and supply. So if generators were to cap all the prices they receive for their production, they run the risk that input prices (coal, natural gas, carbon emission credits) may exceed the revenue generated from sales.

However, fixed prices would be advantageous in some circumstances:

- A generator may feel that electricity prices are relatively high and so may take advantage of this by fixing a price at which they will sell their future output.
- Equally, they could feel that the cost of the requisite energy input for future delivery is low and so there may be merit in locking into a fixed price.
- A consumer or supplier of electricity would have the opposite view – that is, a supplier may decide to buy future consumption at a price that they feel is relatively low.

3. Market participants

It is likely that the larger energy companies will be active along multiple energy supply chains and so may be faced with a variety of different price risks. As a result, it is likely that the all risk management activities for each commodity are consolidated into a single entity. For example, at the time of writing, EDF operates a subsidiary called 'EDF Trading', which deals with a very wide range of market participants:

EDF Trading is a leading participant in the European power market providing wholesale market access to EDF Group businesses, EDF commercial and industrial customers and third party customers such as utilities, generators and finance houses.[1]

One of the key participants mentioned in this definition are the financial market participants. This could include commodity trading houses, investment banks and specialist hedge funds. These entities are an important intermediary in the risk management process. For example, if a producer is looking to hedge future production a bank may be willing to be the counterparty to the trade even though they are not a physical supplier to the wider market. In this case the task of the bank trader is to manage a portfolio of transactions that may differ in terms of volume, maturity and counterparty motivation. Banks can then choose whether they decide to avoid, retain, reduce, transfer or increase their resultant risk exposures with other

1 www.edftrading.com.

market participants. In the absence of such intermediaries, the physical market participants would find it more difficult to hedge their undesirable price risks.

4. Product building blocks

This section covers the main trading products used in the power market.

A forward contract represents a commitment to fix a price for delivery at some agreed time in the future, and we will discuss these type of contracts later in this chapter. A futures contract achieves the same economic result as a forward but is traded on an organised derivatives exchange such as the ICE or the CME group. Futures contracts on power have traditionally suffered from very low levels of liquidity so this chapter will not cover this product. Interested readers who wish to know more about the contract specifications for these instruments are referred to the respective exchange websites.[2]

By convention, forwards on power tend to be physically settled. Physical settlement will involve the receipt or delivery of an agreed quantity of power for a fixed price for an agreed period. Forwards are traded on a bid–offer basis and no fees are payable. The forward bid price represents the price at which the market maker (the quoting institution) will buy power forward, while the forward offer price will be the price at which the market maker is willing to sell power.

A swap contract is essentially a multi-period forward. That is, the swap fixes the price today for multiple settlement dates in the future. However, rather than have different fixed prices for each settlement period, one single fixed price will apply to each period. Swaps are financially settled and so no power is actually delivered; the contract will be settled via an exchange of cash flows. Swaps are quoted in a similar manner to forwards in that no fees are payable and the quotation is expressed as a bid–offer spread. At the bid price the market maker will pay a fixed price while agreeing to receive the agreed floating index price at maturity. The offer price represents the level at which the market maker is willing to receive the fixed price and pay the floating index. Some traders talk about buying or selling swaps, referring to the bid and offer price respectively. The buyer is deemed to be purchasing a stream of variable cash flows for which the cost is a single fixed price. On the other hand, for a swap seller, the fixed price represents the compensation for delivering a series of floating cash flows. However, this language is somewhat ambiguous and so it is often preferable to describe the transaction in terms of whether the fixed price is payable or receivable.

Option contracts are essentially another variant of the forward contract. Whereas a forward represents a commitment to buy or sell power for delivery for a specific date at a specific price, the option contract confers a right but not an obligation to buy or sell the underlying asset at an agreed price which is referred to as the strike or exercise price. The buyer has to pay a fee referred to as a premium to acquire this right. In option terminology a call gives the option buyer the right but not the obligation to buy the underlying asset. A put gives the option buyer the right but not the obligation to sell the underlying asset. As a result, there are four basic permutations:

---

2 See www.theice.com and www.cmegroup.com.

- Buy a call (purchase the right to buy the asset).
- Buy a put (purchase the right to sell the asset).
- Sell a call (confer the right to buy the asset on someone else).
- Sell a put (confer the right to sell the asset on someone else).

Those readers interested in developing a more detailed understanding of options within a commodity context are referred to Schofield.[3]

5. GB electricity market calendar

Traditionally maturities for the GB electricity market had been based on the concept of the Electricity Forward Agreement (EFA) calendar. An EFA day ran from 11pm through to 11pm the following day, with a distinction made between a weekday (WD) and a weekend (WE). Each EFA day was broken down into a series of numbered blocks (numbered 1 to 6), each block lasting four hours. For example, block 1 ran from 23:00 to 03:00, which on a weekday would be designated WD1; over a weekend it would be WE1. From a monthly perspective the calendar worked on a series of 4/4/5 week blocks. So January and February had four weeks while March had five weeks. As an example the following week designations applied in January 2013:

- Week 1 31 December – 6 January
- Week 2 7 January – 13 January
- Week 3 14 January – 20 January
- Week 4 21 January – 27 January

From this it was possible to agree on quarterly periods (eg, quarter 1 was weeks 1–13) or seasons (eg, winter was classified as week 40 in one year to week 13 in the next year; essentially October to March). The EFA year was a 52-week period running from week 14 (April) or week 40 (October).

This particular feature of the GB market differentiated it from the conventions within the continental European markets. These markets have always traded according to the traditional calendar year with a power day generally running from midnight to midnight. However, from the winter of 2014, the GB market has now adopted the same Gregorian calendar-based trading dates as the continental European markets.

6. Physical forwards

A physical forward contract requires the delivery of a fixed volume of power at an agreed price for an agreed period. Consider the following hypothetical transaction:

Trade date	26 June
Effective date	27 June
Maturity	28 June
Buyer	Counterparty A
Seller	Counterparty B
Price	£32.00/MWh

3 Schofield, *Commodity Derivatives: Markets and Applications* (John Wiley and Sons Ltd, 2007).

Volume per hour	50 MWh
Total volume	1,200 MWh
Load shape	Baseload
Delivery point	GB National Balancing Point

A load shape refers to the level of expected demand during certain times of the day. A baseload contract provides for the delivery of a constant volume of power throughout the day. A peak load contract typically runs from 7am to 7pm on a weekday. The other popular standard load shape is offpeak, which is defined as everything except the peak period.

Since this forward is a baseload contract it requires the seller to deliver a constant volume of power for a 24-hour period. In this example the contract covers a one-day period in one day's time but since these contracts are traded on an over-the-counter basis it would be possible for the counterparties to the trade to agree a longer period if necessary.

7. Physical options

Physical forwards represent a binding commitment to make or take delivery of power at an agreed price for an agreed period. By introducing some degree of optionality into the contract the option buyer acquires the right but not the obligation to buy or sell the power. An option is, in essence, a forward contract that allows the option buyer to walk away. A power producer may buy a put on their future production, that is, purchase the right (but not the obligation) to sell their physical production at an agreed price for an agreed period. This type of contract, which would be exercised by the producer if power prices fell below the strike rate, would allow them to sell their production and receive this pre-agreed fixed price.

Having the ability to walk away from the contract means that, unlike forwards and swaps, a fee is payable by the option buyer. Ultimately, the fee is determined by demand and supply in the market although formal models do exist to derive the theoretical value of the instrument. Much has been written about the valuation of options and so here we only present the intuition behind the valuation. There are broadly speaking two different ways to grasp the concepts. The premium can be thought of either as the cost of hedging the seller's resultant exposure or as the expected value of the seller's payout at expiry. To explain this second concept, consider the purchase of a lottery ticket.[4] Suppose that the average payout of a lottery has been £5m and that the odds of winning are 1 in 45 million. The fair value of the ticket is simply the lottery's expected value, that is, £5m × 1/45m – about £0.11. The numbers in the previous example are loosely based on the UK national lottery where the cost of a ticket is actually £2. This example shows not only the intuition behind the pricing of options but also the fact that the public is glad to pay the market price which is greater than the game's fair value.

Using the same principles, it would be possible to derive the premium on a

4 There is no intention to imply that the use of options is inherently a gamble. The analogy is used to convey the intuition that sits behind the formal valuation approach.

financial option. The premium is based on the seller's payout multiplied by the probability that the payout will occur. To calculate the fair value of an electricity option the following inputs are required:

- the underlying price;
- the strike price;
- the time to maturity;
- interest rates; and
- implied volatility.

All of the inputs can be directly observed from the market but the one variable that many market participants struggle to grasp is the concept of implied volatility. A popular approach is to define the concept as the volatility implied by an observed option price. This definition suggests that in order to derive the fair value of the option, a market maker must take a quoted option price and reverse out the implied volatility input in order to price their transaction. However, this is an unsatisfactory circular definition and so an alternative approach is needed.

Implied volatility can be thought of as measuring the likely future realised volatility of the underlying price over some period of time, in per cent per annum. Anecdotally, most options are European in style, which means that they can only be exercised on a single date in the future. The relevant underlying price is therefore not the spot price but a forward price with the same maturity as the option. As a result, implied volatility measures the expected dispersion of prices around this forward price. Implied volatility is equivalent to one standard deviation and so measures the likely fluctuations with a two-thirds probability.

One useful shorthand formula for estimating the premium as a percentage of the strike price is the present value of:

$$\text{Premium} = 0.4 \times \sigma\sqrt{T}$$

Where:

σ = implied volatility of underlying asset

T = time to maturity

One of the issues associated with electricity options is that the underlying prices can be exceptionally volatile and implied volatilities can trade between 10–400%, making the instruments relatively expensive to purchase.

8. Swap structures

8.1 Cash-settled swaps

As entities such as hedge funds do not trade physical power, financially-settled swaps represent an alternative way of taking exposure to the underlying market. These types of swap involve the exchange of cash flows where one cash flow is fixed while the other cash flow is floating. The floating cash flows reference a market index such as the LEBA (London Energy Brokers Association) 'day ahead' index. This index price is constructed as the volume-weighted average of all day ahead baseload trades executed in London by a number of contributing institutions.

GB power swaps settle against the average value of the index through the period being traded, typically months, quarters, seasons or years.

Suppose a hedge fund wishes to express a view on anticipated power market movements over the next winter. They decide to 'buy' 30 MW of winter 15 GB baseload power at £45.50/MWh, referencing to the LEBA day ahead index with monthly settlement covering the six-month period from October to March.

Payments will take place at the end of the month against the average of the day ahead index values published every day throughout the month in question. To illustrate the cash flow amounts let us assume that one of the months has 31 days and that the floating LEBA index has fixed at £40.00. Since the hedge fund has 'bought' the swap they will pay the fixed price and receive the floating index. The cash flows will be:

Fixed cash flows paid

30 MW × £45.50 × 24 hours × 31 days = £1,015,560

Floating cash flows received

30 MW × £40.00 × 24 hours × 31 days = £892,800

Since the timing of both cash flows coincides, it is conventional to make a net payment. Hence the hedge fund will make a net payment of £122,760.

So what would be the hedge fund's motivation for executing this swap transaction? To gain an insight into this we must take a sidestep to consider how the swap price is set, although a full mathematical derivation is beyond the scope of the text. In simple terms the swap price can be thought of as a weighted average of the forward prices for each of the periods that the swap covers. From the hedge fund's perspective, the trade is essentially bullish as they must believe that the actual day ahead price will on average be greater than the individual forward rates used to initially price the swap. So in the previous example the fixed price would be a function of the forward prices for each individual month within the winter period.

This also illustrates another important aspect of trading; forward prices are not a forecast of future spot prices. They simply represent today's prices for delivery at some future time period. For the swap in question, the hedge fund would pay fixed if they believed that on average the actual floating receipts would be greater than their fixed payments. This implies that they believe that actual power prices will be greater than those implied by the forward curve. As such the trader's motivation is simple – they will always aim to 'beat the forward price'!

8.2 Contracts for difference

As a way of encouraging low-carbon power generation, the UK government recently mandated a new product referred to as a contract for difference (CFD), illustrated in Figure 1.

Figure 1: Example of contract for difference

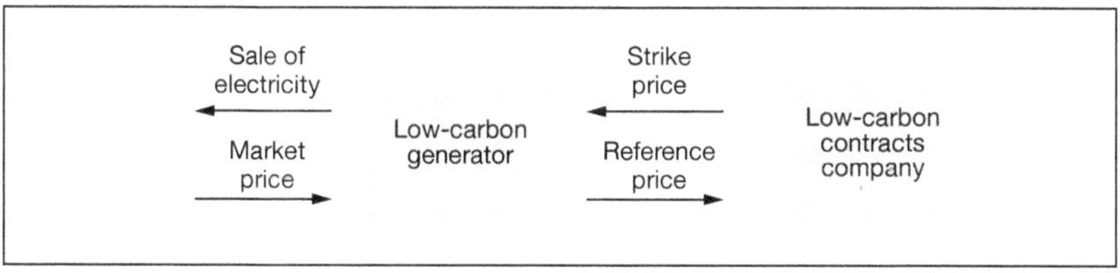

The low-carbon contracts company (LCCC) is a government-owned entity and acts as the CFD counterparty to the generator. The generator will produce its electricity and sell it into the market at the prevailing market price. In order to help it manage market price movements, it could then enter into a CFD for a period of 15 years. Under the terms of the CFD the generator will pay or receive a cash flow based on the difference between a pre-agreed strike price and a variable 'reference price'. The strike price is set by the government and will vary according to the type of technology. For the year 2015/16 the strike price for onshore wind technology (OWT) was set at a maximum of £95/MWh. However, there are circumstances where CFDs are granted on a competitive basis[5] so this strike price acts as a maximum value. For the period 2015/16 the fixed rate payable by the LCCC for OWT contracts was set at £79.23/MWh. The variable reference price payable by the generator is based on the average market price for electricity.

By way of example, suppose an onshore wind generator sells electricity in the open market and receives £70/MWh. Under the terms of the CFD and assuming a fixed strike of £79.23/MWh they will receive a supplemental payment of £9.23/MWh such that their income will be equal to the CFD's strike price. If the price the generator received for the sale of their electricity was, say, £85/MWh, then under the terms of the CFD they would be required to pay £5.77/MWh (ie, £85.00–£79.23). However, in both scenarios the generator's net income from both sides of the transaction would be equal to the CFD's strike price and so they are protected from volatile wholesale prices.

9. Swaptions

A swaption is defined as an option on a swap. Consider the following hypothetical example. A large UK manufacturer is looking to lock in the purchase price of its physical supply of power. Looking at forward prices, they believe the actual price of power will be on average higher than the forward prices currently being quoted in the market. They currently consume about 25 million kWh per month of power and are looking to hedge half this amount. They enter into a fixed price swap with a bank with the following terms:

Swap buyer:	Manufacturing company
Swap seller:	Bank
Volume:	12,500,000 kWh per month

5 See "Implementing electricity market reform", Department of Energy and Climate Change, June 2014.

Term:	12 months
Fixed price:	£50/MWh
Reference price:	GB baseload
Settlement frequency:	Monthly

On the last business day of each month the parties would calculate the reference price which, as we illustrated in the last section, would usually be an average of daily prices observed over the period.

The swap would be financially settled so as not to interfere with the manufacturer's physical supply relationship. To illustrate the impact of the swap, let us consider some possible outcomes. Let us assume that in one particular month the average cost of UK baseload power was £55/MWh. The manufacturer would pay this amount to his physical supplier and receive his required amount of power. Under the terms of the swap the bank would be required to pay this same amount to the manufacturer and in return receive the pre-agreed fixed price of £50/MWh. Since both cash flows under the swap coincide, there would be a net settlement of £5/MWh in favour of the manufacturing company. This means the net cost of buying their power is £50/MWh (£55/MWh paid out to the supplier with £5/MWh received under the swap). If the average price were, say, £40/MWh then the manufacturer would pay this amount to their supplier and be required to make a net payment of £10/MWh under the terms of the swap. The net result in both examples is that the client achieves a fixed price of £50/MWh – the same value as the fixed price in the swap.

Had the trade been structured as a swaption, the manufacturer could purchase the right to 'buy' a swap (ie, purchase the right to pay a fixed price[6]). Similar to the options considered earlier, this transaction would also incur a premium. At first glance it may appear that this transaction would be appropriate if the client believed that power prices were going to rise as they could exercise the option, enter into the swap and then pay a fixed price. However, this is not the case. If they were certain that prices were going to rise they would simply enter into the swap; entering into a swaption will incur a premium whereas the swap is traded on a bid/offer spread. Arguably, the right motivation for the transaction is that the client believes that power prices are going to fall but decides to take out protection in case their view is incorrect.

It is also worth noting that few corporates are willing buyers of options. Anecdotally, their main objection to single option structures is the requirement to pay a premium. As a result, it is most common for banks to structure zero premium transactions where different options are combined such that the client does not incur any upfront charge. A very popular zero premium transaction is termed a 'min–max' structure (sometimes referred to as a zero premium collar). The purchased swaption we considered earlier fixes the maximum price that the client will pay if they decide to exercise the option. To achieve a zero premium, the client not only buys this option but also sells a second option to the bank, which, if exercised, would require the client to pay a fixed price albeit at a lower strike. The strike of the sold

6 This could also be referred to as the purchase of a payer swaption.

option is set at a level such that the premium generated fully finances the cost of the purchased option. The sold option fixes the minimum price that the client will pay and would only be exercised by the bank against the client if the price of power is falling. This will prevent the client from enjoying the benefits of lower prices although it should be remembered that they have protection from prices rising at no premium cost. If the price of power is between the upper and the lower strike prices neither options are exercised and the client buys their power at the prevailing market price. Given many clients' wariness of selling options, the transaction term sheets rarely mention the fact that the structure involves the sale of an option and may simply talk about a 'cap' and a 'floor' price.

10. Cross-commodity trading

Since the production of electricity requires another fuel to be burnt, it is common for traders to express views on the relationship between the cost of the fuel input and the income received from the power output. The relationship between the price of electricity and the price of natural gas is termed the 'spark spread'. The relationship between the price of electricity and the price of coal is referred to as the 'dark spread'. From a view-driven perspective, arguably the most popular trade would be the spark spread as financial natural gas contracts tend to be more liquid than coal. The derivation of the spread is somewhat involved due to different energy units and the fact that one unit of natural gas does not produce one unit of power. Since the convention in the market is to physically settle forward transactions, it is perhaps more likely that these trades will be expressed using financially-settled swaps.

The first step is to take the natural gas price (eg, pence per therm) and divide by 100 to derive the £/therm. The next stage is to convert £/therm into £/MWh by dividing by the applicable energy conversion factor of 0.0293071. To take account of the fact that one unit of natural gas does not produce one unit of electricity, the £/MWh value is divided by a value of 0.49131. This value relates to the typical thermal efficiency of the plant and the market convention is to assume that the power plant is only 49.131% efficient. In simple terms this suggests that 100 units of natural gas will produce 49.131 units of power. The adjustment to take into account the different monetary units, energy units and thermal efficiency results in a value of 1.4399 (100 × 0.0293071 × 0.49131). From this we can derive the spark spread as:

Spark spread = price of electricity (price of natural gas/1.4399)

We can use the same values to determine the relative size of the trade:

- 1 therm per day is equal to 29.3071 kW per day.
- On a per hour basis this would equate to 1.221129 kWh.
- Taking into account the thermal efficiency of 49.131% this would be 0.6 kWh.
- So for every 1,000 therms of natural gas the trader would execute a power trade of size 0.6 MWh.

Since the advent of carbon trading within the EU, it is also possible to calculate the spark spread allowing for the cost of an EU Allowance (EUA). There is a market convention which assumes that 1 MWh of electricity produced by burning natural gas will emit approximately 0.4 ton of carbon. To calculate the 'clean spark spread' we must first convert the price of an EUA from euros into pounds sterling (GBP). We then subtract 40% of this value from the spark spread to calculate the clean spark spread:

Clean spark spread = spark spread – (0.4 × EUA price in GBP)

It is also possible to derive the dark spread using similar principles to those illustrated to calculate the spark spread. The key features are:

- 1 ton of coal provides 7MWh of energy.
- The market convention is to assume thermal efficiency of coal is 36%.
- Generating one ton of coal emits 0.8 tons of carbon.

So the 'clean dark spread' is calculated as:

Price of electricity – (price of coal in GBP/2.52) – (0.8 × EUA price in GBP)

11. Cross-market trading

One type of trade growing in popularity allows a trader to exploit the difference in power prices between countries. Interconnectors allow participants to move electricity across countries but to do so the trader must have purchased the right to transmit the power. The capacity to transmit is auctioned on a regular basis by the grid operator. Cross-market trades are in essence very simple. Suppose a trader sees that the price of power in France is €55/MWh while the price in Germany is €60/MWh. Suppose the trader has purchased annual transmission capacity at a cost of €3/MWh. He agrees a trade size of 100 MW to buy the power in France and sell it into Germany. An annual baseload contract would generate a profit of:

€60 – (€55+€3) × 24 hours × 365 days × 100 MW = €1,752,000

12. Documenting trades

12.1 Introduction

In the previous sections, we talked about the main trading products used in the power market, and we framed them in terms of contracts, such as forward contracts and futures contracts. In this section, we will consider the architecture of the actual contract.

Each country will follow its own approach to this issue, whether mandated by market rules or adopted by industry as 'standard' (or a combination thereof). Broadly speaking, where physical power trading is permitted in a jurisdiction, the arrangements typically comprise: (1) a contract for trading power (which can be a simple one-off trade between two contracting parties, or something more complicated such as a master agreement that governs all power trades between those two parties); and (2) industry rules and arrangements to give effect to that trade (such as procedures to notify the electricity transmission system operator that the trade has been entered into).

Typically, market participants use standardised documentation to document their wholesale power trades. For example, for over-the-counter trading:[7]

7 As discussed earlier in the chapter, it is also possible to trade electricity on power exchanges. These will also be under a form of contract specific to that exchange.

- Physically delivered power trades in Great Britain are usually transacted under a Grid Trade Master Agreement (GTMA).[8]
- Physically delivered continental Europe power trades are usually transacted under a European Federation of Energy Traders (EFET) General Agreement.[9]
- Cash/financially-settled power trades are usually transacted under an International Swaps and Derivatives (ISDA[10]) Master Agreement, irrespective of where they are traded.[11]

Each of the above contracts is a type of framework contract, referred to as a 'master agreement'. By this, we mean it comprises standard terms and conditions that will govern all trades entered into between the two parties. The particular commercial terms (price, date, volume etc)[12] of each trade will be agreed on a case by case basis, usually over the telephone, and these terms will subsequently be documented in writing, on a document called a 'confirmation'. Each trade will incorporate the standard terms and conditions of the master agreement, unless the parties have agreed special terms for a particular trade.

Where two market participants know they are likely to enter into multiple trades with each other, a master agreement can be put in place at the outset to avoid the need to negotiate an entirely new contract each time a trade is proposed. Another key advantage is that if a party is entitled to terminate, it can terminate all outstanding trades together. The outstanding trades will then be valued, to arrive at a single net sum (in the form of a termination payment) owing from one party to the other. This is known as 'close-out netting', and allows the parties to significantly reduce their exposure to the other party for the purposes of credit (and, in the case of parties that are banks, capital adequacy requirements). This feature is particularly important in the context of counterparty insolvency.[13]

It should be noted that even though we refer to such contracts as 'standard form' contracts, this actually refers to the fact that pre-published forms of these contracts exist. In practice, they are then negotiated by the two parties, sometimes at length, and therefore an understanding of these documents and market practice will be important. It will also be critical to undertake due diligence before commencing power trading, so that risks can be understood and informed decisions can be made. In the case of legal due diligence, this should, for example, cover an analysis of the

8 https://fia.org/commodities-agreements.

9 www.efet.org/Standardisation/Legal-EFET-Standard-Contracts-and-Documentation/Electricity-And-Electricity-Annexes.

10 www2.isda.org.

11 Physically settled power trades can also be documented under an ISDA master agreement, by incorporating bespoke annexes to the agreement. For example, ISDA produced a pre-printed form of GTMA annex (Sub-annex G to the ISDA 2005 Commodities Definitions) and this is commonly used where the two trading entities already have an ISDA master agreement in place and choose not to separately negotiate a GTMA. One reason for this approach is to reduce complexity. Entering into more than one master agreement with the same counterparty may create additional risks that need to be considered, such as netting and margining issues.

12 The example given in section 6 sets out a fuller list of terms.

13 Some countries do not permit or recognise close-out netting. In some cases it will depend on the contract drafting. A 'single agreement' clause can be important to the question of recognising close-out netting; this clause states that all trades (including the general terms and conditions) together form a single agreement.

underlying market rules for wholesale trading and physical delivery of power and whether the proposed trading activities are regulated activities in the relevant jurisdiction.

In this section, we will focus on the GTMA, as this is a genuinely industry standard document that has been used in Great Britain since the system of bilateral wholesale trading was introduced in 2000. The GTMA contains key features expected by the market, and this has driven its acceptance within the market. These include effective termination triggers; cross-commodity netting and margining; and effective treatment of issues arising from the physical delivery of power under GB's wholesale market trading rules.

12.2 The GTMA: in a nutshell

The GTMA is a standard form contract that allows two parties to trade wholesale GB electricity from time to time, in agreed volumes and at agreed prices.[14] The transactions can relate to trades (known as 'grid trades') that will occur in the short term, or months or years in the future, with a granularity of half-hourly periods for delivery. In order to give effect to such trades, they must be notified to the electricity transmission system operator's central systems administrator. The parties' energy accounts on the central systems will be credited and debited accordingly, at the agreed time for delivery of the power.

The types of party that will enter into a GTMA will be electricity generators, suppliers and intermediaries/traders. The Electricity Forward Agreement Association published the original version of the GTMA in 2000, to facilitate over-the-counter trading. After industry consultation, the Futures and Options Association released a revised version of the GTMA in June 2004, which (as of the date of this book's publication) is still the latest version.

The GTMA is not a mandatory document, but given its standard form nature, it has almost universal market acceptance in Great Britain and potential counterparties will likely be reluctant to trade on the basis of an alternative document unless there is a good reason to do so. For example, where two parties already have an existing contractual relationship between themselves, such as under an ISDA Master Agreement, they may prefer to adapt that document to apply to GB power trades, rather than negotiate a separate GTMA. Another example is where a generator agrees to sell the entirety of its output to a supplier (ie, the trades only ever flow in one direction); the parties may contract on different terms (such as a bespoke power purchase agreement) rather than a GTMA.

12.3 The GTMA: structure

(a) General structure

Master agreements such as the GTMA, EFET and ISDA all follow a similar basic architecture, although their actual contractual provisions will be very different.[15] The

---

14 The GTMA is available for download at: https://fia.org/sites/default/files/content_attachments/GTMA.pdf.

GTMA is structured as follows:

- general provisions;
- Schedule 1 (definitions and interpretation);
- Schedule 2 (agreement information);
- Schedule 3B (contract party notification agent approach);[16]
- Annexes A, B and C (form of confirmation, notices); and
- options annex (this is a separate document, which allows the parties to enter into options transactions under the GTMA).

(b) ***General provisions***

The general provisions are a set of 23 clauses that will apply to all GB power trades between the parties. These clauses cover:

- Basic terms, such as agreement on contractual interpretation, the provision of representations and warranties by each party to the other party (so that each can be sure that the other is an appropriate party to contract with) and an obligation on each party to comply with all necessary industry rules for trading GB power (including installing the required information technology systems).[17]
- Issues of process, including what practical and physical steps the parties must follow when agreeing trades (for example, it envisages parties will make trades over the telephone and these will later be confirmed by written confirmation).
- Provisions that govern how the trade is given effect. The GTMA's terms in this respect are entirely bespoke to the GB regime for electricity trading. They set out an allocation of risk and responsibility: for example, who will notify the trade to the system operator's central systems administrator, who will check the notifications and what happens if something goes wrong (such as the details of the trade being incorrectly notified or not notified at all) and a party suffers a financial loss. Here, the standard GTMA provides for two alternatives regimes (one set out in clauses 4, 5 and 6; the other provided for in Schedule 3B. The market standard approach is to use Schedule 3B, or a modified version of it).
- Treatment of VAT and other taxes.
- Billing and payment issues (monthly billing, disputes and late payment interest).
- Termination events (such as non-payment, material adverse changes to a party's creditworthiness, insolvency and persistent failure to perform) and liability.
- The governing law, which is English law. Unresolved disputes are settled by

15 There are many useful free resources discussing the ISDA Master Agreement. ISDA also publishes official user guides on its suite of documentation.

16 There is also a Schedule 4 which applied transitional provisions relating to the restructuring of the GB power market in 2000.

17 The GTMA does not have a specified term (duration). It will remain dormant until the parties agree a trade or agree to terminate it.

the English courts (except for certain technical matters, which may be referred to an expert for determination).

- Other provisions, such as *force majeure*, confidentiality, assignment, and other such clauses of a 'boilerplate' nature that can be found in most commercial agreements.

(c) Schedules

Schedule 2 provides a list of mainly commercial options that are negotiated, sometimes at length. These are called 'elections', and cover the following matters:

- How the parties will communicate the written confirmations that record the details of the agreed trade (fax, email or other means).
- Who takes responsibility for notifying trades to the system operator's central systems administrator.
- Commercial terms. These include financial thresholds of losses or indebtedness that will trigger when the agreement can be terminated; what method will be used to value outstanding trades that are terminated; whether one party will require credit support from the other; and what happens if a change in the taxation regime occurs.

The contract provides for default/fall-back positions which apply in the absence of an election.

Separately, Schedule 2 also allows for the parties to document any specific amendments they wish to make to the general provisions. For example, the parties may wish to agree amendments to the standard clause on billing and payment, or introduce entirely new clauses. The desired amendment should be described in Schedule 2 itself, rather than actually amending the text of general provisions.

Larger or well-established trading entities develop their own standard form of Schedule 2, based on their market experience and internal level of risk and comfort. When negotiating a GTMA with a new counterparty, the larger or more well-established entity will prefer to circulate its preferred form of Schedule 2 as a starting position for negotiations. We explored why these contracts are used, how they are structured and the types of issues that they deal with.

13. Conclusion

In this chapter we defined the term 'trading', to incorporate both hedging and view-driven strategies. Although the derivatives market for power is not as developed as, say, crude oil we considered some of the more popular instruments and suggested some possible motivations for their use. The most popular power instruments are:

- physical forwards;
- physical options;
- financially-settled swaps and CFDs; and
- swaptions.

We also looked at how electricity trading can be contractually documented. Cash/financially-settled power trades are usually transacted under an ISDA Master

Agreement. Physically delivered continental Europe power trades are usually transacted under an EFET General Agreement. In Great Britain, physically delivered power trades are usually transacted under a GTMA.

Regulating monopoly infrastructure: an economic perspective

Phil Burns
Frontier Economics

1. Introduction

The chapter on Market liberalisation and organisation looked at how monopoly power can give rise to a need for regulation. In this chapter, we look at what different approaches have been taken to regulate monopolies.

For much of the post-World War II period, the organisation of the power sector in most countries was based on granting monopoly rights to businesses to produce, transmit, distribute and retail electricity. Very often, these monopoly rights were vested in single vertically integrated businesses that undertook all these activities. In many countries these businesses were state owned, meaning the role of owner, manager, regulator and policy maker was bundled together under the umbrella of the state.[1]

During the 1980s and 1990s a wave of reform swept around the world, resulting in the unbundling[2] of businesses; the promotion of competition in power production and retail; and the establishment of regulatory offices to regulate transmission and distribution businesses, which are natural monopolies.[3] Some reforming governments also took the opportunity to privatise part or all of the power sector.[4]

While implicit or explicit regulation of prices and quality had long been

1 The United States was a notable exception to this model. Although the power sector was also monopolised, there was a tradition of investor ownership of the utilities, as well as municipal and co-operative ownership. In addition, these monopoly utilities were regulated by local Public Utility Commissions, or the Federal Energy Regulatory Commission (FERC) in the case of interstate operations.

2 Unbundling refers to the regulatory practice of requiring vertically integrated businesses to unbundle, or separate, their naturally monopolistic network activities from their potentially competitive production and retail activities. This measure was regarded as necessary to ensure that the networks owned by these businesses could not distort competition in the production and supply markets by discriminating in favour of their own production and supply businesses. Different degrees of unbundling were observed in practice, from accounting separation of businesses within the same ownership group, to full ownership unbundling.

3 A natural monopoly exists when it is cheaper for one firm to supply the service than several firms. In the case of electricity distribution and transmission, it is usually more costly to build two networks serving the same geographical area than to build one network. Hence it is more efficient to give one operator the monopoly rights to operate the grid in that area. This is discussed further in the chapter on Market liberalisation and organisation.

4 Chile pioneered power sector unbundling and liberalisation in the 1980s. In 1989, Britain privatised most of the power sector, unbundled the Central Electricity Generating Board (CEGB) into competing generation firms and a separate transmission company, and subsequently unbundled retailing and distribution. During the 1990s, other countries such as Norway, New Zealand and Australia also began to unbundle the power sector and introduce competition. In the European Union, the process of unbundling is now well established, having begun in 1996 with the first Electricity Directive, and continued with two further Electricity Directives (2003 and 2009) which strengthened unbundling requirements and competition, and (amongst other things) required member states to establish regulatory offices.

established in the energy sector to protect customers from abuse of a monopoly position,[5] the structural changes to the sector were accompanied by the development of a radical new approach to regulating monopoly networks known as RPI-X regulation. In this chapter we describe this new approach and how it has evolved over time, and discuss the implementation challenges it has faced and continues to face as networks prepare to facilitate the decarbonisation of electricity systems.

2. The origins of RPI-X regulation

The new system of RPI-X price control regulation was set out in the 1983 report commissioned by Britain's Department of Trade and Industry and written by Stephen Littlechild, a professor of economics at the University of Birmingham, on the regulation of the soon to be privatised British Telecom.[6] This report was further expanded upon in a later joint paper with Professor Michael Beesley that more fully developed the new model of RPI-X regulation.[7] This system of regulation simply required the regulator to set a ceiling on prices determined by the level of retail price inflation (RPI) minus a factor, X, that represented the regulator's best forecast of the productivity gains that he expected the business to achieve in future. This price ceiling would then remain in place for a lengthy period of time, such as five years. This ceiling was intended to protect customers from overcharging and at the same time encourage the regulated business to profit from efficiency savings it could make during the price control period that were not anticipated at the time the price ceiling was set. At the end of the price control period, the regulator would reset prices based on the new information that had been revealed since the last price control review, but would not clawback the profits the business had earned through its efficiency initiatives, since this would damage the incentives to make the efficiency gains in the first place.

This radically simple approach was in stark contrast to the prevailing systems of regulation. The US system, for example, tried to protect customers by limiting the profits that the firm can earn to a 'normal' level, by setting prices on the basis of the firm's own costs. However, being mindful of Hicks' (1935) maxim[8] that the 'best of all monopoly profits is a quiet life', this type of 'cost-plus' or 'rate of return' regime was typically accompanied by ever increasing levels of regulatory oversight, scrutiny and intervention so that the regulators could satisfy themselves that costs were not higher than they should be due to inefficiency, gold-plating of assets, satisficing behaviour or rent-seeking.[9] The heightened levels of oversight and scrutiny created an implicit or explicit culture of intervention by the regulator. However, this did not

---

5 See R Turvey, "The Sliding Scale: Price and Dividend Regulation in the Nineteenth Century Gas Industry" (NERA Topics #16, 1995), for example, on the regulation of electric and town gas utilities in 19th century England.

6 S Littlechild, *Regulation of British Telecommunications' profitability: report to the Secretary of State*, February 1983 (London: Department of Industry, 1983).

7 Beesley and Littlechild, "The regulation of privatised monopolies in the United Kingdom" (1989) 20(3) *Rand Journal of Economics* 454–472.

8 JR Hicks, "Annual survey of economic theory: The theory of monopoly" (1935) 3(1) *Econometrica* 1–20.

9 Rent-seeking is the attempt to capture economic rent (or profit) not through adding value but by exploiting channels of power and influence, resulting in accumulation of benefits for the rent seeker that are not justified by its underlying productivity performance.

adequately address the fundamental efficiency concerns and led to managerial decisions which were heavily influenced by the regulator and the regulatory process.[10]

The source of the difference of approach was a quite different attitude to risk and uncertainty. Uncertainty lies at the heart of the economics of regulation. The regulator may be uncertain about the prevailing cost level, and neither the regulator nor the firm are likely to be well informed about the potential for innovation and efficiency gains in the industry, or the impact of events outside the firm's control. The firm may have better information than the regulator on how to perform more efficiently given the current structure and asset stock of the business – so-called productive efficiency gains; but both the firm and the regulator are likely to be similarly uncertain about how changes to the culture, operations, investment strategy and management of the business could deliver a lower cost outcome over the longer term – so-called dynamic efficiency savings.

The prevailing post-war attitude was that this uncertainty could be resolved if sufficient expert resources were mobilised by the regulator to scrutinise the actions, decisions and operations of the business and intervene when necessary. In contrast, Beesley and Littlechild emphasised that their approach required little, if any, information and expert analysis:

RPI-X ... does not assume costs and demands are given or known: indeed, the problem is to provide adequate incentives for the company to discover them. The aim is to stimulate alertness to lower cost techniques and hitherto unmet demands. The emphasis is on productive rather than allocative efficiency.[11]

This model owed much to the Austrian school, which stressed the limits of knowledge, and implications for governmental control:

If man is not to do more harm than good in his efforts to improve the social order, he will have to learn that in this, as in all other fields where essential complexity of an organized kind prevails, he cannot acquire the full knowledge which would make mastery of the events possible. He will therefore have to use what knowledge he can achieve, not to shape the results as the craftsman shapes his handiwork, but rather to cultivate a growth by providing the appropriate environment, in the manner in which the gardener does this for his plants.[12]

This philosophical position also chimed with a growing body of economic literature, pioneered by the US economist Oliver Hart,[13] which emphasised that a 'contract', such as that between a regulator and a firm,[14] could never be complete except in the very simplest cases. Contracts would be inevitably incomplete since they could not cover every possible eventuality, with the implication that any

10 See, for example, Averch and Johnson, "Behaviour of the firm under regulatory constraint" (1962) 52 *American Economic Review* 1056–69, and Baumol and Klevorick, "Input choices and rate of return regulation: an overview of the discussion" (1970) *Bell Journal of Economics and Management Science*. (1970).

11 Beesley and Littlechild, "The regulation of privatised monopolies in the United Kingdom" (1989) 20(3) *Rand Journal of Economics* 454–472.

12 F von Hayek, *The Pretence of Knowledge* (Nobel Lecture, 1974).

13 See Hart (1995) for a summary.

14 Hart was not just referring to a contract in the legal sense, but also an agreement between two entities.

attempt to try and write a complete contract through an ever expanding regulatory rule book or ever increasing regulatory oversight and intervention would be doomed to failure.[15]

The other dominant form of regulation in the post-war years – that of regulation by nationalisation – attempted to sidestep this problem by internalising all the information asymmetries under the umbrella of the state. In practice, though, this did not deal with the information problem, and it led to managerial objectives in the businesses that were complex, contradictory and *ad hoc* in their formulation. Nationalised businesses were often used as instruments of macroeconomic policy – through public sector wage and price policies, employment and investment policies and so forth. Since there was no clear business focus for managers, they were able to devote their energies to other activities which did not have a clear business rationale, such as unnecessary expenditure on R&D, gold-plating of assets, and other rent-seeking behaviour.

The fact that in many countries the new system of regulation coincided with privatisation implied a significant degree of 'governance unbundling' that separated roles and responsibilities between:

- the policy maker, who sets the legal and regulatory framework within which the other stakeholders operate;
- the regulator, who sets regulatory rules for prices and outputs consistent with the legislative framework and then resets those rules at infrequent intervals and on a forward-looking basis;
- the owner, who puts in place the right management and set of management incentives to deliver shareholder returns within the regulatory framework; and
- the management, to whom operational control is devolved, and who must take responsibility for the investment and operating decisions of the business within this regulatory and commercial environment.

The separation of roles promoted both efficiency and accountability. It promoted efficiency because management would be left to manage the business to deliver shareholder returns within a clear set of regulatory rules. This search for profit is intended to reveal efficiency improvements that would not otherwise be revealed, information which can then be used to set future price controls.

It promoted accountability because the responsibilities of each stakeholder are clear and the tension between the objectives of the shareholder, manager and regulator encourages a mutually reinforcing, disciplining behaviour on all three. In contrast, the conflation of these roles under nationalisation led to a weakening of that discipline and ultimately costly outcomes for customers, at least in the UK.

It was well understood that a regulator operating within a clear legislative remit, but independent of day-to-day governmental control, was an essential ingredient in

15 A lesson that is now being learnt by banking regulators. See, for example, AG Haldane and V Madouros, "The dog and the Frisbee", presented at the Federal Reserve Bank of Kansas City's 36th economic policy symposium, "The Changing Policy Landscape", Jackson Hole, Wyoming, 31 August 2012.

this new policy mix. However, it is less clear whether incentive-based regulation can be applied to a state-owned company. The essence of RPI-X regulation is that profit incentives to improve performance are applied to the business – indeed, it was originally designed to regulate the prices of a privatised company. However, if the business' owner does not value profits, and does not reward management for generating profits, then the regulatory incentives will be ineffective. This phenomenon is more likely to occur with state-owned businesses than private-sector businesses.

To put the point slightly differently, RPI-X regulation is intended to impose a hard budget constraint on the business, which is considerably softened if the state bankrolls inefficiency and under-performance. As a consequence, governments which wish to retain their power networks in state ownership, while at the same time seeking to introduce incentive-based regulation, often recognise the need to create ring-fenced commercial vehicles for the businesses to (imperfectly) mimic the disciplining effect of private ownership on managerial behaviour.

The essence of the original RPI-X model, therefore, is not to second guess or prescribe the business decisions of the regulated firm. Instead, an independent, arms-length regulator should create a simple, well-understood, stable regulatory framework, within which the firm would manage its own risks and have a commercial incentive to make decisions that drive innovation and efficiency.

3. The early death of 'pure form' RPI-X regulation

The original Littlechild model had strong attractions, but it also suffered from a fatal flaw. Regimes which are too 'high powered' – that is, those which allow management extensive autonomy, and which permit firms to keep all the profits of their efforts – are essentially blind to the distributional implications, or 'fairness' of the price control settlement. Starkey and van Pelt[16] draw attention to the key premise underlying high powered regimes, that:

> *increased profits for the firm will be viewed by regulators and their constituency as something other than a failure of regulation itself. If this premise is false then the regulators will be under constant pressure to recontract when the firm reports higher profits.*

In Britain, this intentional design feature – combined with a highly generous set of original price controls implemented at privatisation – enabled the transmission and distribution power network operators to earn very high excess profits without significantly increasing productivity.[17]

Littlechild's 'pure form' RPI-X regulation lasted for just one price control review, that of the National Grid Company in 1992. In that review, a four-page press release announced that the regulator intended to change the RPI-X control to reflect a more

---

16 M Starkey and J van Pelt, "Productivity measurement and price cap regulation: Issues for local exchange carriers in the USA" (1995) 19(2) *Telecommunications Policy* 151–160.

17 In *Regulatory Incentives, Privatisation and Productivity Growth in UK Electricity Distribution* (CRI Technical Paper No. 1. Cipfa: London, 1994) P Burns and TG Weyman-Jones found that productivity amongst the distribution operators in the first three years after privatisation was not significantly different than in the pre-privatisation period; yet, by 1994 these operators were achieving rates of return significantly higher than their cost of capital.

realistic expectation of productivity growth, but would not ratchet down prices to the prevailing level of cost. By 1994 and 1995, the excess profits made by the transmission and distribution businesses alike, accompanied by large increases in remuneration for senior management, created such public disquiet in Britain that the regulatory regime had to be fundamentally modified.[18]

The lesson of the experiment with pure-form RPI-X regulation in Britain was that customers, the public, politicians and the media did not only care about efficiency. They also cared about the fairness of the distributional settlement between shareholders, the executives of the businesses, and customers. For regulators who had been roundly condemned for their willingness to allow the regulated businesses to earn significant excess returns, it was a lesson that was quickly learned. They moved to jettison pure form RPI-X regulation and develop more effective methods of customer protection, while attempting to preserve the efficiency properties of the original Littlechild model.

4. From RPI-X to incentive-based regulation

The root cause of the unsustainability of the original Littlechild model lay in the setting of the cost targets around which those efficiency incentives applied. The cost targets seemed to lack transparent and objective justification, and were ultimately seen as too generous. In addition, while there was general agreement that incentives for performance improvement were a key feature of the regime, there was a lack of transparency, and therefore legitimacy, around the payoffs and profits the business could expect to obtain from its efficiency improvements.

As a result, regulators both in Britain and in other countries sought to retain – and indeed formalise – the desirable efficiency properties of the Littlechild model, but recognised that target-setting needed to be far more rigorous and objective.

Price control regimes continued to attract the label of RPI-X or CPI-X[19] to reflect the fact that the regulated businesses' prices were indexed to an economy-wide price index less an efficiency factor, but the economic characteristics of these regimes were quite different to the original RPI-X model. Indeed, it is more accurate to describe 'pure form' RPI-X as a special case of a more general class of regulatory models that can be described as incentive-based regulation. Incentive-based regulation recognises that a regulatory system is made up of a common set of components, and it is how the regulator puts those components together that determines its efficiency properties, the balance of risk that is shared between customer and shareholder, the distributional settlement and the sustainability of the regime.

The regulatory and institutional ingredients that make up an effective incentive regime are:

- Managerial objectives are ring-fenced from public policy objectives, so that running the business is decentralised to the managers, within a well-defined framework.

18 These outcomes were also observed in other regulated sectors such as the telecommunications, gas and water industries and jointly contributed to public anger.

19 CPI refers to the Consumer Price Index.

- Incentives are provided for managers in the firm to accept cost risk, manage the associated uncertainties, and seek out efficiency savings.
- Credible rules govern the remuneration of long-lived assets.
- The allowable revenue calculations that underpin the price control[20] embody transparent cost targets which are based on exogenous information.
- Targets and incentives are appropriately calibrated to ensure that the financial costs and benefits associated with under- or over-performance by the business are proportionate, and non-distortionary.

No two regimes are identical across each of these ingredients, and these differences will impact to a greater or lesser extent on the economic effect of the regulatory arrangements. The first two of these ingredients have been discussed already. The last three refer to the necessary work that regulators need to do to ensure that the design and calibration of the system achieves its public policy objectives.

4.1 Remuneration of long-lived assets

The application of clear rules for the valuation and recovery of the expenditures incurred in investing in the network is a vital ingredient of regulation. Power system assets can last up to 80 years, so it is usually considered inappropriate for current customers to pay for those assets as the expenditures are incurred. Instead the investment is logged up into a 'rate base' or 'regulatory asset value' to be reimbursed to the business over time. There are many different methodologies that have been applied for the valuation of pre-existing assets[21] and the ongoing updating of the asset base with new investment, but the key point is that the rules governing the valuation and recovery of the asset base over time should be clear and well understood.

The reason for this is that it preserves the credibility that underpins any incentive-based regime. If network operators are concerned that the regulator might make opportunistic regulatory interventions that have the effect of retrospectively stranding sunk investments, then they will be less inclined to make such investments, or would require a higher return to compensate for the risk of opportunistic behaviour. Clear rules for the remuneration of investment must therefore be set in advance, and subject to retrospective review only to enforce proper compliance. For this reason, regulators have tended to be extremely careful to specify the rules for the valuation and updating of the regulatory asset value to avoid creating a commercial climate that discourages necessary investment, or increases its cost.

Alongside this, regulators have also typically developed clear rules for the 'paying down' of the asset value through the depreciation charge that is included in the

20 While the regulatory model is often referred to as 'price control' regulation, in practice regulators determine how much revenue a company is allowed to earn in each year of the price control period, which in turn determines the prices the network can charge.

21 In countries where the business has been privatised, the regulatory asset value is often based on the sale value. In other cases accounting values have been used, ranging from historic cost value to the depreciated modern equivalent value.

allowable revenue calculation. At first sight it would seem sensible to recover the costs of long-lived assets over the lifetimes that those assets are expected to be operational. However, in practice there are two important credibility reasons that would justify adopting a significantly shorter asset life over which customers repay the costs of prior investment:

- to strengthen the credibility of the commitment that businesses will be able to recover efficiently incurred costs; and
- to enhance regulatory discipline and accountability.

Regulators are unable to credibly commit to very slow recovery of costs (through long depreciation periods): the risk that regulatory intervention results in stranding of assets will increase with the effective length of time over which companies are able to recover their costs. Adopting longer depreciation periods may reduce the cost borne by current customers through lower depreciation charges in any particular period, but it may also have the offsetting effect of raising the cost of capital required to finance the assets and/or reducing the investment that is actually made.[22]

The second credibility issue is rooted in the strand of economic theory that emphasises government failure as a source of inefficiency, analogous to the better known problem of market failure. Whereas markets may fail to generate efficient outcomes for a variety of reasons (the presence of externalities, information asymmetries and conditions that give rise to monopolies, etc), governments may also fail to deliver efficient outcomes due to, for example, rent-seeking by government agencies leading to capture by interest groups; and populist or electoral pressure that forces agencies to reject efficient solutions in favour of electorally acceptable ones.

If the speed of cost recovery is too slow, then this can have the effect of increasing the attractiveness of rent-seeking by regulatory agencies because the cost to customers of that behaviour is obscured by the long depreciation period. For example, regulators may have less incentive to evaluate thoroughly the cost submissions made by businesses, or may acquiesce in passing through costs that are not necessary for the provision of the service but are politically convenient to load onto customers. Consequently, a faster rate of cost recovery can have the beneficial effect of disciplining the regulatory agency to act effectively and in accordance with its obligations to customers.

In addition to the valuation of assets and the recovery of that asset base, the regulator also needs to set revenues so as to enable the business to expect to earn a fair rate of return on the investments that are in the asset base. This return is usually estimated by reference to the cost of capital that the firm is exposed to, which reflects both the cost of debt and the cost of equity. The cost of equity is typically estimated using the capital asset pricing model (CAPM),[23] while the cost of debt may reflect the

---

22 See, for example, Brennan and Xia, "Risk and Valuation under an Intertemporal Capital Asset Pricing Model" (2006) 79 *Journal of Business* 1–36.

23 The CAPM attempts to determine the return that the regulated business should earn by reference to the risk it faces. Other models have also been used for this purpose, but the CAPM has proved the most widely used.

business's own 'embedded' debt costs, or a benchmark cost of debt. As with the valuation and recovery of the asset base, consistency and credibility is also important in the return the regulator sets. Regulators have therefore been careful not to undermine their credibility by, for example, opportunistically switching between different debt benchmarks and embedded debt rates simply to find the lowest rate at that point in time.

4.2 Cost targets embodied in price controls

In estimating future levels of operating and capital expenditure, regulators now make increasing use of benchmarking analyses and engineering studies to ensure that prices only cover the estimated level of efficient costs. In doing so, regulators still tend to be careful to recognise the limits of their knowledge. Efficiency estimates, for example, tend to rely on relatively high level benchmarking analyses that seek to answer the question 'is there evidence of inefficiency?' rather than 'how can the firm run its business more efficiently?' Benchmarking has enabled price controls to be set on the basis of more challenging cost targets than would otherwise have been the case, while resisting the temptation to prescribe how the firm could be run more efficiently.

4.3 Calibration of the regime

Regulatory instruments have a powerful effect on behaviour. As we have discussed, even a low powered regime has a powerful impact on behaviour in that it can encourage inertia, risk aversion and rent-seeking behaviour. In contrast, there is a wide consensus that the model of a stable, predictable, transparent incentive-based regulatory framework, in combination with private ownership, has led to productivity gains that would not have arisen otherwise. These productivity benefits have benefitted customers in the form of lower prices than would otherwise be the case.[24]

However, the mix of incentives that make up a higher-powered regulatory regime can also lead to unintended distortions and undermine the sustainability of the regime. Regulatory practice has evolved to both address distortions and to ensure that the price control settlement embodies a fair sharing of risk between the shareholder and the customer.

(a) *Avoiding distortionary outcomes*

Regulatory practice can have distortionary economic effects, on output provision and input choices. In this section, we discuss some common distortions that regulation has induced, and the remedies that have evolved in regulatory practice.[25]

Output distortions: a power network produces outputs that customers value, such as a reliable supply of power, the provision of timely connections services, system

24 See Europe Economics, *Review of Railtrack Efficiency* (ORR/Europe Economics, December 1999) for a review of trends in the costs and productivity of UK utilities in the decade or so after privatisation.

25 See Burns and Riechmann, "Regulatory instruments and investment behaviour" (2004) 12 *Utilities Policy* 211–219 for a fuller description of these distortions.

balancing services, and so forth. Incentive-based regulation can distort output provision in two ways: first, if there are different regulatory rewards for the supply of different services, then this could distort the supply of those services or outputs; secondly, incentives for cost reduction under incentive-based regulation could dominate the incentives for output provision, and lead to a general deterioration in service.

An example of the first effect is where a transmission operator's use of system services are subject to high-powered regulation,[26] but the costs of constraining power plant in order to balance the system are recovered on a cost pass-through basis. In this case, the operator has little incentive to increase investment on the network to reduce constraints because it receives no benefit for doing so, even if it is optimal for it to do so.[27] A balanced set of incentives would encourage the operator to choose the solution that minimises the total cost of investment and constraint costs.

The second concern is that a network operator might be able to reduce costs by 'cutting corners', resulting in decreased delivery of outputs. This is despite the fact that in the power sector, typically there are onerous statutory requirements applied to the network operators to deliver outputs, at least to a minimum standard.[28] To address the concern, additional quality targets are applied to distribution and transmission businesses, relating for example to the number of supply interruptions and the number of customer supply minutes lost due to power cuts. Bonuses and payments are associated with performance around these targets, subject to caps and collars.

However, these quality indicators are not ideal because in general there is a time-lag between reduced investment and reduced reliability. Ideally, quality regulation should expose current management to the implications of its investment and maintenance decisions even if these may arise in the future. This could, for example, take the form of a regulatory regime based on 'leading' indicators of the level of quality that can be expected in the future, given the current state of the assets. Ofgem (2009) has begun to use asset health indicators for this purpose. These metrics are designed to give the regulator early warning that the network may face quality issues in future.

However, although this may be seen as a sensible way to set cost allowances, there is a clear associated danger. The regulator may use out-turn performance on asset health indicators to judge *ex post* whether the business has (or has not) maintained the underlying reliability of the network at a level consistent with the funding provided at the price control review. If the business is penalised or rewarded for this performance, a number of problems arise. This is because the health of the

---

26 That is, the regulatory regime is constructed to expose the firm's financial performance to its efficiency and operational performance.

27 The experience of the National Grid Company in England and Wales provides an interesting case study of this effect, which led to Ofgem (2002) changing the balance of incentives across services: see Ofgem, *NGC System Operator Incentive Scheme 2003/04–2005/06: Initial Consultation Document*, 68/02, 18 October 2002.

28 These rules embody serious penalties for breach, which may include financial penalties, revocation of licences or criminal penalties. Where a quality regime is applied by the regulator, it will complement these statutory requirements.

individual assets does not determine the reliability of the network as experienced by customers. Reliability is also driven by other inputs such as automation, planning of restoration activities, investment in related parts of the network, and so forth. By penalising or rewarding businesses on the basis of their performance on one input, the regulator would inadvertently send a very strong signal to manage reliability through the use of that input, even when others would be more efficient. In other words, the regulator risks creating a boundary that distorts behaviour towards potentially inefficient outcomes.[29]

As a consequence, there is a danger of a creep into input based regulation, where the indicator of success is not the output being delivered, but performance against one particular input.[30] This would undermine innovation and raise costs.

Input distortions: as noted earlier, when setting price controls, regulators will typically evaluate what operating and capital expenditure (capex) costs (which might broadly be termed 'inputs') are expected to be in future. In doing so, regulators may set targets for different categories of costs in different ways, and this can signal implicitly or explicitly where network operators should focus their cost efficiency efforts. For example, regulators will often undertake a benchmarking analysis for operating expenditure, but tend to shy away from undertaking a similar analysis of capital expenditure on the grounds that the lumpy profile of capex, the different investment cycles of the businesses, different topology and other factors make like-for-like comparisons across networks a more challenging exercise. The result of this process is therefore to expose operating expenditure to a more high-powered regime, allied with tougher targets, than capital expenditure. Naturally, this can lead to incentives to capitalise operating expenditures, or even distort input choices to prefer an investment solution where a maintenance solution would have been optimal.

Another example of an input distortion is due to the application of the so-called ratchet effect when price controls are re-set. If prices are ratcheted down to the new, observed level of costs at the end of the (say) five-year price control period, then this creates stronger incentives to make cost reductions at the beginning of the price control period than at the end.

Both these examples are due to the existence of boundaries – in the first case in the definition of costs, and the regulatory treatment of these costs (which may be substitutable for each other) depending on which side of the cost boundary they fall; and in the second case, a timing boundary. While the second of these is easier to resolve than the first, it highlights the point that apparently simple and superficially sensible approaches to setting up regulatory mechanisms can have inefficient distortionary effects.

---

29 Unfortunately, the application of the DPCR5 price control and the subsequent RIIO framework in the UK, which is intended to be output based, embodies precisely this arrangement whereby the licence conditions under which the electricity distributors operate are highly prescriptive and permit the second guessing of the works programmes of the operators at the end of the price control period, leading to a potentially significant distortion of input choice.

30 See Frontier Economics, *RPI-X@20: Output measures in the future regulatory framework*, a report prepared for Ofgem in 2010 for a further discussion of this problem.

Regulation is evolving to deal with the problem of cost boundaries, and total cost approaches are now becoming increasingly common. In the Netherlands, for example, a yardstick competition regime[31] has been in place since 2000. This regime indexes the price that any individual distribution operator can charge to the change in industry average total costs. This has very strong efficiency properties but also encourages distributors to find the right mix of inputs to minimise total costs. Other European countries such as Sweden, Norway, Austria, Belgium and Germany all embody increasingly strong elements of yardstick competition.

Achieving a fair settlement: as well as encouraging regulated businesses to choose the most efficient operating solution, yardstick regimes have the very attractive property that they have an in-built risk allocation: customers are exposed to cost shocks that affect the industry as a whole, but businesses are exposed to the risk that their performance may be better or worse than the industry average. As a consequence, and in the absence of collusion, each business has an incentive to reduce costs by more than the average, which accordingly lowers the industry average cost, and therefore the prices paid by customers. The key to the efficiency properties of the regime lies in the fact that the price control for each individual business is set on an exogenous benchmark, rather than its own costs, which reduces the scope for strategic gaming behaviour. The key to the efficient risk-sharing properties is that the benchmark is not some arbitrary index, but a benchmark made up of the individual businesses' peers.

However, the implementation of a yardstick regime is difficult. The starting level of prices and costs is not necessarily the right starting point for the benchmark, as it embodies differential levels of efficiency across the peers. Statistical analysis is therefore required to adjust for these factors to set the right benchmark. Moreover, imposing this type of regime requires the cooperation of the businesses, which can be challenging when the businesses know that they will be placed in direct competition with one another. In the Netherlands, for example, the introduction of yardstick competition in 2000 was highly contentious,[32] but the regime was eventually established, and a review of the regulatory model after ten years suggests it remains a sustainable regulatory model.[33]

Yardstick competition represents a very natural way of returning efficiency gains back to customers in a way that does not distort behaviour, and which maintains a fair distributional settlement. In contrast, other mechanisms such as fixed term price controls, sliding scale arrangements,[34] re-opener clauses, uncertainty mechanisms

---

31 See A Shleifer, "A Theory of Yardstick Competition" (1985) 16 *Rand Journal of Economics* 319–327 for a description of the economic properties of yardstick competition.

32 See P Burns, C Riechmann, C Jenkins and M Mikkers, (2006) "The role of the policy framework for the effectiveness of benchmarking in regulatory proceedings" in T Coelli and D Lawrence (ed) *Performance Measurement and Regulation of Network Utilities* (Edward Elgar Publishing, Cheltenham, 2006) and P Nillesen and M Pollitt, *The consequences for consumer welfare of the 2001–2003 Electricity Distribution Review in the Netherlands* (Cambridge Economics Working Paper No 0446, 2004) for a description of the introduction of yardstick competition in the Netherlands.

33 See Netherlands Competition Authority (NMa), *Taking care of optimal energy-distribution networks* (2010) for a summary of three separate research evaluation exercises conducted by Movares Nederland, Kiwa Gas Technology and PricewaterhouseCoopers Advisory (PwC).

and so forth, are more arbitrary and require the regulator to make two important judgements. First, it must strike the right trade-off between providing the business with insurance against unexpected events and with incentives to improve performance and manage risk. Too much insurance against cost shocks weakens incentives on the firm to manage those shocks effectively and manage its own costs efficiently, while too little insurance can expose either the customer or the business to windfall gains and losses. Secondly, the regulator should ensure that the wider group of stakeholders find the balance of risk reasonable, in order that the regime as a whole retains its legitimacy, which is the source of its sustainability and credibility.

Most regulatory regimes now contain a myriad of targets and incentive mechanisms that apply to, *inter alia*, costs, different reliability metrics, customer services, network losses, connections service, the volume of low-carbon generation, and business carbon footprints. As well as ensuring that these regulatory instruments line up with one another, regulators are also now careful to ensure that the overall package represents an appropriate balance of risk and reward between customers and shareholders.

At the fifth distribution price control in Britain, for example, Ofgem developed a methodology to assist it in calibrating the regime to achieve a fair sharing of risk.[35] The methodology essentially analysed the financial impact of over- and under-performance against the full set of incentive mechanisms, given the cost targets and the allowed weighted average cost of capital (WACC[36]) that the regulator had established. In this sense it represented a holistic assessment of the overall package of targets and incentives. The results of this analysis were used to both sense-check the value of the WACC and also to establish that the rewards and penalties for different levels of performance were proportionate to the performance levels that were actually achieved.

5. From RPI-X to RIIO in the UK

In March 2008, Ofgem announced a review of RPI-X regulation. It finalised its review in October 2010 after the publication of over 100 consultation and decision documents, and extensive engagement with the regulated companies and other stakeholders to refine the model. The first price control review using the new approach was implemented in 2013 for the electricity and gas transmission businesses, with the gas distribution networks review also completed in 2013 and the electricity distribution price control completed in 2015.

The review gave rise to the RIIO model of regulation – setting Revenue using Incentives to deliver Innovation and Outputs. Space considerations preclude a full description and assessment of the numerous features of the RIIO model, but three features are worth highlighting in the context of this chapter.

34 See JJ Laffont and J Tirole, *A Theory of Incentives in Procurement and Regulation* (MIT Press, 1993) and P Burns, R Turvey, and TG Weyman-Jones, "Behaviour of the Firm under Alternative Regulatory Constraints" in Scottish *Journal of Political Economy* (1998) for separate analyses of sliding scale arrangements.

35 Ofgem, *Electricity Distribution Price Control Review, Final Proposals* (2009).

36 The WACC is the average of the regulator's estimate of the cost of debt and the cost of equity, weighted by the share of each of these two types of finance.

First, Ofgem took the very sensible step of reversing the burden of proof on future cost levels. It required all companies to produce so-called Well Justified Business Plans, that contained the outputs they proposed to deliver (not just reliability and safety, but also environmental, connection, social and customer service outputs); the process by which those outputs were determined (which had to include meaningful stakeholder engagement); and the costs associated with meeting those outputs, and the extent to which the plan was robust to uncertainty. These plans were then assessed, and if the plan passed certain criteria the company was allowed to be 'fast-tracked', meaning that the price control could be imposed on the basis of the plan, and that the company would earn a modest premium on the allowed rate of return (the architects of the review also envisaged that companies that had just failed to be fast-tracked would remain in the slow-track price control process, but would be subject to a more proportionate review). Part of the assessment involved the benchmarking of the future costs that the company expected to incur. Consequently, for the first time, there was a formal process of competition in the development of the plans with meaningful rewards for submitting a good plan. In principle, and indeed in practice, this change should improve the quality of the plans and diminish the degree of information asymmetry between the regulator and the companies.

Secondly, in its development phase, the architects of RIIO clearly saw the relevant outputs as those that the customer experiences, and that these should be wider than simply reliability and safety. It was clear that how the companies managed their inputs to achieve those outputs was of secondary importance to Ofgem, although an explanation of how the plan would be delivered was rightly a key indicator of the robustness of the plan. In principle, this should encourage innovation and efficiency in the production of outputs, rather than creating input distortions.

Thirdly, Ofgem wished to encourage longer-term decision making and so extended the price control period from five years to eight years.

In practice, these desirable features of the RIIO model were undermined, and this was particularly clear by the time of the electricity distribution price control review, the last review in the cycle of price control reviews for energy networks.

In respect of information revelation, there is little doubt that competition to produce better business plans had the desired result. At the transmission reviews the two Scottish companies were fast-tracked to reflect their better quality business plans, and to enable Ofgem to focus on NG, the transmission operator in England and Wales. Although no gas distribution network got fast-tracked at the gas distribution review, Ofgem did praise the quality of the plans. It was during the final price control review of the cycle, ED1, that significant problems arose, and it is this experience that is likely to send the strongest signal to management teams and investors across the sector. As with the earlier reviews, there was little doubt that the quality of the business plans had significantly improved. Three of the six operators produced particularly good plans, with one being fast-tracked on the basis of benchmarking analysis that showed it to provide the most efficient use of resources. In contrast, the remaining three operators appeared to adopt a more 'wait and see approach' to future cost revelation.

However, the fast-track assessment exercise was faulty, and the company that was fast-tracked was found to be inefficient once the data, calculations and models had been refined and corrected during the slow-track process. Moreover, the fast-tracked company benefitted not only from the uplift in the required rate of return, but also by not being exposed to changes in Ofgem's view on costs that applied to the whole sector (such as the cost of capital) because it had already exited the price control process. The eventual benefit to the fast-tracked company of nearly £1bn was far in excess of the intended reward for a good business plan. Moreover, Ofgem adopted a 'cliff-edge' rather than graduated rewards for business plan quality, so that the two companies that narrowly missed out on fast-track status received no benefit at all. Given that the object of the competition was to encourage good business plans, this 'winner takes all' model diminishes incentives for information revelation in future because Ofgem revealed that there are significant risks attached to the distribution network operators for doing so.

In respect of outputs, by the time of the electricity distribution price control review, Ofgem was clearly more focused on price reductions for customers rather than output enhancements outside of reliability and safety. However, the more worrying departure from the stated intent of RIIO is that the regime was intended to be output based, whereas in practice it evolved towards input based regulation. The original intention was that the outputs would be determined through stakeholder engagement and the means by which those outputs would be delivered would be by the operators in the best ways that they saw fit, through the optimisation of investment and operating costs over time, and given the spatial characteristics of the network. In the slow-track process, however, Ofgem effectively over-wrote the work activities required to deliver those outputs that the customers actually value with the results of its own models. Moreover, the licence conditions that enforce the price control give Ofgem a highly significant ongoing role in ensuring that the operators stick to those input plans for the duration of the price control period, including enforcement of financial penalties if particular inputs are not delivered. In other words, the effect of the regime was to shift towards input based regulation, rather than output based.

In part, a significant source of these problems lies with the institutional weaknesses within Ofgem, which are not unique to Ofgem, and so this experience contains lessons for other regulators. First, there needs to be a critical mass of the original architects of the regime to implement the new regime at the major reviews, particularly if the changes to the regime are significant, as they were in this case. By the end of the cycle of price control reviews, most of the staff who had had a strategic role in the development of RIIO had left the organisation, and the few that remained were not responsible for the implementation of RIIO at price control reviews. Those that were left to implement the reviews had either no association with the design phase or were sceptical of many of the architects' objectives and the means to achieve them. This meant that the effect of the price control reviews in practice became disconnected from the original intentions of the architects.

Secondly, a regulatory office needs to assure itself that its functional capability is well-equipped to handle the demands of the new regime. For example, it has long been true from previous price control reviews that Ofgem's Initial Proposals have contained data and modelling errors which can be cleaned up in time for Final Proposals. The fast-track decision was made at a similar stage in the process to the Initial Proposals at previous reviews, and on an evidence base that contained many of the types of errors and problems observed at the Initial Proposals stage in previous reviews. Ofgem seemed to be unaware that its models and data needed to be 'decision-ready' far sooner in the price control process than they had been historically.

In summary, the RIIO model in principle is one that had very good properties, and contained genuinely valuable innovations that would have benefitted customers in the longer term. In practice, it has fallen short of the original intention, and the key lesson for why that has happened lies in the failure to address the internal challenges faced by the regulator itself in implementing the model.

6. Conclusions and challenges for the future

Incentive-based regulation today differs quite considerably from the original Littlechild RPI-X regime. Having been the forerunner of incentive-based regulation, it is now a special case of it, as incentive regimes of many different economic characteristics can be found around the world. This history of radical change and then subsequent evolution and innovation in regulatory custom and practice provides a rich source of experience to enable regulators and policy makers to meet their biggest challenge yet.

Over the next 10–20 years, power networks will have to spend enormous sums of money to facilitate the transition to a low carbon economy. In Britain alone, it is estimated that transmission and distribution networks will need to spend £35bn (approximately US$53bn) for this purpose over the next decade. Yet how that money will be spent, at what time, in which parts of the network and at what scale is highly uncertain. This is not only because the scale, timing and location of low carbon generation is uncertain, but also because it is difficult to predict how customers will behave in respect of the take-up of electric vehicles, for example, or in response to the installation of smart meters that should give them the ability to manage their load more effectively.

In order to respond to these challenges at least cost, network operators will need to innovate across a wide set of their current activities: for example, their network planning will need to not only make plans but also contingency plans to ensure that sunk investments to anticipate changes in user behaviour are made on a 'least regret' basis;[37] they will need to optimise their use of resources to be able to ramp up and down to a higher and more uncertain rate of connections requests and associated reinforcements; and they will need to invest in automation to make the networks smarter. At the same time, regulators will need to develop regulatory frameworks that encourage network operators to meet these challenges efficiently.

---

37 See A Burger, M Huggins and A Rodgarkia-Dara (2012), *Taming the Beast – Regulation under Uncertainty*, European Electricity Market (EEM) conference, Florence, for a discussion of the use of real option theory in network planning under conditions of acute uncertainty, and the implications for regulation.

There are a number of lessons from the past experience of incentive-based regulation that could be relevant to guide regulators to enable network operators to meet these challenges efficiently.

First, policy makers and regulators should promote a commercial regulatory environment where the network operators are encouraged to find solutions, rather than these being prescribed by the regulator.

Secondly, the regulator should focus on outputs and outcomes, rather than on how they have been or could be achieved. This is not straightforward, and at times it will be necessary for regulators to focus on inputs where the uncertainty is so acute, or the specific investment need so strategic, that an input focus is the most efficient course of action. So long as these departures are isolated and ring-fenced, and undertaken under pre-specified conditions, the scope for any creep into input based regulation will be limited.[38]

Thirdly, with these two rules in mind, the complex work of defining the specific targets and incentive rates can proceed, with rigorous assessment of the package of incentives to ensure that it is coherent, minimises distortions, promotes innovation, encourages operators to manage their operational risks, and represents a reasonable sharing of risk with the customer.

Fourthly, commitments should be made to confirm the principle that investments cannot be written out of the rate base simply because they are no longer used and useful. In such an uncertain environment as the one currently being faced, it is inevitable that investments will be made that will be, with the benefit of hindsight, unnecessary. However, if there is a risk that these will be struck out, then the costs of raising finance to fund the investments will rise considerably. In any case, if the first three lessons set out above are adhered to, there are likely to be fewer unnecessary investments and they will be likely to have been undertaken more cheaply than if the regulator prescribes the investments and provides a complex and contradictory commercial environment.

Regulatory theory often focuses on the asymmetry of information between the network operator and the regulator. The practical reality has been that the greatest successes of regulation have been when it has provided a stable commercial framework within which businesses can find innovative and efficient solutions to problems where previously these solutions were not imagined to have existed at all – by either the business or the regulator. Over the next one or two decades that attribute of incentive-based regulation will be of great value, if put to full effect.

38 See Frontier Economics, *RPI-X@20: Output measures in the future regulatory framework*, a report prepared for Ofgem in 2010 for further discussion of the criteria that should be adopted.

Power to the people: the Smart Grid and the democratisation of energy

Thomas Leonard
Frits Verheij
DNV GL Energy
John Scott
Chiltern Power

1. Introduction

The energy landscape is changing as long established priorities and stakeholder roles and responsibilities shift and re-align. Electrification of transportation and greater demand from domestic appliances will increase the need for power quality and security of supply at a time when power flow is becoming more complex due to distributed renewable generation and smaller domestic producers. The energy market is changing into a system which is more complex and diverse but also much more flexible.

The Smart Grid will play a major role in this global transition, which should be understood within the context of a greater change. The Smart Grid is the next generation of transmission and distribution in which the network is monitored and controlled so as to react to electricity flows. This technological revolution is still in its early stages and many challenges must be overcome before this vision of a balance between environmental and economic sustainability and security of supply is realised.

These challenges are not only technical, but also regulatory and, possibly most importantly, social. The new energy market will see devolution of responsibility for the control of the means of power generation from large integrated utilities to individual commercial and domestic customers. As will be shown in this chapter, it is a vision which will come about through industry and private sector collaboration, societal support and the exploration of real world solutions.

2. The energy generations

In 1920 Vladimir Ilyich Lenin declared that "Communism is Soviet power plus electrification of the whole country!". As a talented propagandist, Lenin understood perfectly the value of an integrated, national transmission system as a symbol of national unity and technical and social progress. If the previously existing archipelago of self-sufficient generators and loads could be described as a collection of 'Grid Villages', Lenin's vision was for the implementation of a united, centrally planned and national 'Grid Kingdom'.

By 1920, the Grid Villages had been in existence for almost a century in a number of countries. The development of equipment to generate, transmit and consume electricity had been underway throughout the 19th century.[1] However, at the end of the 19th century, electrical loads could not be far from the generators. For example, by 1896, the world's longest commercial electrical power transmission circuit could move power at 11.2 kV only 35 miles (56 km) across the San Joaquin Valley in Fresno, California.[2]

In the years immediately after World War I, these distributed networks started to join together to form the first national Grid Kingdoms.[3] The mechanism which caused this shift differed from country to country and could take the form of central diktat or local evolution. This did not produce in all cases the complete state monopoly on the supply and transport of power which was imposed in the Soviet Union. However, generally the change was, by its nature, a move from local, parochial control of the means of power production to a more centrally planned and integrated system, raising both cost-effectiveness and security of supply.

The Grid Kingdom has proven to be a remarkably resilient innovation. The electricity networks we enjoy today are in principle not very different from those which developed in most industrialised nations of the 1930s. Electricity is still, mostly, generated at large centralised power stations and distributed around the country via a national grid to passive consumers, who simply 'take and pay'.

In the coming decades, the global electricity industry will experience a technological revolution no less tumultuous than that experienced almost a hundred years earlier with the advent of the Grid Kingdom. The 'Grid Democracy', or Smart Grid, will combine many of the aspects of the Village and Kingdom Grids. Like the Grid Kingdom, it will span large contiguous areas. However, as with the Grid Village, control will be increasingly devolved from the centre to localities, communities and even individual businesses and households.

- Grid Village – small generators connected to nearby loads via short distribution networks.
- Grid Kingdom – large, national scale integrated generation and transmission and distribution.
- Grid Democracy – the Smart Grid, which allows comprehensive grid integration to co-exist with small, distributed, often renewable energy.

3. The Smart Grid generation

There is no universally agreed definition of a Smart Grid, although many have been suggested. It is, in any case, perhaps more helpful to try to understand what a Smart Grid does than what it is. The Smart Grid functions can be grouped into four categories:[4]

1 R Kennedy, *Modern Engines and Generators* (D Van Nostrand Company, New York, 1903).
2 EJ Houston and AE Kennelly, *The Electric Motor and the Transmission of Power* (WJ Johnston Company, New York, 1896).
3 TP Hughes, *Networks of power: electrification in Western society, 1880–1930* (Johns Hopkins University Press, Baltimore, 1983).
4 P Nabuurs, "'A defining moment', Understanding what a smart grid is means understanding what a smart grid does" (Global Contact 2010/2011, DNV GL (formerly KEMA)).

- Energy management: allowing domestic customers and small businesses to make efficient use of energy.
- Energy sales: allowing consumers to also be producers, generating and selling power.
- Grid optimisation: improving the efficiency and effectiveness of the distribution grid itself.
- Renewable integration: integrating large scale, renewable generation into the system.

Like all revolutions, the Smart Grid will come about due to a combination of perceived necessity and the availability of means. A principal source of necessity will be the pressure to decarbonise national energy consumption. In 2008, the European Union set a target of reducing carbon dioxide emissions levels by 20% (compared to a 1990 baseline) by 2020, with some individual countries choosing to reduce levels by as much as 30%. By the middle of the 21st century, carbon dioxide emissions levels are set to have been reduced by 80%.[5]

This will lead to the building and connection of national volumes of dispersed, often small scale and, to an overwhelming degree, fluctuating electricity generation. Some projections foresee up to 80% renewable energy generation in Europe by 2050.[6] According to these scenarios, up to 30% of power could come from wind, 24% from solar and 26% from other renewable sources.

This future energy system will require more flexibility, which can be provided by:

- adding more flexible power generation;
- increasing interconnection capacity;
- Smart Grid services, such as demand response; and
- energy storage.

4. What are the parts of the Smart Grid?

The Smart Grid is not any specific item of technology. It is rather an energy generation and distribution philosophy that brings together and coordinates a raft of technologies, many of which already exist but are not yet deployed and integrated. The Smart Grid is not just about inventing new devices but also the large scale implementation and integration of these inventions, together with their supporting commercial systems.

The part of the Smart Grid most visible to the average consumer will be smart meters and intelligent domestic appliances. Smart meters can record consumption in half-hourly or hourly intervals and transmit that information remotely. They differ from traditional meters which need to be read manually and give little or no information on precisely when the electricity was consumed. Intelligent domestic appliances will be able to react to the availability of cheap electricity at times of low demand, or at other times of the day when there may be a surplus of, say, wind or solar generation.

Smart meters and intelligent appliances are important building blocks of the

5 "2020 climate & energy package", European Commission, accessed 23 April 2016 from http://ec.europa.eu/clima/policies/strategies/2020/index_en.htm.
6 www.roadmap2050.eu.

Smart Grid as they are central to the ability to monitor data and control energy usage in real time. However, the Smart Grid is more than a collection smart meters and appliances. Physical activities in a typical electricity system comprise four distinct parts:

- generation;
- transmission and distribution;
- consumption; and
- storage.

All of these functions will continue to exist under the Smart Grid, but should progressively interact with each other in a more intelligent manner. Furthermore, the boundaries between the functions will start to blur as consumers start to take on a greater responsibility for demand management, local generation and local storage.

5. Unity, power and control

Much Smart Grid philosophy is concerned with making the best use of already existing transmission and distribution infrastructure, as well as the implementation of already established technologies. A key principle is the aggregated monitoring and control of ever more distributed power generation, storage and consumption. Consumers will be able to generate, store and sell electricity. Electricity supply companies will need to be able to monitor and react to the intentions and actions of their numerous and dispersed end customers. The control of these Distributed Energy Resources (DERs) will take place via the creation of so-called Virtual Power Plants (VPPs). A VPP is an aggregation of small power generators, storage sites and controllable loads which, for the purposes of supply of power to the grid, are controlled as a single entity.

Consumers will also increasingly be in a position to provide to grid operators ancillary services which would traditionally have been supplied by generators. For example, generators may be required to increase or decrease generation in order to allow grid operators to balance the network, so that supply consistently matches demand. However, a similar effect can also be achieved by use of demand response (DR). This is a service whereby grid operators offer consumers a financial incentive to be allowed to have an element of control of their electrical loads, for example time-shifting the heating of water. The grid operator may contract this service directly with the consumer or via a third party. Third-party 'Curtailment Service Providers' have long been established in the USA and are becoming increasingly active in Europe.[7]

Much proposed new renewable generation capacity may comprise large projects which are distant from the intended loads. For example, some ambitious scenarios call for Europe to be supplied by, amongst other things, a combination of large scale solar plants in North Africa and Southern Europe and huge offshore wind farms in Northern Europe.[8] This technical vision is mirrored by a political drive to create a single contiguous energy market across the EU.

---

7 "Demand Response Markets in Europe Begin to Blossom", GreenTech Media, 8 March 2015, accessed 23 April 2016 from www.greentechmedia.com/articles/read/restore-raises-7m-for-europes-growing-demand-response-markets.

8 www.roadmap2050.eu.

These scenarios envisage a huge expansion of the pan-European transmission grid, in order to balance these disparate and less controllable power sources. They will require more efficient transmission equipment, such as high voltage direct current (HVDC) lines as well as high temperature conductors for overhead transmission lines. There will need to be €70–80 bn of investments by 2030 to build up to 200 GW of cross-country interconnectors by 2030.[9] Knitting together this vast, complex continent-wide disparate system of generation, transmission and load will require a raft of smart technical solutions. For example, dynamic circuit rating will allow the operator to monitor in real time how the current-carrying capacity of a line changes with variations in ambient temperature and wind speed, whilst electronic equipment will automatically stabilise line voltages.

6. Electricity storage

Because of the planned larger volumes of renewable energy, it will also be necessary to store energy in much greater amounts. The Smart Grid is likely to become an integral part of the process by which this storage capacity is coordinated with the transmission networks.

Central control of the grid will still be necessary in order to ensure that inputs and outflow from the grid remain in balance, although the means of doing this can vary radically. The traditional electricity market has always operated as a 'just-in-time' supply chain. Large scale storage of electricity is expensive and complex and stored electricity capacity has tended to be small compared to generation capacity. Large power storage has mostly been based on large hydro-electric pumped storage. Most countries have limited available sites for such projects.

Consequently, power grid design has always been based largely on the assumption that power generation and consumption need to be matched in real time. In order to achieve this, it has been necessary for the grid to be equipped with fast-reacting generators which are able to respond to peaks in demand. This is typically provided by generators operating at part load, or by stand-by plant such as Open Cycle Gas Turbines (OCGT) or Internal Combustion (IC) engines. These peaking plants are often small and relatively cheap to install. They are however dependent on fossil fuels and are less efficient than larger, more complex base load plant. As well as providing peak load generation, these plants may also be required to provide a number of other ancillary services. This can include frequency response, where quick acting generation is needed to respond to fluctuations in grid frequency. In some cases, larger generators are run at lower than their full capacity, so as to form a spinning reserve which is able to react quickly to the sudden loss of another generator or other disturbances. This tends to result in a reduction in efficiency, increased emissions, fuel price risks and higher costs as equipment utilises operating hours at sub-optimal loads.

As variable renewable generation sources come increasingly online, the need for such ancillary services is only likely to increase. There are many advantages to having fast-reacting sources of stored energy easily accessible to grid operators. A number of

9 ENTSO-E TenYear Development Plan, accessed 18 August 2016 from http://tyndp.entsoe.eu/.

large new potential storage solutions are already under development, including batteries, flywheels and compressed air.

Part of this need for storage could be filled by an aggregation of a large number of individual embedded power storage devices, such as fuel cells or lithium-ion batteries. There are potential financial and environmental advantages to providing ancillary services in this way. Assuming that power can be stored efficiently, it will be possible to operate base load plant at a constant rate. This means that the large base load generators will be able to maintain a steady state of operations using fuel in the most efficient manner and producing a minimum of emissions. It will not be necessary to bring on line expensive-to-operate peaking plant, thus reducing the total cost of generating electricity.

Fast-response storage devices used in ancillary services applications may tend to operate for a lower duration than traditional generation assets. They are however more effective than traditional generation methods at reacting to demands for ancillary services. It has been shown that a 30 MW to 50 MW storage device is at least as effective as a 100 MW combustion turbine used for regulation purposes.[10]

7. Information is power

Smart Grids are not only concerned with the movement of kilowatt-hours from one place to another and their consumption when they get there. The Smart Grid will be as much a revolution in communications, data processing and control as it will be in power distribution hardware. The Smart Grid involves the flow of information and the control of equipment from the largest generator down to individual domestic appliances. The principal feature that will differentiate the Smart Grid from the existing electricity grid will be the two-way flow of electricity, information and control. This can range from the household smart meter to a grid-wide automated network management (ANM) system. It is a new business proposition which is encouraging companies not necessarily associated with the energy industry, such as Cisco and Google, to enter the market.

There are advantages to both the utility company and to the consumer in allowing this degree of closer oversight of consumption. Smart grids should facilitate more control over outage management and allow the operator to see where an outage is occurring and which customers have been affected, thus allowing them to respond to customers much more promptly and with detailed recovery times. Grid operators and suppliers will be able to gather information about customer consumption patterns. This will allow utility companies to plan their network operations and retailers to have greater foresight over the wholesale markets, thus allowing them to more effectively plan their power purchase arrangements and offer more attractive commercial deals to consumers.

This has been enabled by the remarkable explosion of information processing power and communication. In the time it has taken a generation to grow to property owning age, the expensive house-brick mobile phone has transformed into

---

10 R Masiello *et al*, "Research Evaluation of Wind Generation, Solar Generation, and Storage Impact on the California Grid", CEC, June 2010.

something quite different. A relatively cheap device the size of a cigarette packet can turn its owner into a post office, journalist, cameraman, author, publisher, event organiser, political activist and much else besides. Is it so strange to imagine that our houses and those of our neighbours could be turned into community scale power utilities?

8. The electric vehicle: consumer and storage

The most powerful driver of the Smart Grid may prove to be the latest incarnation of that other great emblem of individual empowerment and independence, the automobile. The impact which electric vehicles (EVs) will have on the power grid cannot be overstated. A UK household typically has an average demand of approximately 0.5 kW, rising to more than 6 kW for short peaks. However, these peaks do not occur simultaneously for all households, so reducing the overall demand on the local network. An EV would need to draw about 3 kW for up to eight hours in order to recharge; this will summate with neighbours doing likewise. Thus, a householder who buys a new EV effectively builds up to two new house loads on top of their property the moment they plug their new car in. Alternately, charging may take place at 'fast charging stations' at public car parks, resulting in even higher peak loads. This evidently has the potential to create demands far in excess of the capacity of the local networks, depending on the degree of EV clustering.

The UK's National Grid Future Energy Scenarios[11] assumes that electric vehicles could account for 14 TWh per year of additional residential electricity consumption by 2035. It is estimated that in 2050 as much as 800 TWh per year (16.7%) of European power generation could be directed towards feeding EVs.[12] The additional load on the distribution system which will result from these vehicles can be handled in one of two ways: grid reinforcement or smarter use of the grid we have (or in practice, a combination of the two approaches).

The EV has the potential to be the answer to its own problem. Each vehicle will be fitted with a battery with sufficient capacity for reasonable length journeys. Many drivers on most days do not need anything like the full potential range of their car. So, the car could be configured to draw power in periods of low demand, and therefore low electricity cost, and to sell electricity back to the grid when prices are high (vehicle-to-grid or V2G). It has been suggested that the introduction of a relatively simple two rate tariff could encourage EV users to charge their vehicles in the off-peak period, thus providing smoothing to the off-peak period whilst avoiding an increase in peak loads.[13]

There are, however, obvious societal problems with this scenario. The purchaser of a brand new EV wishes presumably to control his or her own vehicle and expects the battery to charge when it is plugged into a charging point. What incentive should a grid operator or energy supplier offer to encourage a car owner to charge their car during periods of low demand? A further consideration is the effect on battery life of

11 Future Energy Scenarios 2015, National Grid, accessed 23 April 2016 from http://fes.nationalgrid.com/.
12 www.roadmap2050.eu.
13 D Densley, "Electric Vehicles and the Grid", SSE presentation to the Institute of Engineering and Technology, 2 June 2011.

continuous charging and discharge. What compensation will the vehicle owner want for any reduction in battery life and the inconvenience which results from this? No doubt the answer here lies in the commercial deal – and its marketing!

9. Unwilling revolutionaries?

Paradoxically, the Smart Grid will place ever more control into the hands of individual consumers, who will in turn need to hand over more control to automated systems and to electricity service provider companies. In order to take advantage of optimum opportunities for the purchase or sale of power, consumers will need to allow individual appliances to turn themselves off and on in accordance with pre-set instructions. According to the VPP concept, this could also be the result of a direct request by or instruction from the power supplier.

This is a change that will necessitate a new view of the energy system and the role within it of consumers, generators and those that do both. Overcoming the technical challenges to achieving this state is only a part of this story. At least as complex will be the reprogramming of human 'software' in order to turn passive consumers of electricity into CEOs of miniature integrated utilities with service companies acting as their 'management'. In order for customers to fully engage with the Smart Grid, they must have time, ability and inclination. Until now consumers have had little incentive to understand the way in which electricity makes its way from the generating stations and into their homes.

Some consumers may take easily to the new regime. Younger people who have grown up in the multi-media age may feel comfortable with, and may actually expect, the opportunity to seize control of electrical power. A growing understanding of the environmental dangers in the coming years will also tend to encourage consumers to adopt such measures, if it can be shown that the Smart Grid represents a real contribution to solving the problems facing the planet and addressing dependency on energy imports.

The relatively cash-rich but time-poor middle-class and older customers may be less likely to embrace the new ways without a significant incentive. Consumers are more likely to engage fully with the Smart Grid if the effort of doing so leads to sufficient financial compensation and/or other benefits, such as greater convenience. Currently standard consumer electricity tariffs are based on meter readings taken many months apart from each other. The supplier has no way of knowing exactly when the electricity was consumed and tariffs are normally charged at a flat rate. Smart meters will allow the consumption of electricity to be monitored, and thus billed, in real time. Consumers will then have the ability to buy power at periods of relatively low demand and, thus, low price.

10. The role of government in the Smart Grid revolution

Whilst the Smart Grid revolution may well devolve power into the hands of consumers and small generators, it is fairly certain that the initial impetus for progress will need to come from government bodies. Society has an inbuilt inertia and many of the drivers for change, such as environment and security of supply, are either too abstract or too distant to provoke a rallying cry to direct action. Whilst the free market may be an efficient method for bringing about system optimisations, it is less effective at provoking revolutionary change.

Few are calling for a return to central control of the power industry, but it will be necessary for the state to accept at least part of the risk associated with the transition. In order to achieve critical mass, it is almost certain that subsidies, investment-friendly regulation and the establishment of new standards will be needed to support the early implementation of Smart Grid technology. Government and regulators do not need to become central planners, but they will need to be a catalyst for change.

There is a need for large investments in energy infrastructure across the developed world in order to meet the needs of the low carbon future. Ofgem, the energy regulator for Great Britain, has estimated that the UK will require up to £200 billion worth of investments by 2020. This includes a £32 billion investment in upgrading the gas and power transmission and distribution networks.[14] In 2014, the European Commission presented an investment plan intended to facilitate energy infrastructure investment of €315 billion in the following three years alone.[15] It has been estimated that the rate of US investment in energy infrastructure will need to increase from $62 billion to about $73 billion per year to avoid a funding gap of $732 billion by 2040.[16]

Regulatory methods need to adapt to meet the changing needs of the industry. For example, since 1990, the UK has used the RPI-X model where network operators were entitled to increase network charges annually in line with the Retail Price Index (RPI) with a reduction (X) to promote increased efficiency. The RPI-X model was successful at reducing costs to consumers whilst still delivering a reliable network, but there is evidence that the method does not encourage long-term investment in R&D for innovative grid technologies. Ofgem has refined the RPI-X model and describes its new framework as RIIO (Revenue = Incentives + Innovation + Outputs) which rewards network companies who improve efficiency, promote innovation and deliver measurable benefits, whilst penalising those that overspend on infrastructure projects.

In addition, Ofgem's Low Carbon Network (LCN) Fund provides £500m worth of funding to promote projects in the UK which encourage the use of low carbon technologies, including smart meters, smart domestic appliances and EVs.[17] Funding is allocated on the basis of a competition and is not used to support specific research and development activities, but rather activities which investigate practical ways of implementing technologies and encouraging consumers to use them.

In the USA, legislation has promoted the rollout of Smart Grid technologies to federal government sites. The Energy Policy Act 2005 mandated federal facilities to

---

14 Ofgem, "Britain needs rewiring to the tune of £32 billion", press release, 4 October 2010.

15 European energy infrastructure opportunities, Norton Rose Fulbright, September 2015, accessed 24 April 2016 from www.nortonrosefulbright.com/files/european-energy-infrastructure-opportunities-connecting-the-dots-131696.pdf.

16 ASCE, "Failure to Act: the Economic Impact of Current Investment Trends in Electricity Infrastructure", American Society of Civil Engineers, 2011, accessed 24 April 2016 from www.asce.org/uploadedFiles/Issues_and_Advocacy/Our_Initiatives/Infrastructure/Content_Pieces/failure-to-act-electricity-report.pdf.

17 Ofgem, Low Carbon Network Fund, accessed 24 April 2016 from www.ofgem.gov.uk/electricity/distribution-networks/network-innovation/low-carbon-networks-fund.

collect hourly consumption data and to install appropriate metering into new and existing buildings above a specific consumption level. The subsequent Energy Independence and Security Act 2007 and the American Recovery and Reinvestment Act of 2009 have set levels for emissions from federal buildings, promoted the modernisation of the electricity grid and have funded the mandates of previous legislation.[18] This has included the Smart Grid Investment Grant (SGIG) programme, intended to modernise the nation's electric transmission and distribution systems. This scheme covers 50% of the costs of 99 projects through federal financial assistance.[19] A stimulus package of $3.4 billion was earmarked for advanced power grid projects, including grants of up to $200 million to support smart meter installations.[20] In 2015, the US Energy Information Agency stated that more than 50 million smart meters had been installed in the USA by 2013, of which more than 46 million were in residential premises.[21]

11. Transnational cooperation on standards

The Smart Grid must necessarily be able to operate across borders as electricity networks become more integrated. Some activity is already underway to try to establish a set of global standards for the development and operation of Smart Grids. The International Electrotechnical Commission (IEC), an international standards authority, has highlighted a lack of awareness of existing standards when designing Smart Grid systems.[22] In addition, there is a need to harmonise standards which have been established by different groups or technical committees, such as the US National Institute of Standards and Technology (NIST) and the EU Smart Grid Coordination Group (SG-CG).[23]

A helpful comparison is perhaps that of the experience of mobile phone operators in establishing the standards for network roaming. A tourist from Moscow who wishes to visit the site of the historic San Joaquin Valley transmission line can call home on his Russian mobile phone without having needed to think about how this connection is achieved. This was enabled through global standards of telephone communications which were established in the 1980s and 1990s. In the same way, global Smart Grids will have to achieve comparable levels of standardisation.

Transnational coordination on Smart Grid implementation has been emerging gradually. It has long been recognised that Smart Grids will not be a purely technical venture and that commercial and regulatory issues must also be addressed. The European Union has raised the profile of energy and the need for policy development to address supply security, strengthen markets and regulations and

18 "The Recovery Act Made The Largest Single Investment In Clean Energy In History, Driving The Deployment Of Clean Energy, Promoting Energy Efficiency, And Supporting Manufacturing", White House, Office of the Press Secretary, 25 February 2016.

19 www.smartgrid.gov/recovery_act/overview/smart_grid_investment_grant_program.html.

20 "Obama Trumpets Energy Grants", *Wall Street Journal*, 28 October 2009.

21 "How many Smart Meters are installed in the United States, and who has them?", US Energy Information Administration website, updated 1 May 2015, accessed 24 April 2016 from www.eia.gov/tools/faqs/faq.cfm?id=108&t=3.

22 "IEC Smart Grid Standardisation Roadmap", SMB Smart Grid Strategic Group (SG3), June 2010.

23 www.nist.gov/smartgrid/grid-091311.cfm.

promote environmental sustainability. This has been underpinned by substantial research programmes and the creation of stakeholder technology platforms.[24]

12. Real Smart Grid applications

A number of Smart Grid demonstration sites and trials are already in existence, such as the PowerMatching City in the Netherlands and the Cities of the Future programme and the US Navy Advanced Metering Infrastructure Programme.

The PowerMatching City was implemented by a group of organisations, including DNV GL (formerly KEMA), TNO, HumiQ, Essent and Enexis, as a Smart Grid market model under real operating conditions.[25] It is a living community as well as a Smart Grid laboratory. Twenty-five regular households in the Dutch town of Hoogkerk have been equipped with micro-cogeneration units, hybrid heat pumps, PV solar panels, smart appliances and EVs. Additional power is produced by a 2.5 MW wind turbine and a gas turbine. Energy demand and use is balanced by use of PowerMatcher software, which aims to simultaneously meet the needs of generators and consumers in the most optimum way.

Each house in the PowerMatching City is equipped with an Energy Service Gateway (ESG). This ESG monitors the supply of energy and the demand. At low electricity prices, the system buys electricity and sells when prices are high. Pre-programmed software ensures that household appliances, such as washing machines and dishwashers, start and electric vehicles charge up when local power prices are low. Low cost electricity is also used to run heat pumps in order to heat water for central heating and domestic use. Excess hot water is stored in vessels. Each house has the ability to sell excess power to neighbouring houses or back to the grid. Residents can buy electricity from the grid when there is an excess of available power, such as when high winds or sunshine are causing surplus renewable power to be generated.

In response to federal energy independence and security legislation, the US Navy is implementing an Advanced Metering Infrastructure (AMI) programme. The Navy is installing advanced electric, water, gas and steam meters across 120 naval bases worldwide. All metering data will be collected and archived in a data acquisition system (DAS), where an operator can view and remotely analyse the data. The central meter data management system (MDMS) can conduct data analysis, process billing and provide data to the customers through a web portal.[26]

13. Conclusion

A technical and, even more important, a social revolution is needed to ensure secure, cost-effective and sustainable energy for nations, communities, industries and households. The triple challenges of security of supply, affordability and environmental sustainability will cause a dramatic change in the way in which electricity is made, transported and consumed. International pressures on primary

24 "State of the Energy Union 2015", Commission Staff Working Document on the European Energy Security Strategy, European Commission, 18 November 2015.

25 www.powermatchingcity.nl/site/pagina.php?id=41.

26 JH Edwards and GJ White, "Leveraging Advanced Metering", *The Military Engineer*, Society of Military Engineering, 25 April 2014.

fossil fuel sources, as well as efforts to decarbonise generation, will result in a higher proportion of our power coming from variable renewable sources as well as smaller embedded generators. In addition to this, the increasing take-up of electric vehicles has the potential to quickly place an additional heavy load on the network.

The cost-effective solution to these challenges could take the form of the Smart Grid, in which communications and control equipment is used to allow a market of smaller units to band together into larger aggregated power supply, storage and consumption entities. These aggregated entities will give grid operators the flexibility to react to the more unpredictable demands and sources.

Consumers will have more engagement with the flow of their electrical energy and new services offered to them, but they will in turn become increasingly reliant on automated systems which may at times come under the operational control of energy companies. These companies may, with our consent, have the ability to switch our appliances on and off and to gather detailed data about our electricity usage.

Much of the technology to achieve this already exists, but there are many other barriers before the Smart Grid can be realised. Common national and international standards must be established and regulatory measures must be put in place to ensure sufficient investment is available to achieve this transition.

Possibly the greatest challenge will be to bring the people along with the revolution. There may be strong resistance to the concept from individuals who object to this level of direct control of the loads in their homes. Indeed, if the incentive to participate is not strong enough, there is an even greater danger that the project will fail due to user apathy. There is a need to win social acceptance for the fundamental changes to the way in which we view our electricity and how we interact with it. Individuals will need to raise their understanding of the technical and economic practicalities of power supply in order to be able to gain the full advantage of this revolution.

Controlled pilot projects have shown that it has been possible to implement this technology in real communities. Lack of engagement by individuals and communities would risk losing the benefits of the revolution – bringing additional costs to all parties and the loss of new services. The real challenge will come as the Smart Grid revolution moves out of these model sites and into the unpredictable world.

About the authors

Marianne Anton
Associate, CMS London
marianne.anton@cms-cmck.com

Marianne Anton is an associate in the energy, projects and construction team at CMS in London, advising on electricity regulation, projects and transactions. She holds a law degree from Oxford University.

After training and qualifying as a solicitor at CMS, Ms Anton spent some time at Ofgem, the energy regulator, gaining deep industry knowledge and expertise in regulation of the electricity industry with a particular focus on offshore transmission and competitive networks before returning to CMS. She advises on a wide variety of domestic and international matters, ranging from corporate and commercial to regulatory matters in the electricity, gas and renewables sectors. She also has experience of advising on wholesale electricity market reforms, liberalisations, regulatory frameworks and compliance and EU law.

Phil Burns
Director, Frontier Economics
phil.burns@frontier-economics.com

Phil Burns is a director at Frontier Economics specialising in regulatory and competition analysis in the energy sector. His work on monopoly regulation, both for clients and in published papers, extends across price cap and sliding scale regulation, finance issues, comparative efficiency measurement and incentive design. In the energy sector he has worked on regulatory reviews across Europe – including advising on the pioneering yardstick competition regime in the Netherlands – and virtually all the energy price control reviews in the UK since the sector was privatised. Recently, he has worked on Ofgem's RPI-X@20 review, and Northern Powergrid at the commencement of RIIO-ED1, and Phoenix Natural Gas Ltd, NIE and NPg before the Competition Commission.

Phil has also worked extensively in postal markets over the past 10 years on a variety of issues including price control design, the cost of the universal service obligation, and competition issues raised by the liberalisation of postal markets. He has also worked on many wholesale and retail market analyses, both to support specific competition investigations and to inform the scope of regulatory frameworks and business strategies.

Hugo Coetzee
Energy finance partner, CMS London
hugo.coetzee@cms-cmck.com

Hugo Coetzee is a project and energy finance partner in the infrastructure and project finance team at the international law firm CMS based in London. He advises private and public sector clients on strategy as well as the acquisition, development, restructuring and financing of projects in the infrastructure, energy and natural resources sectors.

Hugo works on a wide range of energy and infrastructure (greenfield as well as operational) projects where he represents infrastructure and renewable energy funds, senior debt funds, developers, contractors, utilities, banking institutions and the public sector.

He has advised a number of utilities on the disposal of their wind farm portfolios and the project financing aspects of their energy efficient asset bases.

Hugo has led a number of CMS teams on energy finance transactions in the renewable and conventional energy industries including in the following sectors: wind, solar, waste/energy from waste and gas and electricity meter financings.

Rupert Cowen
Commercial and nuclear energy lawyer, Prospect Law
rcc@prospectlaw.co.uk

Rupert joined Prospect Law from Dentons where he specialised in energy projects, construction and infrastructure. He has a master's degree in construction law and specialises in power generation, transmission and nuclear projects. For the last 12 years Rupert has concentrated on the renewable and nuclear generation and decommissioning industries. He has developed procurement strategies, encouraged outsourcing, and explained nuclear law, insurance transport regulations and licensing regimes to Tier 1 contractors and their suppliers responsible for delivering the UK's civil decommissioning effort. Rupert is currently assisting participants in renewable energy to navigate the electricity market reforms and in nuclear decommissioning to reduce the nuclear inventory. Rupert is married with eight children and lives in Hertfordshire with his wife, some of his children and various animals.

Ian Dalley
Partner, Dentons
ian.dalley@dentons.com

Ian Dalley is a partner of Dentons in Abu Dhabi, where he has been based for a decade. He is dually qualified as a lawyer (English solicitor) and a professional engineer. He holds a master's degree in engineering and is a professional chartered engineer, a fellow of the Institution of Engineering and Technology and a fellow of the Energy Institute. He specialises in major international engineering projects and related matters such as public procurement, long-term supply agreements, concessions and operations and maintenance. This has included drafting and negotiating an engineering contract with a contract sum in excess of US$4 billion.

Ian plays a leading role on the drafting panel of the MF/1 standard form contract for electrical/mechanical plant, which was first used for a power station in 1916. He has a strong grasp of local laws and has been commissioned by Middle East government entities to prepare drafts of a number of laws and regulations.

Nick Elms
Associate director, Frontier Economics
nick.elms@frontier-economics.com

Nick Elms is an associate director at Frontier Economics. Nick holds degrees in management science and engineering, and has specialised in the economics of electricity, gas and the environment for over 20 years while based in London, Madrid and Wellington.

He has advised on the design of wholesale markets and rules for transmission access and pricing for both electricity and gas in many countries. He has also worked on many power station, electricity interconnector and underground gas storage projects and transactions. In addition, he has advised on the design of network regulation, assisted clients to gain regulatory approval for the access regime to several LNG import terminals and advised on the competitive effects of mergers and possible remedies. Most recently he has developed expert reports for a number of disputes related to power purchase agreements, gas supply agreements and network regulation. Nick's clients include governments, regulators, competition authorities, investment funds, utilities and traders.

Angus Evers
Partner, Shoosmiths
angus.evers@shoosmiths.co.uk

Angus Evers is the head of Shoosmiths' national environmental law practice, based in London. His experience also covers related areas such as planning and health and safety law. His work is a mix of transactional work on energy and infrastructure projects and corporate and real estate transactions, as well as regulatory and compliance work. His clients include operators and developers of infrastructure projects, property investors, property developers, private equity funds, and public sector and government organisations.

He has an LLM degree in environmental law and has been rated for his expertise in energy and infrastructure in *Chambers UK*, which stated that: "He is utterly dependable, unflappable and you can guarantee he will always take care of anything that comes up."

Munir Hassan
Head of clean energy, CMS London
munir.hassan@cms-cmck.com

Munir Hassan has been advising the power sector for 19 years and heads up the active clean energy practice at CMS in London. He is a regular speaker, commentator and recognised international legal expert in the field. He is the consulting editor of *Wind: Projects & Transactions* by Globe Law and Business, and has published over 100 articles on specialist energy matters.

Munir advises across the range of electricity generation technologies, from wind and solar through to biomass, wave, tidal, gas, carbon capture and storage and nuclear. He also has significant experience in the electricity sector of advising on or writing the rules for subsidy arrangements, wholesale market reforms, regulatory frameworks, privatisations, regulated electricity networks, independent power producer procurement programmes, emissions trading, EU law, grid codes, and offshore transmission and connection arrangements.

Nicholas Hilder
Counsel, Ashurst LLP
nicholas.hilder@ashurst.com

Nick Hilder is of counsel in the Corporate Projects group of Ashurst in London. He has extensive experience advising lenders, sponsors and the supply chain on the construction and operational aspects of international project finance infrastructure and power transactions.

Nicholas Kelly
Principal, Kelly Legal
ntk@kellylegalservices.co.uk

Kelly Legal provides legal advice for oil and gas, utilities, power, renewables and commodity trading companies. Nick has over 17 years' experience in the energy sector, having advised Shell, E.On E&P, RWE npower, EDF Energy, ONGC, CNPC, Fortum, Ofreg and the Commission for Energy Regulation on energy-related matters. As well as advising clients across the energy spectrum, Nick acts as General Counsel to Sindicatum Sustainable Resources, a Singapore-based fund investing in clean energy projects in Southeast Asia.

Jonathan Leech
Commercial and nuclear energy lawyer,
Prospect Law
jrl@prospectlaw.co.uk

Jonathan is a commercial, regulatory and projects lawyer, with particular emphasis on the energy and nuclear sectors. He was admitted as a solicitor in 1998 and began his legal career resolving construction disputes. His work includes advising on legal and contracting strategies and regulatory issues associated with major nuclear development, decommissioning, waste and reprocessing projects, energy infrastructure and other utility and infrastructure related projects. Jonathan also works extensively on procurement strategies for development and renewal of UK electricity and gas network infrastructure, including development of multi-party alliance structures and innovative incentive models. Jonathan joined Prospect Law from Dentons, where he was a partner in the energy team. He is married with two children and lives in Leicestershire. He plays the violin when in need of a diversion from nuclear law.

Thomas Leonard
Senior consultant, DNV GL Energy
thomas.leonard@dnvgl.com

Thomas Leonard is a senior consultant within the DNV GL Energy Smart Energy Advisory (SEA) team in London, specialising in energy development projects, including conventional and renewable generation, transmission and distribution, storage and retail. He has more than eight years' experience working directly in the energy industry and a further three years' experience of managing process consultancy projects. Prior to this he was a marine engineer in the British Royal Navy for five years. He specialises in helping institutions with an interest in project development to understand the value of energy investments. He has worked for government and non-government organisations, fuel suppliers, developers, network operators, retailers and investors.

Dalia Majumder-Russell
Managing associate, Linklaters
dalia.majumder-russell@linklaters.com

Dalia is a managing associate in Linklaters' Energy and Utilities Global Project Finance group in London.

Dalia's specialism is the electricity sector where for several years she has advised a wide range of stakeholders in the UK and overseas on conventional as well as renewable power projects. In particular, she advises governments and industry on all aspects of the regulatory frameworks supporting electricity markets, interconnectors and contractual matters. Dalia has been deeply involved in the commercial and legal issues for novel technologies, such as the first commercial-scale carbon capture and storage project in the UK, smart metering and developments in the UK offshore wind sector.

Rajan Phakey
Partner, Dentons
rajan@phakey.com

Rajan Phakey leads the Middle East Energy and Projects practice at Dentons, the world's largest law firm. He has advised on transactional and regulatory projects in over 20 countries since 2000, while based in London and Abu Dhabi. These projects span all areas of the energy industry, for both the public and private sector, and many have been the first of their kind. Mr Phakey is a solicitor (England and Wales) and obtained his law degree from the University of Oxford.

Milagros Miranda Rojas
Former policy director at the
World Coal Association
milagros.miranda@gmail.com

Milagros is a professional diplomat with over 16 years' experience in international trade and sustainable development issues. She has substantial involvement in the negotiations of the United Nations 2030 Sustainable Development Agenda, the Sustainable Development Goals and Financing for Development issues.

Before her last diplomatic position in the Permanent Mission of Peru to the United Nations, Milagros was a WTO representative and negotiator. She also negotiated numerous free-trade agreements.

Milagros holds a Juris Doctor, a master's degree in International Law and Economics and a master's degree in International Relations.

Milagros wrote the chapter on Conventional Power while working as policy director at the World Coal Association. She has now left that organisation to move into legal private practice in London as an international trade expert.

Neil Schofield
Managing director, Financial Markets Training Ltd
neil.schofield@fmarketstraining.com

Neil is the managing director of Financial Markets Training Ltd and offers training services in the areas of treasury, derivatives, capital markets and risk management to financial institutions, central banks and corporations worldwide.

Neil was global head of Financial Markets training at Barclays Capital from 2001 to 2008. Before joining Barclays Capital, he was a director at Chisholm-Roth Training for four years, where he was responsible for the provision of training services for a number of blue chip global investment banks. He has also held positions with JP Morgan Chase Security Pacific Hoare Govett (now trading as Bank of America) and Lloyds TSB.

Neil holds a BSc in Economics from Loughborough University and an MBA from Manchester Business School. He was elected as a fellow of the IFS School of Finance (formerly the Chartered Institute of Bankers) in 1999. He is also a visiting fellow at the University of Reading ICMA centre having been appointed in April 2007.

John Scott
Director, Chiltern Power
john.scott@chilternpower.com

John Scott is an independent consultant with 40 years of experience in electricity distribution, transmission and regulation. His previous roles include director of engineering for National Grid, technical director for Ofgem, and director, network innovation for KEMA (now part of DNV GL Energy).

He takes a particular interest in innovation and sustainable energy systems, and factors critical to successful deployment of innovation on power systems. He is a founder member of the government's Smart Grid Forum and undertakes a number of roles including non-executive director at Smarter Grid Solutions and adviser to Pearlstone Energy. He is an active Fellow of the Institution of Engineering and Technology and has served as a member of the board of trustees.

Frits Verheij
Director Smart Green Cities, DNV GL Energy
frits.verheij@dnvgl.com

Frits Verheij has been working in the renewable energy business, and related areas like smart grids and energy storage, since the start of his career in 1987. Prior to joining DNV GL (then KEMA), he held various positions at the research organisation TNO and was programme manager at the Dutch energy agency, Novem. Currently, Frits is director Smart Green Cities for DNV GL Energy. He is vice-chairman of the board of Top Consortium on Knowledge and Innovation (TKI) Urban Energy, and member of the executive board of USEF (Universal Smart Energy Framework).

Frits is an expert in working at the crossroads of innovation, energy policy and strategy. He works for governments, utilities, industries and other organisations in the energy sector.

Related titles in energy

Globe Law and Business

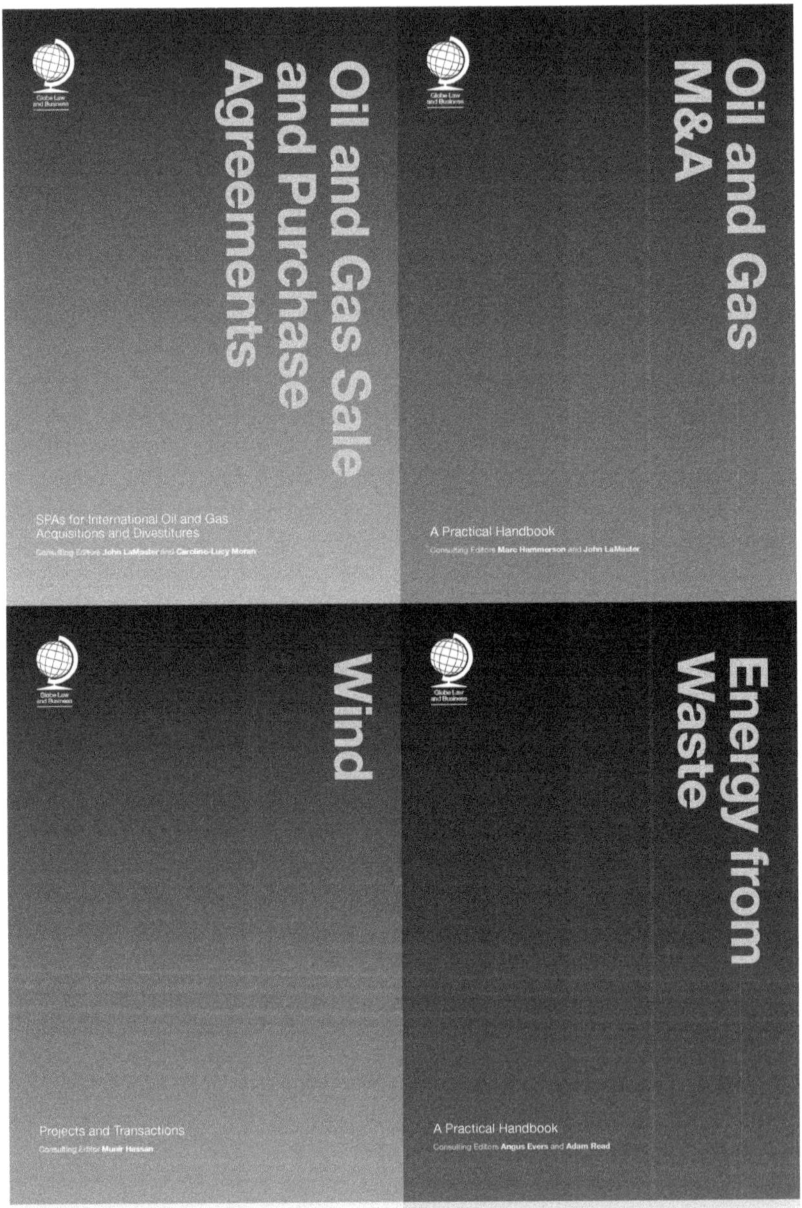

Go to **www.globelawandbusiness.com**
for full details including free sample chapters

www.ingramcontent.com/pod-product-compliance
Ingram Content Group UK Ltd.
Pitfield, Milton Keynes, MK11 3LW, UK
UKHW062251150926
8656IPUK00007B/41

9 781905 783854